THE UNACCEPTABLE FACE

THE UNACCEPTABLE FACE

The Modern Church in the Eyes of the Historian

JOHN KENT

SCM PRESS LTD

BR
290
.K46
1987

© John Kent 1987

All rights reserved. No part of this publication may be reproduced, stored in a retrieval system, or transmitted, in any form or by any means, electronic, mechanical, photocopying, recording or otherwise, without the prior permission of the publisher, SCM Press Ltd.
Cataloging in Publication Data available

British Library Cataloguing in Publication Data

Kent, John, *1923–*
The unacceptable face: the modern church
in the eyes of the historian.
1. Church history—Modern period, 1500–
—Historiography
I. Title
270′.09 BR290

ISBN 0–334–01712–2

First published 1987
by SCM Press Ltd
26–30 Tottenham Road, London N1

Phototypeset by Input Typesetting Ltd, London
and printed in Great Britain by
Richard Clay Ltd, Bungay, Suffolk

Contents

Foreword

This book developed out of an essay on modern ecclesiastical history which I contributed to the second volume of the *Pelican Guide to Modern Theology*, published in 1969, and edited by R. P. C. Hanson. I am grateful to Penguin Books Limited for the return of the copyright; I have retained a few pages of the earlier work, but have placed them in a new context.

To the extent that this is a book about Roman Catholicism and its relations with other Christian bodies, I owe a great deal to Günter Biemer, Derek Holmes, Nicholas Lash, the late Nicholas Theis, and above all to John Coulson, who has constantly stimulated my interest in modern Catholic history. On a personal level, I would like to acknowledge help and encouragement from many scholars, more especially from Clyde Binfield, David Jasper, Stuart Mews, Henry Rack, John Walsh, Haddon Willmer, Terry Wright, and my colleagues at Bristol, Dennis Nineham and Sean Gill. None of them, of course, is necessarily in agreement with the arguments advanced here. I have also benefited very much from my wife's understanding of the kind of problems which fascinate me. Finally, I am much indebted to Mrs Anne Cade, who typed (and retyped) most of these pages.

Introduction:
To Serve, rather than Seduce, Mankind . . .

The history of modern Christianity, a period which stretches from the Reformation and the Counter-Reformation to the present day. ought to be studied not in terms of the Christian church only, as though such matters as the amazing resilience of the papacy, the constant Anglican need for self-definition, or the disastrous rise and fall of Calvinism exhausted the story. The recent history of the Christian religion is part of the history of the religious life of modern Western man and his former subjects and clients outside Europe, a history which shows signs of culminating in a mainstream culture whose choices, styles and myths will owe very little to the various religious sub-cultures, including Christianity, which struggle to survive in an institutional form. If the Christian religion sometimes seems essential to the nature of Western civilization, this is because Christianity played a vital role (though never to the total exclusion of the classical tradition in philosophy and ethics) in the building-up, after the collapse of the Roman empire in the West, of a new society in which art, science and literature all drew on Christian sources. In the turmoil of the sixteenth century, however, institutional Christianity split between Catholic and Protestant, lost much of its intellectual and spiritual authority, and could not prevent the growth of an alternative culture which was to make decreasing use of Christian ideas, symbols and rituals. New societies take time to develop, however, and the churches, as economic, political and legal dependencies and assistants of the state, retained something of their former social ascendancy at least until the French Revolution of 1789.

During the nineteenth century the economic and political bases of organized Christianity declined rapidly, and by 1900 both Catholicism and Protestantism had to face a critical encounter with 'modernism', a situation which has been described as 'the encounter and confrontation of a religious past long established in its mould with a present which had found elsewhere the vital sources of its inspiration'.[1] At the same time as the traditional forms of Christianity were being subjected to moral and religious criticism in Western society, nineteenth-century imperialism and commercial expansion were carrying a largely unmodified Christianity into Africa, India and the Far East, where the missionaries in their turn assumed the role of moral and religious critics of the other great religious sub-cultures of the world. They had already failed to come to terms with the survival of Judaism in the West, in the sense of accepting its right to an existence independent of Christianity. One of the changes which is recorded in this book, which discusses the church history which has been written in the past fifty years, is the rapid disappearance of the old-style missionary history which reflected the mistaken belief that Western Christianity was about to sweep all other religions out of human history. In the last year of the nineteenth century 'the evangelization of the world in our generation' had become a popular slogan among Protestants.

The modern professional study of history started in the eighteenth century as one aspect of the growth of the non-Christian society, and historical study helped to generate the crisis of modern Christianity. Twentieth-century professional history is effectively secularized, in the sense that no specifically religious or Christian understanding of the past or the future underlies either its methods or its products.[2] Most professional historians take for granted a concept of the possible which excludes events like the resurrection stories about Jesus in the New Testament; in any case, these stories do not enter into their usual subject-matter. When they have to deal with more recent claims to supernatural intervention they prefer to treat the events described – miracle stories from the medieval period, for example, or the alleged appearances of the Virgin Mary at Lourdes in France in 1858 as what certain individuals and groups of people believed to have happened.

For example, the historical problem is not whether Berndadette thought that the Virgin Mary appeared to her on eighteen different occasions between 11 February 1858 and 16 July in the same year, and said on one occasion 'I am the Immaculate Conception', but rather in what kind of community such stories came to be told, how they took the form in which they were recorded, how they affected the behaviour of those who accepted or rejected them, why and how they became the basis of an international pilgrimage-cult, and on what grounds later healing stories became attached to Lourdes. (The secular historian is not obliged to deny the possibility of healings as such.) This is not to say that the study of history can generate its own criteria of what is ultimately possible, but that the professional historian is entitled to ask on what grounds some Roman Catholic scholars accept that, for example, the Virgin Mary said that she was the Immaculate Conception, and that he is also entitled to offer alternative explanations of the report. He is not obliged to accept the appeal to the supernatural as somehow foreclosing the discussion.

In Christian apologetic the matter tends to end there. On the one hand, there is the Christian historian, and especially the church historian, who says – usually on philosophical grounds – that one should not rule out supernatural intervention in history on principle, and who may therefore interpret Lourdes as a case of direct action by the Virgin Mary; and on the other, there is the secular professional historian who dismisses the possibility of supernatural intervention before he starts work, and who therefore attaches no transcendent importance to the suggestions of a Marian action at Lourdes. In practice, there is at least a third position, that of the historian who regards himself as religious but who does not think that the concept of direct divine intervention is essential to a religious outlook; he usually regards the kind of historical evidence which has been collected at Lourdes, when looked at in the context of the overall history of Roman Catholicism, as being adequate ground for rejecting the idea of an objective presence of the Virgin Mary. This third position became increasingly influential in the later nineteenth and early twentieth centuries, at first through Liberal Protestant writers and then through the Roman Catholic Modernists, and it largely destroyed the ground for the comfortable orthodox belief that the historical examination of the New Testament would sooner or later arrive at 'agreed results' which would confirm traditional Christian doctrines, such as the divinity of Christ. The disintegration of New Testament criticism did not take place because historians ruled out in advance the idea of supernatural events, but because they were able, without recourse to the idea of supernatural intervention, to give adequate and plausible accounts of how the biblical documents reached their present form. At this stage the discipline of history had become the chief tool of a modernizing movement whose supporters thought that if Christianity were to survive as a religion deeply involved in Western society and not just as a sectarian resistance movement it would have to drop most, if not all, of its claims to divine intervention in history, whether these were based on what was said in the Bible or on what was said to have happened later in the history of the Western churches.

The success of the modernists and the historical critics obscured the survival of the traditional Christian philosophy of history, according to which divine providence presided over the broad sweep of events and guided it towards its goal in the final triumph of creative love over evil, a goal which was bound to be attained because God willed it and which, in a theological sense rarely clarified for laymen, was said to have already been achieved by Christ in his death and resurrection. These ideas of Providence caused less intellectual difficulty in the late nineteenth century because it seemed as though they could easily be reconciled with the Victorian idea of progress, an idea which owed more to idealist philosophy than to Christian theology, and more to economic and imperial expansion than to either. A non-Christian writer like Friedrich Nietzsche might declare that man 'was not the result of a special design, a will, a purpose; he was not the subject of an attempt to attain to an "ideal of man" or an "ideal of happiness" or an "ideal of morality" ';[3] but the church historian was tempted to say that he could see the traces of God's working in the world;[4] and the famous Roman Catholic historian, Lord Acton, held that belief in God's government of the world necessitated belief in progress.

In the twentieth century the climate changed abruptly. The expansion of Europe, which had for so long seemed – in the West, at least – to be of unquestionable benefit to humanity, slowly came to be seen from the point of view of the conquered, the colonized, the exploited, the culturally invaded. Non-Christian cultures which seemed to be crumbling away, as in China and India for example, now found the power to transform their situation. Neither in the constant major wars, nor in the use of atomic weapons by the West, in the East in 1945, nor in the competitive atomic deterrence which has followed has there been any sign that the Christian churches had significant influence on the political and military behaviour of states, on the emotions released by nationalism, or on the ends pursued by individuals in the cumulative waste of the earth's resources. However powerful it might have been in the past, a religious myth needs at least some apparent confirmation from what happens in the present if it is to retain its liveliness in the imagination. Appalled by the new situation, theologians gave up the combination of providence and progress and tried to turn disaster and weakness into an argument in favour of the Christian understanding of history. In the 1920s German theologians like Karl Barth reacted fiercely against the modernist conviction that one could find God at work immanently both in the individual and in human society. By the 1940s there was a revival of Augustinian images of the church as a divine society, a City of God which lived its more than earthly life side by side with the city of destruction: the evil which dominated this earthly city, the *civitas terrena*, might be negative and parasitic but it was at the same time so tenacious and effective that no power in history could overcome it. 'The Antichrist who appears at the end of history', wrote Reinhold Niebuhr, 'can be defeated only by the Christ who ends history.'[5] The suffering of the innocent, which might seem to a humanist to be the fundamental objection to the idea of divine providence, was identified with the death of Christ himself as an innocent victim, and so transformed into 'the ultimate answer of history' to the ambiguities of human behaviour and its relation to God.[6] This stubborn reaffirmation of traditional piety had its own pathos; Niebuhr even presented it as 'Christian realism'; but such theologians seemed to lack an imaginative grasp of human, as distinct from divine, suffering.

Niebuhr was not a professional historian like Herbert Butterfield, whose widely-read *Christianity and History* (1949) expressed a post-war mood of exhaustion and despair. Christians who had shared the Enlightenment's faith in rationality, toleration and time, or who had believed in liberal theology and the modernist concept of divine immanence, or who had worked for political change as the natural outcome of Christianity, all responded eagerly to Butterfield's exhortation that they 'hold to Christ, and for the rest be totally uncommitted'.[7] This Christian romanticism, however, was not incompatible in Butterfield's mind with the belief that there was a 'providence, in fact, which moves over history with the function of creating good out of evil'[8] – a belief which implied that the divine set limits to the destructive freedom of the human, an assumption which perhaps rested too heavily in Butterfield's mind on the premise that Hitler's final defeat squared an abominable account. The Christian philosopher of history, it appeared, could dispense with 'progress' more easily than he could dispense with 'providence', perhaps because he has always felt the pressure to make a case for the overall influence of Christianity on history. Butterfield, for example, having deplored the political record of the Catholic and Protestant churches in European history, tried to balance his account by saying that 'if people would turn, however, from politico-ecclesiastical history to the intimate life of the church throughout the ages, and the spiritual work done by humble men over the face of the continent for fifteen hundred years, they would find it the most moving spectacle that history presents, and would see how the spread of piety does mean the growth of charity'.[9] This was special pleading: the central, arresting images of the providential pattern might seem distorted, pathological, but nevertheless, almost hidden from sight in the margins of the spectacle there lurked a compensating health and grace. The spread of piety, however, is as closely linked to intolerance, cruelty and warfare as it is to any growth of charity, and charity will grow as vigorously from humanist as from Christian soil. It is no answer to this objection to talk about the evils of Stalinism:

Marxist humanism is as rare as Christian charity; it is the shortage of both that is the major problem of the late twentieth century.[10]

Although theologians and church historians could not decide whether to dismiss human history as parasitic and negative, or to look for traces of providential action in it, the years between 1918 and the 1960s saw a new theological emphasis develop on the importance of the church, an attempt to reassert the indispensability of an apparently declining institution, and this in turn affected the attitude of some church historians to their work. They rejected the nineteenth-century liberal individualistic view of the 'church' which had found classical expression in Adolf von Harnack's *What is Christianity?*:

> We are well aware that in the interests of order and instruction outward and visible communities must arise . . . but we do not hand our hearts upon them, for they may exist today and tomorrow give place, under different political and social conditions, to new organizations; let anyone who has such a church have it as though he had it not.[11]

What was affirmed was the direct opposite: the idea of the 'church' as a corporate necessity, supernaturally founded and endowed, with a right to claim obedience from each individual member, and assured of historical survival and final triumph.

> It is a distortion of the apostolic doctrine to say that men are first united to Christ through faith within an invisible society of the truly faithful, and then find admission to the visible Church. The right order is not: Christ – faithful individuals – the Church; but: Christ – the Church – faithful individuals. It is Christ in his body who justified men, and their justification is their deliverance into his body. The visible Church is a part of the Gospel . . . [12]

The Anglo-Catholics who wrote this in 1947 were consciously contradicting the tradition which the Lutheran but liberal Harnack had represented. For them the 'church' was 'a divine fact',[13] episcopally defined and not at all Protestant, though the ecumenically-minded Protestants who formed the World Council of Churches in 1948 were equally willing to put the visible, institutional church at the centre of their understanding of Christianity. This change of mood produced no decisive action, however; Catholics and Protestants remained disunited even after the Second Vatican Council, summoned by Pope John XXIII in 1959, had added Catholic weight to the idea of reunion. Nevertheless, the intense theological and ecclesiastical stress on the 'church' as a supernatural body was bound to affect orthodox church historians, leading them to think yet again that the 'church' was a special case, an institution somehow existing on two levels, the natural, visible and historical level, and the supernatural. This general campaign for reconciliation also prompted some historians to rewrite the story of past conflicts, particularly those of the Reformation and the Counter-Reformation, as though the conflict had been more apparent than real. One climax of this process was the work of the French Catholic historian, Jean Delumeau, for whom the Reformation and the Counter-Reformation became different aspects of a major Christian effort to convert the less than Christian culture of medieval Europe.

Since the 1960s, however, there have been signs that the study of modern church history is becoming less introverted. Slowly but surely the social historians, whose presuppositions are often secular, began to interest themselves in the history of religion, and in the part which religion had played in the formation of the modern world. Such scholars did not regard the 'church' as a special case in any theological sense, but approached the role of religion from a more anthropological point of view which sought to construct a model of the whole society under observation, and to situate religious beliefs and rituals within this totality. This change of interest also affected Christian missionary history, where the study of the impact of Christianity on Africa, China and India passed from the hands of Western missionaries concerned to justify the evangelical past into the hands of historians who thought of the history of Christian missions, not as part of a divine plan which deserved approval and support, but as the record of an alien invasion of communities which had valid religious traditions of their own. These new missionary historians interpreted Western religion as first and foremost an intrusive political element in rapidly changing societies.

Social historians working on the history of modern Western cultures took a different line, because for them religious belief and ritual (more especially ritual) were a formative part of what would have otherwise have been incompletely developed Western societies. They regarded religion, including Christianity, as stimulating and sustaining community. In eighteenth-century Brittany, for example, according to Donald Sutherland, the church had a unique socializing role. 'The parish, rather than the village assembly or the municipality became the centre of community life. Churchgoing thus allowed the parishioners to express themselves as a group, govern relations outside the hamlets, satisfy their gregarious instincts, gain a sense of human dignity.'[14] This at least helped to explain why the Civil Constitution of the Clergy in 1791, a Republican scheme for 'modernizing' the French Catholic Church, provoked peasant counter-revolutionary revolts in Western France which dragged on for years. A similar attitude underlay John Morrill's discussion of the causes of the outbreak of the English Civil War:

> By 1640, Charles' government was profoundly unpopular, and above all for its religious policies. Innovation in religion (Morrill meant Laudian, not Puritan innovation) was even more compulsively listed in the petitions and addresses to the Long Parliament than was Ship Money. Yet England was psychologically far from civil war in 1640. . . . It is my contention that what made civil war possible in 1642 was a crisis of religion.[15]

Disagreement about religious issues, and the impact of imposed changes in the local community, rather than the more secular, central controversy about the forms of political power, provided the 'ideological dynamism' which compelled minorities to fight. This change of emphasis is important, and appeals to commonsense, as when another historian asked:

> Can all those thousands – hundreds of thousands – of Europeans who rose in the name of their faith (in the Catholic counter-revolutionary movements which erupted in various parts of Europe between 1789 and 1815) really have been the dupes of

their own misinterpreted needs and/or the manipulated puppets of their selfish élites?'[16]

The reinstatement of religion as an autonomous source of causation did not necessarily imply a return to the traditional church historian's 'providential' understanding of the past. Religion, after all, was now presented as the set of beliefs and emotions which tipped the political balance of seventeenth-century England and precipitated civil war; or as the energy which fomented and sustained widespread armed resistance to the Revolutionary politics of the later eighteenth century; or, to go further back, as the root-cause of the bitter cruelty which characterized the French Religious Wars of the sixteenth century. Religion emerged from the background as the cause of division and war, perhaps a providential instrument but hardly a creative one. This was not the image which the church historian or the theologian wanted: they preferred to think of war as the result of human sinfulness and to advocate Christianity as the means of reconciliation and peace. They would have rejected the possibility that an increase in religious intensity might also increase the chances of social division and even violence.

If the church historian was embarrassed by some of the results of social history, the social historian was also in some difficulties with his interpretation of historical Christianity in terms of 'community'. The social historian resembled the church historian to the extent that both pursued a private vision of a social state of grace. Interpreting religion in terms of Durkheimian social emotion, social historians valued ritual and symbolism as alleged generators of an intense, creative common life. Unfortunately they also found that socially-binding emotions often found expression in aggression and conflict.

Nevertheless, familiar subjects were treated with fresh brilliance: witchcraft and superstition, for instance, from the sixteenth to the nineteenth centuries; ideas about death, especially against the background of the French Enlightenment. James Obelkevich, in *Religion and Rural Society in South Lindsey, 1825–75* (1976) thought that the changes which he detected in Victorian, rural, non-institutional religion constituted 'probably the most important set of changes in popular religion since the Reformation'.[17] Revivalism and adventism became almost respectable subjects, and scholarly works were written on topics like Joanna Southcott, Swedenborgianism and the Plymouth Brethren.[18]

Over all hung the concept of 'secularization', much used by sociologists of religion. Should the essential subject-matter of modern church history be understood as the decline of the Christian churches, and if this decline (which seemed to be established statistically for Catholics as well as Protestants in the West) were accepted as the central event which needed analysis, was it evidence for a more significant drying-up of the individual religious consciousness? Or was institutional decline evidence that modern societies had been turning away from traditional methods of generating socially-binding feelings? If it was the first of these, a profound transformation was taking place; if it was the second, other methods would no doubt be found for working up similar social effects. (In neither case was there much to be said about the so-called 'new religious movements', which were really no more than marginal examples of routine religious eccentricity.)

Both the conservative church historian and the social historian were left with the further question, as to whether historians of religion could provide explanations of this decline from their own resources, or whether one had to argue, as for example Obelkevich did, 'that the secret of theology is anthropology, and, by extension, the secret of religious history is social history'?[19] However, that thumpingly Feuerbachian assumption begged the question as to whether social history had a coherent secret to impart. Was social history, in this limiting sense, an adequate explanation of why the English Civil War began; why the Bretons fought so long against the Revolution and its religious reforms; why the conflict between the Catholics and Protestants in sixteenth-century France reached repulsive depths of cruelty? Social historians like Obelkevich eliminated supernatural forces from history, and then assumed that what remained was 'social history', to which traditionally 'religious' behaviour could be reduced. This looks like a modern simplification, part of the constant academic war on most forms of psychology, and on the idea of 'personality' in general. Granted that supernatural intervention may be ruled out of human history (and only the most naive of conservative ecclesiastical historians can rule it in by this time) there may still remain sources of human feeling which do not simply reflect changes in social structures, but manipulate them: it is highly implausible, for example, to argue that all forms of nationalism, the most powerful emotional imperative of the last two centuries, can be explained by saying that the secret of nationalist history is social history. Whether such sources of emotion are full of grace and truth is another matter. Nationalist emotions have been powerful enough to destroy societies, as Nazism did, and as Persian nationalism has done. Mass revivals of religious excitement must remain under suspicion and be treated, on sound historical grounds, as potentially undesirable. The highly politicized American 'religious Right' is an example of the danger of allowing religion into contemporary politics, and Roman Catholicism has an equally bleak record. If religion is to serve, rather than to seduce mankind, we need to examine its historical record, its unacceptable face, much more critically than has been done by either the ecclesiastical or the social historian.

1

Acceptable Faces of the Church: General Histories

General histories of the modern church, and even histories of the church in a single country, have not enjoyed great popularity in the post-war period. Perhaps publishers wonder who reads them, apart, that is, from professional historians in search of generalizations which can be criticized, and students looking for a bibliography or the background of an essay. In general histories, where the emphasis must fall on the interpretation of detail rather than on the details themselves, everything depends on the underlying structure of interpretation. Church history itself originated in the impulse to record and celebrate what God was said to have done and still to be doing for the redemption of the human race. The 'miraculous spread of Christianity' used to be a staple article of Christian apologetic, and so the occupational temptation of the church historian used to be optimism, or a pious sentimentality. General histories have become much harder to write in a period when professional historians cannot agree as to whether or not Christianity is suffering from a terminal illness, and when Western secular culture seems to have lost its self-confidence.

Nevertheless, optimism died hard. For example, America's most widely read church historian,[1] Kenneth Scott Latourette, advocated a wave-theory of Christian history according to which, after an unpromising beginning, Christianity had progressed by a series of pulsations of advance, retreat and advance.[2] According to Latourette each advance had carried the tide of Christianity further than its predecessors, whereas each recession had been shorter and less marked than the one which had preceded it.

In the mid-twentieth century, in fact, Latourette thought that Christianity was more of a force than it had ever been before, a view which now seems to reflect not only the traditional, aggressive optimism of American Protestantism in a country in which classical Christian institutions still appeared to flourish, but also the momentary self-confidence of the United States as a world-power in the interval between its victory over Japan in 1945 and its defeat in Vietnam in the early 1970s. World Protestantism caught this feeling of confidence and superiority, and the founding of the World Council of Churches in Amsterdam in 1948 seemed briefly to foreshadow a Western Protestant world-culture, but the victory of the Chinese Communists in 1949 should have put all this in its proper perspective.

Latourette chose the wrong moment at which to proclaim that Christianity was gaining strength and influence in human society. The structure of his general history depended on the simple principle that God willed the final triumph of the visible church, and the wave-theory was meant to cope with the historical evidence, which suggested that failure was now more obvious than success. No secular historian has accepted the conclusion that in the long run the Christian church has steadily increased its influence on human history; this is because the secular historian interprets the concept of a 'revolutionary age', which Latourette incorporated into the title of his later study, in a more drastic sense altogether. Most professional historians would prefer, for example, E. J. Hobsbawm's understanding of what is meant in the religious context by talking about 'revolution' in the eighteenth and nineteenth centuries:

> The bourgeoisie . . . remained divided in its ideology between a minority of increasingly frank free-thinkers and a majority of the pious, Protestant, Jewish, and Catholic. However, the new historic fact was that of the two the free-thinking sector was immeasurably more dynamic and effective. Though in purely quantitative terms religion remained immensely strong and . . . grew stronger, it was no longer (to use a biological analogy) dominant but recessive, and has remained so to this day within the world transformed by the dual revolution in France and

> America. The most obvious proof of this decisive victory of secular over religious ideology is also its most important result. With the American and French revolutions major political and social transformations were secularized. The issues of the Dutch and English revolutions of the sixteenth and seventeenth centuries had still been discussed and fought out in the traditional language of Christianity, orthodox, schismatic or heretical. In the ideologies of the American and French, for the first time in European history, Christianity is irrelevant.[3]

What was said here of America and France was to be even truer of the Russian and Chinese revolutions in the twentieth century. The general church historian cannot conjure out of existence, as Latourette sought to do, a fundamental change which has taken place over the past two hundred years in the relationship between Western society and what has become in that time a Christian sub-culture;[4] the survival and significance of a more vaguely defined 'instinct of religion' is a different issue, of which I shall say something later.[5] Unsuccessful attempts to fuse Catholic and Marxist thought in what is now usually called 'liberation theology' suggest the Christian sub-culture's awareness of the danger of being finally excluded from influence on what happens in the future; on the other hand, the revolutionary tradition which Hobsbawm was describing has failed to unite Western society in a new common culture, and to the extent that Christianity is politically organized this offers dangerous choices.

With this in mind we may look at Catholic versions of the general history of the modern church. The standard history has been the *Histoire de l'Eglise*, planned in twenty-six volumes in the 1930s; there is no English translation of the modern volumes; the most relevant from our point of view is *Le Pontificat de Pie IX (1846–78)* by Roger Aubert,[6] who was also one of the editors of *The Christian Centuries*, a five volume history of the Catholic Church begun in the 1970s.[7] Aubert faced the problem of how to present the pontificate of Pius IX, which the secular historian might interpret as the defence of the Roman Catholic Church against being reduced to sub-cultural status. Such an interpretation would emphasize Pius's rejection of the principle of intellectual freedom which had been at the heart of the eighteenth-century Enlightenment, his opposition to the democratic and laicizing tendencies of the French Revolution and of the revolutions of 1848 which stemmed from it, his resistance to the aspirations of Italian nationalism – he did not consent to the absorption of the Papal States into the new, unified Kingdom of Italy but struggled instead to recover the lost territories. At one point, in the Syllabus of Errors in 1864, he seemed to be pitting Catholicism against modern civilization *in toto*, and had to be rescued by subtle commentators who lifted the Syllabus on to a plane where it had few serious cultural consequences. Pius also asserted the absolute certainty of the dogmas of the Immaculate Conception of the Virgin Mary (1854) and of Papal Infallibility (1870). Pius was vainly resisting the shift away from the use of Christian systems of reference which we have been describing; he could magnify the office of the Pope but he could not alter the social reality of the church's changing status outside Rome.

For Aubert, Catholicism was still a special case, and he did not accept such a translation of its nineteenth-century fate in terms of social history. Nor did he have to reckon with the Second Vatican Council, which some were to interpret as siding with Pius IX's more moderate critics, especially over the question of freedom of religious belief outside (but not inside) the institutional church as such. Aubert presented Pius IX's policies as *spiritually* appropriate to an age of revolution and nationalism, because the Pope's aim was to defend revealed truth against a rising tide of human error, social as well as intellectual; but as *politically* misguided, because the Pope became obsessed with the loss of the papal states after 1870 and sacrificed the best interests of Catholicism in France and Germany to the vain hope of their recovery. These political mistakes were of only temporary significance, however; his more diplomatic successor, Leo XIII, restored the image of Rome by softening the manner rather than by altering the long-term programme. Pius's spiritual success was much more important. He helped to foster 'a rediscovery of Christ in the nineteenth century' which was naturally accompanied by a new growth of piety towards Mary. 'God encouraged this movement of devotion' Aubert said, 'through various appearances . . . The Virgin, who had appeared in 1830 in Paris to Catherine Labouré and in 1836 to the curé of Notre-Dame des Victoires, l'ábbé Desgenettes, appeared on September 19, 1846, to two young Savoyards, Maximin Giraud and Mélanie Calvat.' These appearances, and the pilgrimages which followed them, were eclipsed by the events at Lourdes in 1858, of which Aubert wrote that

> the miraculous facts of Lourdes were only a privileged case. One would say that God was taking pleasure in reacting against the positivist rationalism of the time by multiplying supernatural interventions: around the curé d'Ars and Don Bosco miracles occurred which yielded nothing in comparison with those of the past . . . and in the life of many other humbler heroes of sanctity, poor religious, heroic curés, founders of hospitals and orphanages, one sees the same solid evidence of supernatural action. Canonisations, which Pius the Ninth liked to surround with extraordinary brilliance, and the number of which struck contemporaries after the caution of earlier popes, contributed to draw the attention of the faithful to the permanent presence of marvels of divine grace in the Church.[8]

In paragraphs like these the church still appeared as a unique institution which fulfilled a transcendent will in history; Aubert did not describe clearly how sacred and secular history intermingled but he left no room for doubt that the church was essentially supernatural.

A generation later, in *The Church in a Secularised Society*,[9] the atmosphere seemed less confident. The Second Vatican Council dominated the structure, but the authors, who included Aubert,[10] were less certain of their position than Aubert himself had been in 1952, when he had even said that after Vatican I those bishops who had at first opposed the proclamation of the dogma of papal infallibility had finally accepted it because they felt that their objections had been met. The volume covered the period from 1848 to 1965, but it was perhaps the negative aspects of the years after Leo XIII's death in 1903 which subtly depressed the record. In his foreword Aubert admitted that more space might have been given to ecumenical affairs and to the increasingly similar problems confronting the major Christian confessions, but (he said) 'it should be remembered that the period running from Pius IX to Pius XII was probably the one in which confessional barriers were at their most impermeable ever as far as the Roman Catholic Church was concerned'.[11] This feeling that Pius IX and Leo XIII had left a situation which had deteriorated during the reigns of Pius X, Pius XI and Pius XII permeated the whole account, while the section on the Second Vatican Council was probably affected by the growing realization that the expectations of change which the Council had raised were being disappointed. Aubert and his collaborators responded by attempting what they called 'a more sociological approach to church history', which meant that they gave more space to the spiritual life of the faithful and less to theological controversy and relations between church and state. This did not conceal their uneasiness about the numbing effect of ecclesiastical centralization on the ethical, political and theological sympathies of the church. Perhaps it was also true that the brief pontificate of John XXIII from 1958 to 1963 left the reputation of the other twentieth-century popes more vulnerable than would otherwise have been the case. Aubert said that the church was an organism in which believers recognized the action of the Holy Spirit but which nonetheless was subject to the laws and contingencies governing any association of human beings. This was an elegant way of saying that if the church historian concluded that the church had failed to meet the repeated challenges of the twentieth century, he was not obliged to surrender the theory that the church was an institution grounded in the supernatural. The secular historian might add that in that case the theory lost its relevance.[12]

Neither *Le Pontificat de Pie IX* nor *The Church in a Secularised Society* expressed the sort of optimism characteristic of the Protestant Latourette.[13] A new *Oxford History of the Christian Church*, which drew on both Catholic and Protestant writers, was started in the 1970s, and one of the early volumes, on the papacy in the eighteenth and early nineteenth century, was by the Anglican historian, Owen Chadwick.[14] Chadwick switched the centre of interest from the France so familiar to British historians to Italy, Spain, South Germany and Austria. His subject naturally fell into three sections: a gentle picture of Catholicism in the first half of the eighteenth century; the impact of revolution; and the post-1815 church of the

Restoration, haunted by memories of the recent upheavals. The Revolutionary period showed the frailty of faith, or, if true faith could not have been shaken, how insecure the social structure of the church was in a divided country. Chadwick did not draw the theological conclusion, that one could exaggerate the sense in which the church's allegedly supernatural being guaranteed it a permanent existence within Western society, but he pointed out how the widespread temporary collapse of Catholicism affected the whole later attitude of the church to the modern world. At the same time, however, tempted perhaps by the spirit of Barchester, he argued that revolution usually achieved less than the revolutionaries believed, and that much of what emerged as permanently changed in the Catholic Church and in its relationship with society in the nineteenth century did so because movements in favour of such change had started long before in a Catholic Enlightenment which was distinct from the better-known anti-Christian Enlightenment. Monasticism, for example, had begun to decline before the Revolution, states were already trying to redirect some of the church's money into what seemed to be more useful channels, and toleration was becoming a public ideal. At the level of popular religious behaviour, public processions of flagellants, and the ringing of church bells in a thunderstorm would have ceased, revolution or no revolution, because sensible people preferred lightning-conductors and were learning to link flagellation with the sexual instinct.

In France, the Revolution discredited the reformers, as in more recent times Eastern European revolutions have discredited socialist reformers. The papacy, partly because of the deadweight of the Papal States in Italy which the popes could neither rule well nor relinquish, emerged from the Napoleonic Wars associated with the political Right in a way which (according to Chadwick) had not been typical of its past. The Vatican supported parties of 'order' against 'liberalism' and nationalism, because these parties offered support for the claims of the Roman Church in society. 'This link with order, and stance against "liberalism", was the curse which the Revolution bequeathed to the Popes.' This position was reinforced by the papal preference for censorship:

> a teaching office which *felt* toleration to be wicked was supreme governor of a Church where most of the members knew toleration as a necessity of life, German states, France, Holland and Belgium, some of the Latin American republics.[15]

The practical effect of the Revolution was to increase the power of the papacy within the Roman Church. At this point one would have liked a comparison, which Chadwick was well-equipped to make, between Catholicism and Anglicanism, which also moved closer to the political right after 1789 and also tried, as late as the 1860s, to censor the spread of new theological ideas, as in the case of Colenso, the bishop who doubted the Mosaic authorship of the Pentateuch. Throughout the nineteenth century, however, the papacy was more effective than the Anglican hierarchy in censoring new ideas, and part of the explanation may lie in the deeper anxiety left in the Catholic Church's consciousness by its disastrous experiences in the Revolutionary period.

Although Chadwick did not ignore the institutional church as itself a source of problems for Christianity, he preferred to think of the 'true ecclesia' as a remnant of pious and sensible men and women who understood the church less as the ruler than as the servant of people. He asserted a continuity of Catholic reformers which persisted almost in spite of the popes. These men and women were not 'liberals', but they wanted a stronger parish life and worship, better educated priests, and improved public education freed from Jesuit dominance. These changes came in the nineteenth rather than in the eighteenth century, and revolution delayed as much as it facilitated them. The growth or decadence of piety, the rise or fall in the quality of the priesthood, the degree of freedom and toleration for fresh theological exploration, emerged as the 'true' history of the church as far as Chadwick was concerned. Everything else was almost as secular as the truly secular events which interrupted this spiritual history and sometimes seemed about to annihilate it. Chadwick's reformers were aware that in the course of the eighteenth century the forms of Catholicism, as structure, doctrine and moral system, had been knocked about and found to be more brittle than anyone had expected; therefore the church, (here essentially the pious remnant), must penetrate behind the forms and renew its contact with its divine sources. Chadwick did not bring out the intellectual problems of such a renewal, because his separate treatment of Catholicism, looked at apart from Protestantism and without much mention of the anti-Christian enlightenment, meant that the intellectual history of eighteenth-century Christianity was bound to be described incompletely. He left the impression, however, that despite the efforts of the saving remnant the institutional Roman Church approached 1848, another year of revolution, as the prisoner rather than the redeemer of a society which held it locked into a right-wing political stance which fitted only too well with ideas of papal infallibility, order, and doctrinal intransigence. He found the reforming Catholics sympathetic, but the future lay more than he suggested in the hands of what he himself called popular Catholicism. This it was that produced the cult of the Sacred Heart in the eighteenth century, was to do equally creative things with Marian devotions in the following years, and which saw itself as the 'saving remnant' of the Catholic Church. Anglican church historians dislike a picture of the church as a conflict of religious forces; even Aubert and his associates preferred to see the pontificate of Pius IX as a conflict between Catholic truth and secular error; but the secular historian might say that the major struggle lay inside the Catholic Church itself between different forms of Catholics, and that in both periods the reforming party lost the contest.

This overall view of eighteenth- and nineteenth-century Catholicism was partially confirmed by the other important modern history of the church, the *Handbuch der Kirchengeschichte*, edited by Hubert Jedin and John Dolan. Contributors to the 'Church in the Age of Absolutism and Enlightenment',[16] the volume of the series which covered the eighteenth century, suggested that, taking the period from 1648 to 1789 as a whole, historians had put too much emphasis on factors which pointed toward the emergence of a secular society in which Christianity had lost the intellectual and moral leadership which it had still possessed at the beginning of the seventeenth century. This emphasis had meant the neglect of the history of spirituality, a field in which the *Handbuch* included popular Catholicism. Jansenism, for example, had originally protested against the purely political ecclesiasticism of the rulers of the French church, and had sought compensation in a new, Christocentric piety.[17] It was a tragedy for the church, the *Handbuch* said, that the religious energies generated in seventeenth-century France had been squandered in the Jansenist controversy of the following century. The political power-structure of the church had reacted brutally, causing Jansenism to take a more political form, especially when it expanded into Italy. As for the liturgy, what happened liturgically between the Council of Trent and the reforms of Pius X was now dismissed, and in a Catholic history at that, as decline. In the eighteenth century the Mass, out of touch with popular religion, was said to have become a spectacle in magnificent churches, where priests and acolytes performed a courtly ritual before a monstrance suspiciously like a sun. One cannot avoid the thought that liturgical fashions do not cease to change, and that something like the style of the eighteenth century will sooner rather than later return to favour, and that this adverse judgment is too obviously in line with mid-twentieth-century ideas about how the liturgy should be celebrated (or performed).

The *Handbuch* did not provide much more than a useful bibliography of the history of spirituality, and perhaps the unhappy influence of Pourrat, 'the first historian of spirituality', may be detected here. Pourrat laid down that whatever the various forms in which the religious life manifested itself, the same spiritual doctrine was always to be found. No doubt there had been schools of spirituality, such as the Dominican, the Franciscan and the Augustinian; and when Counter-Reformation Europe became more nationalistic, national schools of spirituality also developed – but all these schools, in so far as they were 'Catholic', taught the same fundamental spirituality, whatever the differences in style and presentation. Pourrat's theoretical stand-point made for monotony, and begged the question as to whether or not the seventeenth and eighteenth centuries saw attempts at a radical reappraisal of Catholic ideas of holiness.[18] As a result, the contributors to the *Handbuch* gave most of their space to the sophisticated teaching of individual mystical theologians, ignoring the powerful currents of popular religious feeling and practice which continued to express themselves through the Catholic Church.

More usefully, parallels were drawn with Protestantism,

particularly with the Church of England and Methodism, as part of a common search for Christian answers to the emergence of modern society. Methodism, here interpreted entirely in terms of its founder, John Wesley, and as though popular religion did not exist in Hanoverian England, was described as creating an attractive, if fragile, synthesis between the Catholic ethic of sanctification and the Protestant doctrine of grace.[19] This view might perhaps be traced back to the Jesuit, Maximin Piette who, in *La réaction Wesleyenne* (1926, ET, *John Wesley and the Evolution of Protestantism*, 1937), interpreted Wesleyanism as an inevitable reaction in the direction of Catholicism from the extreme individualism which Protestantism had reached by the end of the seventeenth century. Piette said that the vital conversion-experience of John Wesley's life was that which happened in 1725, and that it could be attributed to his study of Catholic authors like Thomas à Kempis.[20] On the other hand, the Anglican historian, V. H. H. Green regarded Wesley's development as the natural outcome of his 'Anglicanism', and said that in 1738 (the date of the 'evangelical' conversion preferred by Methodist writers) 'in the Moravian sense of an instantaneous change and renewal Wesley was not indeed converted . . . the ideas and habits of the next fifty years were already fixed'.[21] This inter-denominational struggle for the soul of Wesley is not very convincing. The wisest interpretation of eighteenth-century Wesleyanism may be in terms of the way in which religious divisions reflected the social divisions made in English society in the first half of the sixteenth century and perpetuated into the eighteenth by the Civil War and its aftermath. Piette, Green and others have concentrated on John Wesley's personal development as though this provided the key to the formation of the Wesleyan societies, but they were more than a reflection of Wesley's personality, they expressed deep-rooted passions of a social kind with which Wesley himself had little to do. The 'church-history' style of the *Handbuch*, and of the authorities on which it largely relied, was too enclosed within an ecclesiastical sub-culture to capture the complicated origin and growth of Wesleyanism.

This impression of the *Handbuch's* limitations is confirmed by looking at the ninth volume of the Jedin-Dolan *History*, which covers the years from 1878 to 1914.[22] Here the contributors did their best to measure the impact of nineteenth-century social and industrial change on the Catholic Church. For them, however, the question took the form: had Catholicism successfully offered an alternative form of society – in effect, a return to some form of Christendom – or had the church only 'asserted itself defensively against modern society, whether 'liberal' or socialist? Oskar Kohler admitted that there was a degree of hysteria in the Vatican's fanatical opposition to Freemasonry, which was denounced as part of an international 'liberal' conspiracy against Christianity, but his apology for Catholic antisemitism, which he explained by saying that 'a subcutaneous antisemitism in the history of the Church surfaced because of the animosity of liberal, Jewish writers against the Church',[23] effectively repeated the kind of language familiar in the late nineteenth century and after. What was characteristic here was the extension of 'liberal' as a pejorative term from the economic 'liberalism' of the nineteenth century to 'liberalism' in general, meaning all ideas which could be said to have stemmed from the eighteenth-century Enlightenment, which had replaced the Reformation as the chief source of the modern troubles of the church. Paradoxically, Catholics influenced by this antiliberalism sometimes ended by associating with Marxism, if not with Marxists: the lines of authoritarianism lay close together. But the *Handbuch* failed altogether to analyse the problem as to how this defensive-aggressiveness became the dominant Catholic attitude to the modern world down to the Second Vatican Council, and seems to have recovered its nerve, if not all its old ascendancy, under Pope John Paul II.

The role of the papacy in the process was another factor which the *Handbuch* under-examined. There was the apologetic implication that the strengths of one pope balanced the weaknesses of another, so that Leo XIII corrected the mistakes of Pius IX and Benedict XV those of Pius X. This idea permitted the church historian to retain a vestige of the theological premise of providential direction. Yet Roger Aubert conceded that the Holy See did not try seriously enough to curb the general tendency of European Catholics to fall under sway of nationalist movements, and he left the impression that the papacy was ready to tolerate extremist groups if they offered support of some kind to the church. This impression was only increased by the Holy See's benevolence towards Action Francaise and the non-Catholic Charles Maurras, a bitter pioneer of racialist politics. In an interesting discussion of events leading up to the outbreak of the First World War Roger Aubert said that Pius X, who died on 19 August 1914, deeply sympathized with Austria's intransigent policy towards Serbia, not least because the Austro-Hungarian Empire was by that time the only large Catholic state in Europe.[24] Pius X was also criticized by Jakob Baumgartner for his comparative indifference to the missionary activity of the Catholic Church outside Europe.[25] It is difficult, in reading this volume of the *Handbuch*, to believe that Pius's policies were divinely overruled for good. One feels that the contributors to Jedin-Dolan would like to believe, with Owen Chadwick, that the work of a chosen few justifies the existence of the ecclesia in history; but that even the thought of Vatican II, far out of mind when Pius X died in 1914, offered them inadequate compensation for the shortcomings of the past.

2

From the General to the Particular: Early Modern Europe 1500–1800

The historiography of 'early modern Europe' – the historical period invented to cope with the slow detachment of the nineteenth century from the history of its predecessors – is best approached by making a distinction between 'committed' and 'uncommitted' historians. By 'committed historian' one means here historians who take a specifically 'Christian' view of their material, who accept in advance the primacy of ideas in history, especially when these ideas are religious: who say, in effect, that 'religious' events require a 'religious' explanation. This means that if the historian is Protestant, for example, he assumes that the driving force behind the Reformation was what he might call the 'openness' of Luther and Calvin (about Zwingli he tends to have doubts) to the prompting of spiritual forces, more specifically the urging of the Holy Spirit. In the past Catholic historians, however, have tended to regard the Reformation as a disaster to the extent that it succeeded; in the case of the English Reformation Catholic historians still argue that the Protestant triumph was the result of governmentally-applied compulsion. Still other Catholic historians subsume the Protestant Reformation as a whole in a general and essentially Catholic movement of European 'christianization', which began in the fifteenth and extended well into the eighteenth century. 'Committed' history is still deeply rooted in much of the academic world, above all in Germany, where a recent commentator said that 'the strength of the theological faculties, their explicit confessional allegiances, and the tight grip which they have exercised over ecclesiastical history has prevented the emergence of a confessionally neutral, sociologically informed, history of religion'.[1]

This distinction between 'confessional history', and historical writing which is 'neutral, sociologically informed', is one way of contrasting what I have in mind by separating the 'committed' from the 'uncommitted', though apart from the inevitable hesitation about the possibility of 'neutrality', one has also to beware of the dangers of combining 'confessional' and 'sociological' into what French historians call 'religious sociology', a methodology which is far from being uncommitted, but suborns sociology to the task of rescuing institutional Christianity from decline. In general, uncommitted historians are either indifferent to the religious content of events – for example, they treat the Protestant and Catholic Reformations as of no great significance in the history of Early Modern Europe, or else they are committed to some specifically non-Christian philosophy of history. On the one hand, they may try to produce 'neutral' narrative and explanation; on the other, they may, for instance, work out a Marxist interpretation of the apparently religious past.

We shall look at the Marxist understanding of the Reformation first, because committed historians cold-shouldered it for most of the century: this was not an attitude peculiar to church historians, but one aspect of the neglect of Marxist analysis in Western universities down to about 1945. Marxist historians rejected any idealist interpretation of the Renaissance/Reformation. A 'religious' event did not require a 'religious' explanation, because the religious system of ideas and actions was the intellectual and emotional, or ideological case for what happened on other grounds. The early modern period, as it came gradually to be called, produced an early bourgeois revolution, whose ideology was Protestant. Luther represented a bourgeois attack on the power of the clergy, and he was supported by territorial rulers whose own interests coincided with change. Then, in 1525, came a popular movement, the Peasants War, which radicalized the situation: a deeply alarmed Luther, realizing that the bourgeoisie had lost control of the situation, shifted his support to the princes, who institutionalized a new politically harmless Lutheranism at the same time as they crushed the revolution itself. This argument, which can be found initially in Friedrich Engels's remarkable work, *Der Deutsche Bauernkrieg* (1850, ET 1926) reached an orthodox climax in a book by a Russian historian, M. M. Smirin, *Die Volksreformation des Thomas Munzer und der grosse Bauernkrieg* (1956[2]). Smirin said that the goal of the early bourgeois revolution was the formation from below of a unified national German state, but East German scholars interpreted the movement in more strictly economic terms, as the overcoming of the restrictions which feudalism placed on private property: the 'peasants war' involved the well-to-do peasantry, and drew support from similar groups in German cities. The Marxist point of view was powerfully reinforced in the course of the commemoration of the four hundred and fiftieth anniversary of the Bauernkrieg in 1975, when it was clear that the East German régime would be happy to incorporate Luther into its own recreation of the German past which culminated, of course, in present-day East Germany. Up to this time committed historians had largely ignored the Marxist version of the Reformation, and had concentrated on Luther as a *religious* hero, treating his behaviour during the Bauernkrieg as an eccentric event of no religious or political significance, like the extraordinarily fierce, apparently unmotivated, attacks which he made on the Jews towards the end of his life, attacks which nevertheless had a tragic influence on the development of antisemitism in Germany.

German Marxist scholarship became available in English rather slowly, especially when compared with the steady flow into English of German studies of Luther's theology, but R. W. Scribner and Gerhard Benecke edited a useful survey in *The German Peasant War of 1525: New Viewpoints* (1979). Orthodox historians now found Luther contrasted unfavourably with Thomas Munzer, the unflinching leader of the people's revolution. The new approach violated the purity of the concept of a 'religious', Protestant Reformation, but committed scholars increasingly admitted that powerful waves of German nationalism and anti-papal feeling, together with the number and military strength of German cities, played a vital role in the Reformation's actual survival.[2] An excellent account of the problems involved was given by Peter Blickle in *The Revolution of 1525* (1977)).[3]

Blickle was sceptical of any deep-laid connection between the Lutheran Reformation as such and the Bauernkrieg: he saw the war as first of all the result of a complicated pattern of long-standing socio-economic grievances, though he admitted that it was not easy, from the existing records, to establish what the pattern had been. Blickle tried to clarify the question as to whether 'the peasants falsely understood the central assertions of the Reformation in a "carnal" sense, or whether they only wanted to improve their economic and social position under the pretext of the Gospel'. This interpretation (which protected Luther from responsibility for the outbreak of violence) employed the distinction between élite religion (the Reformers) and popular culture (the peasants), according to which the élitists had lofty religious motives, whereas the peasants combined superstition and self-interest. 'The only way to keep this interpretation afloat', Blickle wrote, 'would be to affirm the Lutheran Reformation as the only Reformation'. Lutheran (and Calvinist) scholars have always left the impression that only the kind of Protestantism which derived from their Reformer was true Protestantism: the rest was deviation. Blickle continued: 'As soon as one certifies Zwingli and the South German humanists as independent reformers – and there can be no doubt of that – then one has to agree that the Revolution of 1525 was an unfolding of the Reformation itself.' The peasants acted within the Zwinglian-Humanist understanding of the Reformation; they were quite capable of criticizing their socio-political environment in the light of what they believed to be reformed Christianity. 'Just because the Reformers could derive their ethics from theological premises and then tell the state how it would have to change is no reason to value their deductive procedure more highly than the thought of peasants', Blickle said. And he went on, 'To the contrary. The relatively loose and arbitrary nature of the reformers' arguments is obvious if one considers that from the same theological starting-point the dialectical encounter with the real conditions of life could produce completely divergent ethical and political ideas.'[4] The peasants had genuine grievances, and could find a valid theological language in which to express them: Luther's reaction against them was not the betrayal of an early-bourgeois revolution, it was the horrified anger of the priest-intellectual when he finds that he no longer controls the behaviour of the laity, and it was not an event which can be regarded as extraneous to the Reformation.

The long-delayed effect of Marxist interpretations of the history of Europe in the sixteenth century has been to make much of the committed writing on the Reformation look anaemic and one-sided. Nevertheless, the campaign to convert the Reformation into a by-product of the slow change from the feudal to the capitalist form of society, ingenious though it was, has run out of steam. That does not mean that the shift from theology to social politics, from the excessively-studied personalities of Luther and Calvin to the problem of what human life, religious and secular, was remotely like in the sixteenth century can easily be reversed. Historical attention has been swinging away from the Reformation-as-theology to the examination of such concepts as 'popular religion', 'anticlericalism', 'secularization', and so forth.

The shift which has been taking place in Reformation studies (outside Germany) can be illustrated by Thomas Brady's criticism of what he called 'romantic idealism' in the more traditional scholarship of the period. By 'romantic idealism' he meant the view

> that behind the phenomena of history there lies an unfathomable essence whose progressive self-unfolding constitutes the true meaning of history, and these essences or ideas can only be suggested, intuited, contemplated, or wondered at, not understood. Applied to [the sixteenth century] this means the hegemony of theology over history in the form of the belief in the Reformation as the 'breakthrough' of an eternal 'Reformation-principle', rather than the appearance of new forms of European Christianity whose character and destinies have to be explained by historical causes . . . Reformation history raised Luther's theology above mortal time.[5]

The committed church historian is wide open to criticism for the 'hegelianism' latent in his belief in the essential unity of Christian history, and in the eternal truth of Christianity's central propositions. He becomes even more vulnerable if it appears that the 'hegemony of theology' has been made to serve more time-bound purposes. Brady suggested that the twentieth-century Luther-renaissance was 'basically a special form of ideological warfare against the Weimar Republic, in the government of which the two chief enemies, Catholicism and Social Democracy, were allied'.[6] This suggestion was a broad one, but ever since the German revolutions of 1848 Protestantism and German Nationalism had moved steadily towards one another, their meeting facilitated by the Prussian (Bismarckian) absorption of the other German states by 1870. A 'timeless Luther' was one of the guardians of what was, in the end, a Protestant definition of Germanness, seen at its starkest in Bismarck's late nineteenth-century campaign to shatter the political influence of Roman Catholicism and of working-class socialism in Germany. The collapse of the German Empire in 1918 left power temporarily in the hands of the previously excluded groups, and the Luther-renaissance played its part, as Brady implied, in the struggle to restore right-wing Protestant nationalism to power. The extension of the new interest in Luther to England after 1945 (see, for example, *Luther's Progress to the Diet of Worms* (1951), and *The Righteousness of God* (1953), both by E. G. Rupp), was more a matter of ecclesiastical than of secular politics. The British Protestant Free Churches were in decline after 1918, and the contemporary image of Luther was distorted by almost a century of Anglo-Catholic propaganda against the Reformation.[7] *The Catholicity of Protestantism* (ed. R. N. Flew, R. E. Davies, 1950), was an official Free Church symposium which tried to rehabilitate Luther (and Calvin) as essentially 'Catholic' in their understanding of the doctrine of the church, in the hope that this would strengthen the hand of the Free Churches in their ecumenical negotiations with the Anglican Church. The revival of Reformation scholarship in Britain came too late, however, to affect the ecclesiastical conflict, because Catholic polemic increasingly traced the ills of modern civilization not to the sixteenth, but to the eighteenth century, a change of direction which embarrassed English Protestant intellectuals, many of whom felt obliged to defend the Enlightenment against its new critics.

Not all of the uncommitted social historians who were interested in the history of Western religion between 1400 and 1800 were primarily Marxist in orientation. Some of them showed the influence of the French *Annales* tradition, a school of historians which had its roots in early twentieth-century sociology (especially the work of Durkheim), and which emphasized the study of what were called 'mentalités' – roughly, the study of the total state of mind of a given period or group, but with an additional attention to economics and to quantitative research which might seem to reduce the historian's ability to analyse distinctively *religious* phenomena – always supposing that these occurred.[8] Transferred to the study of the history of religion in the Early Modern period, the *Annales* method has tended to produce generalized images of an alleged collective psychology in a decidedly static society, and these images are easily, but not always convincingly, manipulated against a background of vast stretches of time. The approach may be described as radically different from the study of the past as the search for a significant stream of events, or for a description of 'what happened', or for narrative.

The link with the history of religion came about through the growing interest in 'popular culture'. 'Popular' is not a term easy to define in this context, and it must be kept in mind that here the word excludes, strictly speaking, modern 'mass-culture', the product of an entertainment industry which has grown prodigiously in this century, but which many of these scholars would describe as inferior to the 'popular culture' of the Early Modern type. The use of the word 'popular', however, does suggest both 'widespreadness' and some degree of social inferiority as between subject and ruling groups; another phraseology, deriving from the Italian Marxist political philosopher, Gramsci, distinguishes subordinate from dominant classes. In effect, the validity (or the usefulness) of the concept of 'popular culture' depends upon the alleged existence (for, in the form alleged, it may not have existed at all) of some alternative, less widespread, perhaps more highly intellectualized and internalized, certainly more expensive, and in any event *different* culture. As such, the idea has been more popular among secular historians with a political bias than among committed church historians. Secular historians do not need Marxist promptings to sympathize with the idea of an unofficial, deep-rooted and popular culture which at least to some extent was alienated from the culture of the dominating groups in Western society. Secular historians do not, of course, take the history of Western religion at its own orthodox valuation; they are bound to regard 'religion', to the extent that it is an identifiably separate area of human behaviour, as a matter of the satisfaction of subjective psychological needs which have no supernatural significance.

'Popular religion', for historians like, for example, Peter Laslett, really meant an aspect of the behaviour of a rural society which has now disappeared in the smoke of industrialization (see his *The World We Have Lost*, 1965). For an equally romantic, but more politically-minded historian like Edward Thompson, 'plebian religion' seemed still to exist as a potential source of strength for the revolutionary people; in Thompson's *The Making of the English Working-Class* (1965) the workers were described as being betrayed by a debilitating version of official evangelical Protestantism in the shape of Wesleyan Methodism. This resembles Roger Mandrou's picture of France in *De La Culture populaire en France au 17e et 18e siècles: La Bibliotheque Bleue de Troyes* (1964). Mandrou suggested, on the basis of an analysis of the kind of literature supplied in this period by colporteurs to ordinary people, that popular culture helped to impose on the subordinate classes an escapist world-view compounded of fatalism, the occult and the marvellous, a mixture which encouraged them in political docility. Similar material was used a few years later, however, by another French scholar, Geneviève Bollême, to argue the existence of a spontaneous popular religious outlook deeply attached to the image of the poverty and humanity of Jesus (see her *Les Almanachs populaires au 17e et 18e siècles*, 1969). This technique has been criticized. It involves the assumption that one may correlate the mentality of publishers and vendors with that of their readers or hearers; and although one can isolate themes in popular literature, it does not follow that these themes really existed as part of a structure of popular thought.[9]

Nevertheless, the concept of conflict between an 'official' religion and an unofficial, or 'popular', religion, itself sometimes presented as largely autonomous, is deeply embedded in the secular historian's treatment of European religion between 1500 and 1800. This can be seen in Peter Burke's influential book, *Popular Culture in Early Modern Europe* (1978). Burke, who was an admirer of the French historian, Lucien Febvre, an important figure in the *Annales* mythology, said that in the late sixteenth and early seventeenth centuries an élite group, which for these purposes consisted chiefly of Catholic and Protestant clerics, tried systematically 'to reform the culture of ordinary people'.[10] On the secular side, this meant an attack on the theatre, on popular preaching, on carnivals (whose 'significance seems to have got a little out of hand recently'), and on any kind of feast-day which brought the common people together to enjoy themselves. The religious element of the campaign was the gradual disappearance of religious plays, a change of preaching-style (the late medieval popular sermon was inherently theatrical, and the 'reformers' distrusted the sermon as a branch of the entertainment industry), and a more specifically Protestant abolition of saints days which was echoed in a Catholic drive to reduce their celebration to a strictly pious form. At the same time, the Protestants made the Bible available in the vernacular as far as possible, adding vernacular catechisms and hymns. The overall effect was that, whereas in about 1500 there had been a popular culture in which the educated shared, by about 1800 the nobility, the professional groups including the clergy, and the merchants had largely withdrawn from the popular culture, abandoning it to the poorer classes. Once the élite had downgraded the popular culture they then started to take an intellectual (or antiquarian) interest in what now became the strange customs and beliefs of the lower orders, and to collect folk stories and folklore. Peter Burke did not identify 'popular culture' with anything in the nature of a distinct, unofficial 'popular religion'. He had the obligatory chapter on 'Carnival', but he followed the general line of scholars like Roger Caillois (*Les Jeux et les hommes*, 1967), that the apparent disorder of the carnival-season was a source of social order; similarly, Keith Thomas, in *Religion and the Decline of Magic* (1971), thought that carnivals operated as safety-valves for the disadvantaged in a hierarchical society. That a comparatively small group of men and women, Catholic and Protestant, seeking to impose what may be called 'the godly discipline' on whole societies, restricted carnivals and charivaris and other occasions of communal pleasure as much as possible seems to be agreed by both secular and committed historians; but why they did so, what sort of resistance they encountered, and how far they were successful are matters of greater uncertainty.

Generally speaking, secular historians of religion have worked with a ready-made theory about the development of European religious culture.[11] Obviously, they have to account for the presence of religious language and ritual without recourse to the idea of the supernatural. They have therefore supposed, with some help from the anthropologists, the existence of a predominantly peasant society, technologically backward down to the end of the eighteenth century, and imprisoned psychologically (so it is claimed) in states of anxiety and fear. The appearance of ritual, religion, magic and superstition can then be interpreted as ways of (*a*) providing what was bound to be a spurious supplementary technology, and (*b*) more genuinely emotional release and consolation. This ignorant, illiterate, and religiously 'prechristian' peasantry did not constitute the whole society; the slowly growing towns contained a slightly more educated population, which in its turn accepted the hegemony of a small élite, within which the Christian priesthood had found their place. The psychological make-up of the élite was presumably similar to that of the peasantry, but they were much more sophisticated linguistically, and from time to time were tempted to criticize what seemed to them a strain of crudeness and materialism in Christian liturgy and symbol. This is sometimes called a two-tier theory of culture, and in some versions there is no question of a two-way cultural exchange or any positive 'peasant' influence on the 'dominant' clauses. However, in *The Cheese and the Worms* (ET 1980), Carlo Ginzburg, regarded his Friulian miller, Menocchio, who was executed as a heretic in North Italy in about the year 1599, as a representative of an ancient peasant oral culture which carried, in its religious outlook, a distinctly non-Christian streak of pantheism. This tradition, however obscurely, had provided food for a dissident element in high European culture, which in its turn produced unorthodox books, a few of which Menocchio seems to have read, in whole or in part. The Russian structuralist, Mikhail Bakhtin, also thought that peasant culture could be creative; he interpreted Rabelais' writings as emerging from an optimistic, critical background located in the subordinate culture (see *L'oeuvre de François Rabelais et la culture populaire au Moyen Age et sous la Renaissance*, French tr. 1970).

These scholars shared Peter Burke's view of how the relationship between these distinct cultures changed after 1500. Ginzburg said that the German Peasants War and the Anabaptist occupation of Münster in 1525 were the decisive events; Muchembled[12] thought that the change took place in the fierce excitement of the Catholic Reform movement later in the sixteenth century, but both saw the élite as rejecting any further positive contact with the culture below, and seeking to change, and in its own view, to raise, the moral perceptions and the religious behaviour of the peasant communities and their equivalent in the cities. The word 'acculturation' has sometimes been borrowed from anthropology to describe this social aggression on the part of an élite which seeks to impose its own socio-religious system on a subject population. The 'acculturation' analogy is not well taken,[13] because anthropologists normally use the term to cover encounters between races, not between classes within what would usually be thought of as a single society, but there is no doubt that between the early sixteenth century and the early eighteenth century the dominant classes in Europe made a deliberate effort to modify popular religious behaviour so that it conformed more closely to their own pattern. In fact, though the historians we have been discussing regard the French Revolution as a kind of ultimate disaster, the End of Early Modern Europe, nevertheless the nineteenth-century bourgeoisie vigorously renewed the campaign to enforce the 'godly discipline', this time on a predominantly urban working-class, but also on rural workers.

A committed historian, like Jean Delumeau in *Catholicism between Luther and Voltaire* (1971, ET 1977), accepted many of these assumptions and used them to propose the hypothesis that on the eve of the Reformation Europe was only superficially christianized, and perhaps not Christian at all. Delumeau belonged to what he felt was a new school of church historians, who had largely abandoned the traditional emphasis on the study of the history of 'belief', i.e. theology, in favour of the employment of the methods of 'religious sociology'; they were much more interested in religious behaviour, individual and social, than in the abstract history of religious ideas. This approach also meant playing down what may be called the 'high politics' of the churches, their involvement in the secular politics of their time; Delumeau himself regarded the Catholic Church's appetite for social and political power as the tragic error of Christian history down to the sixteenth century. He interpreted the Protestant Reformation and the Catholic Counter-Reformation as forming together, despite their evident conflicts, a single process which aimed at 'spiritualizing' Western religion by removing from it magic, superstition, 'paganism' and so forth. It is significant that when another Catholic historian, John Bossy, introduced Delumeau's book to English readers, he objected to the French writer's dismissal of medieval Christianity. There had been, he said, 'a Christianity of the illiterate', a sensible reminder that an oral culture is not bound to be ignorant and irrational, and he added that there was evidence that despite their shortcomings 'the unreformed Church and uninformed Christian of pre-Reformation days had some sort of grip on the idea that Christianity meant loving one's neighbour'.[14] Bossy was perhaps more sensitive than Delumeau to the point that if the medieval Catholic Church had not succeeded in christianizing Europe, then the Protestant Reformers had a powerful case for making a fresh start: the Catholic Counter-Reformation then becomes not only a Catholic revival but, as Delumeau was himself ready to admit, part of a movement of evangelization shared with a Protestantism which would have to be regarded as more than a historical aberration, a blind-alley.

In practice, Delumeau and Bossy were in disagreement not only about the nature, but also about the consequences of the Catholic renewal. For Bossy, the eighteenth century was a period of sound if slow Catholic growth in England, a positive recovery from the shock of the loss of social acceptance in the Tudor and Stuart epoch, and a laying of foundations on which Newman and Wiseman would build further in the nineteenth century. For Delumeau, looking at the eighteenth century on the basis of French experience, 'dechristianization', the collapse of later eighteenth-century Catholicisim in France, was an undeniable event, which had to be explained. It is interesting to compare his view with that of another distinguished French historian, Michel Vovelle, the author of *Religion et Révolution: La Déchristianisation de l'An II* (1976). Delumeau did not want to accept that this dechristianization was the work of a deeply anti-Catholic popular mood: instead, he said that the Catholic revival which had begun in the aftermath of the Council of Trent had gradually slackened in the late seventeenth century, so that dechristianization meant no more than the break-up of an imposed Catholic conformity in the wake of war and revolution. Vovelle, on the other hand, very much the uncommitted historian, rejected the position of what he called 'conservative' historians – that is, committed Catholic writers – that dechristianization was just a campaign launched by a small group of impassioned revolutionaries in the delirium of the initial triumphs of the new order. Vovelle argued that dechristianization spread on a large scale, that its real centre was not in Paris but in rural France. Dechristianization evolved its own language and liturgy. Vovelle commented:

> The promenade of the charivari, the incineration of Caramentran, the carnivalesque banquet, derision and a mixture of genres: we really have the impression from these examples of taking part in a revenge of popular culture on the constraints of the discipline imposed by the Tridentine reconquest.[15]

Vovelle regarded dechristianization as 'one of the last expressions (and the last in violent form) of a subordinate culture which refused to disappear'.[16]

Committed Catholic historians, who used to trace all modern calamities to the Protestant Reformation, now prefer to blame them on the Enlightenment, and Immanuel Kant has often replaced Martin Luther as the ideological enemy par excellence. They write as though the French Revolution should not have happened, and as though, even if it did happen, it was never really to be accepted as a revolution. Forced, nevertheless, to account for the continued decline of Catholic social power in modern Europe, Catholic historians constantly invoke the image of a sudden, unforeseen, irrational and revolutionary irruption which seized political power and imposed a secular culture, from which Europe has never quite succeeded in liberating itself.[17] In this version of the past, the French Revolution becomes an unacceptable, almost extra-historical event, demonic perhaps, which somehow shattered a divinely underwritten, though not apparently permanently guaranteed, pattern of society. (For it is certain that the revolutionary society itself cannot have been divinely underwritten – and the same goes for Soviet Russia in the late Modern period.) Transformation of the holders of power released forces which had been held in check, beneficially, by the traditional religio-political system of the *ancien regime*. Committed historians may, of course, retain the triumphalist position, and say that the Enlightenment and the revolutionary movements prove the accuracy of the older judgment that the Protestant Reformation destroyed the proper balance of Western society. Delumeau, however, in his sketch of modern European history, interpreted the sixteenth century as a time in which the various Christian institutions, Catholic and Protestant, strove to master those forces in society which had never fully internalized Christianity – there was opportunity rather than disaster.

In the eighteenth century, however, Catholicism in Europe paid (in the shape of the revolutionary triumphs) for the church's obsession with power, wealth and, paradoxically, an ascetic style of self-destructive piety which, for all its undoubted heroism (some part of which was either sadism or masochism) centred on a God of fear, not on a God of love. The revolt against Christianity which grew in the seventeenth and eighteenth centuries was essentially a protest against the image of a cruel God which had been spread by a long-standing Augustinian orthodoxy. 'Have we not for long called "Christianity" ', he said, 'what was in fact a mixture of practices and doctrines with frequently but little connexion with the gospel message? – which should have been about a God of love'.[18] On this basis dechristianization would become a misnomer, because even in the eighteenth century Christianity was still, apparently, rather hard to find, and certainly not to be loosely identified with the visible Catholic worshippers of the period. Delumeau quoted with approval the words of Gabriel le Bras, the father of 'religious sociology':

> We must insist on this frequently neglected truth: the fulfilment of periodic (religious) duties does not constitute genuine, deep-rooted Christianity. The man who believes in the divinity of

> Christ and eternal life, the man who observes the commandments even by habit, is better than the regular mass-goer who observes the law by habit but does not practise the virtues. Attitudes like these can characterize entire populations. To be dechristianized, they must at some stage have been christianized.[19]

The dangers of Le Bras' position are obvious. He could say that 'attitudes like these can characterise entire populations', but he could not demonstrate such a judgment sociologically. The religious sociologist can measure the figures for mass-attendance, or at any rate he can do so to the extent that statistics, which may or may not have been entirely trustworthy, have survived from earlier centuries, but he cannot establish figures for mass-devotion, so to speak, still less the figures for any effective influence of mass attendance on individual behaviour. A recent American study of Lutheran education in the sixteenth century has given added point to this criticism. Gerald Strauss, in *Luther's House of Learning: Indoctrination of the Young in the German Reformation* (1978), used Lutheran visitation records to argue that Lutheran education failed, by its own sixteenth-century standards, precisely in the task of indoctrination, so that the level of popular religious commitment remained much as it had been before 1500. And R. W. Scribner, in *For the Sake of Simple Folk: Popular Propaganda for the German Reformation* (1981), shifted attention from the 'high art' of the period to what was aimed at a wider audience, and concluded that although Lutheran visual propaganda successfully reflected popular anticlericalism and the widespread desire for a less institutionalized and more lay religious style, and shaped an image of Luther as the German prophet which lasted well into the nineteenth century, it also failed to transform popular culture, to give it what a modern middle-class historian would recognize as deep religious commitment. There is perhaps a trace of naiveté in a historical approach which supposes that mass-religion (not quite the same as popular religion) could be more than a matter of ceremonial, but historians influenced by anthropology are apt to exaggerate the positive content of ceremonial (ritual) in any case.

The 'religious sociologist' is, in fact, in a difficult position. If one appeals to a 'hard-core' definition of religious institutions in periods of decline (after all, what matters, as Le Bras said, is 'the quality of those who attend mass, not the quantity'), then one should also abide by it in periods of apparent growth; one is not entitled to chop and change in order to protect the prestige of the institution. There is little hard evidence, in historical terms, that the 'hard core' has varied substantially between one period and another, though kinds of religious activity may have changed. But the behaviour of the church-as-an-institution has to be described and analysed by using the surviving evidence of the visible behaviour of the hard core and soft majority taken together. Jean Delumeau wrote recently that

> one can grant that it is necessary to intergrate statistics into the history of religion, and yet at the same time feel that faith and love will always retain an unquantifiable character. At best, one measures outward indications of faith and collective attitudes, not states of soul. In any case, what did mass church-attendance signify in times of compulsory religion? Voltaire communicated more often than Pascal. More generally, one must underline the shortcomings of statistical totals when one is trying to assess the condition of Christendom.[20]

These are two quite different things: to treat 'dechristianization' as the breaking-down of a hard core, a rare event in theory and one for which we perhaps lack evidence in modern Western religious history; and treating 'dechristianization' as the dissipation of the 'soft majority', a possible event which can be seen to have happened in practice, but one for which, with every respect to Gabriel Le Bras and others, 'dechristianization' is a perfectly proper description.

The hard core may be thought of as those members of a religious institution for whom the institution has become the existential centre of attention, as distinct from the soft majority, for whom the relationship to the institution is essentially social. The hard core is not necessarily an élite; indeed, the idea of an élite group, including many ecclesiastics, seeking to reform the culture – including the religious culture – of ordinary people, has a dubious ring about it. The brutal witch-burnings of the sixteenth and seventeenth centuries did not happen because either Protestants or Catholics disbelieved in the Devil or rationally condemned the concept of witchcraft, but because the persecutors felt a need (which might elsewhere be classed as 'primitive') to destroy what they regarded as hostile. The act of destruction was not rational. Even Carlo Ginzburg, in his otherwise subtle study of the Friulian miller, Menocchio, who was also destroyed – in his case for talking heretically – misses the enormity of what took place. Ginzburg concluded:

> The supreme head of Catholicism, the pope himself, Clement VIII, was bending towards Menocchio, who had become a rotten member of Christ's body (Ginzburg did not, of course, mean to accept this judgment), to demand his death. In these very months in Rome the trial against the former monk, Giordano Bruno, was drawing to a close. It is a coincidence that seems to symbolize the twofold battle being fought against both the high and the low in this period by the Catholic hierarchy in an effort to impose doctrines promulgated at the Council of Trent. This explains the persistence of the proceedings (against Menocchio), which are otherwise incomprehensible, against the old miller.[21]

Here the secular historian (Ginzburg) did his best for the committed historian, implying that the judgment, in effect the judicial murder, of Menocchio (like that of Servetus or Bruno) made sense when placed within the impersonal frame of ecclesiastical high politics. The committed Delumeau inevitably fell back on the defence of 'mentalités': during the Reformation and Counter-Reformation, he said, the promoters of christianization, following the lead of Augustine, called Satanism (witchcraft) what was really residual paganism; he also claimed, however, that fear of the Devil decreased as the effects of the Protestant and Catholic revivals worked down to the parish-level in the second half of the seventeenth century. This argument seems confused. It was presumably 'christianization' which stimulated the sixteenth and seventeenth-century witch-hunts and which provided an ideology which justified the burning of women (after all, they were not in any meaningful sense 'witches', and the significant act was not the alleged witchcraft but the actual incineration). The Reformation and the Counter-Reformation went hand in hand with the French Wars of Religion, the Dutch-Spanish War, the Catholic conquest of South America and the Protestant invasion of North America, both of which had destructive results for the indigenous populations, the German Thirty Years War and the English Civil War (which was more of a war of religion than seems to have been noticed by two generations of secular historians obsessed with the far from gripping tale of the economic fortunes of the landed classes). One could perhaps say that fear of the Devil declined as the influence of the various religious reformers declined at the parish level, and that influence declined as the contradictions between Christian peace and Christian war became more glaringly evident. It hardly follows that this gradual amelioration (unless religious romanticism really wants to restore both suburban witchcraft and suburban witchburnings) was brought about by a religious élite which 'purified' popular religion. Neither official nor unofficial religion was 'purified'. R. C. Trexler, an American historian of sixteenth-century Florence, has sharply criticized historians of religion who have interpreted the period since 1500 as one in which rational, reflective religion gradually replaced an earlier irrational mixture of ignorance and superstition.[22]

Perhaps it is partly because professional historians easily became authorities in limited fields and so contributed to the inward-looking nature of the present-day academic culture, but there is a strange reluctance on the part of those concerned to recognize the importance of a Western classical ethical tradition which never combined completely with Western religion in its Christian post-classical forms, but which had at least as much influence on the changing moral perceptions of the élite in Early Modern Europe (Montaigne seems an obvious example) as had either official or unofficial religious movements. Social historians, however, dislike the contemplation of what may be represented as chains of ideas, preferring to stress the survival of rituals (which include, of course, the much romanticized carnival and charivari), because ritual is a group-activity and in the Durkheimian tradition to which so many of these scholars consciously or unconsciously belong, the significant elements of religious experience are to be found in the behaviour of groups rather than in the verbal articulation of doctrine. Such analysis skirts the possibility that most repetitions of a particular ritual may generate no common experience worth study at all, that ritual is, most of the time, a non-event. In the longer perspective of the late twentieth century, however, the prestige and influence of ideas like tolerance are seen, after their brief prominence in and after the *Siècle des Lumières*, to have faded, so that our communal behaviour, with its repeated return to savage warfare, resembles that of the later sixteenth and seventeenth centuries, rather than that of the eighteenth century. One guesses that our fresh emphasis on the value of ritual reflects the social need to bind local communities and battle-groups tighter together in order to reduce non-conformity, in war as well as in peace. Religions do not have to be true, in order to serve these purposes.[23]

These unhappy thoughts bring us back to the question of the Reformation and Counter-Reformation, and especially to the way in which committed historians have studied them. Perhaps the most striking change of the last twenty years has been the decline in interest in the history of the doctrinal disputes of the sixteenth century. This decline followed a period in which, in Britain, there had been a revival of enthusiasm for Luther and Calvin, which had produced, for example, E. G. Rupp's *Luther's Progress to the Diet of Worms* (1951) and *The Righteousness of God* (1953); *Calvin's Doctrine of Man* (1949) and *Kingdom and Church* (1956) by T. F. Torrance; and a long series of translations which made both men much more accessible to the English and American reader.[24] For all these writers what counted was not so much 'church history' as the attempt to restore the theological standing of the orthodox Protestant tradition, and especially of Calvinism, whose prestige had been irreparably shattered in the eighteenth and nineteenth centuries by the long sustained pressure of the kind of ethical tradition to which reference has been made above. For almost a generation, say from 1930 to 1960, the intellectual pietism of the Barthian school of theology and the soft-centred ecumenism of the 'biblical theologians' coincided with the anxieties of the Reformed Churches to forge a fresh image of John Calvin as at any rate a god-intoxicated man whose thought offered a basis for resistance to all kinds of modernism. In the 1930s orthodox theologians felt that what was required was a reassertion of the absoluteness of God, of the final divine authority of the Christian revelation, of the unquestionable need for everyone to belong to the Christian church in order to be saved. Theological, ethical and biblical criticism had made these assertions less plausible; an appeal to the authority of the great Reformers seemed a possible solution. The campaign sputtered out, however, and one can see why if one examines the standard biography of Calvin, by François Wendel: *Calvin, The Origin and Development of his Religious Thought* (1950, ET 1963).

Wendel repeated the stock defence of Calvin's share in the execution of the Unitarian intellectual, Michael Servetus in 1553,

> that it is contrary to a sound conception of history to try to apply our ways of judging and our moral criteria to the past. Calvin was convinced, and all the reformers shared his conviction, that it was the duty of the Christian magistrate to put to death blasphemers who kill the soul, just as they punished murderers who killed the body. [25]

There was more than one weakness in Wendel's position, beginning with the fallacy of 'mentalities', according to which the historian could confidently say that 'all the reformers' shared Calvin's point of view, when Sebastian Castellio, who must be thought of as a Calvinist theologian, condemned the execution of Servetus and pleaded for absolute toleration of opinions. Behind this lay the assertion, taken for granted in the Luther-Calvin revival, that these men defined the 'Protestant' theology, and that those who disagreed with them were deviant. But the problem is not only with the Calvin of the sixteenth century: one can understand, in a strictly external sense, how Calvin came to have Servetus eliminated. Wendel, however, was not only reconstructing, as far as that was possible, a 'Calvin of the sixteenth century', but, like other committed historians to whom I have referred, was recommending Calvin as a religious teacher for the twentieth century. Now it is not unreasonable to say that we should not take too seriously the claims of a religious leader who was willing to put men and women to death for their allegedly blasphemous views. And one does not shield Calvin from that objection by talking about a sixteenth-century 'mentality', because the problem of intolerance does not only belong to the past. Calvin's fusion of divine sovereignty with human power in the theocratic city-state of Geneva is a vision not too easy to revive in a society which has seen, only too frequently, the outcome of yielding to the coercion of ideological absolutism. Nevertheless, Calvin's assertion of divine omnipotence, of the right of the priesthood to a kind of political hegemony, and of the duty of the church to impose the so-called 'Godly discipline' on people in private life, has been a constitutive element in the formation of the nineteenth- and twentieth-century evangelical pietist sub-culture, which never ceases to pursue power with which to enforce its code of behaviour on society at large. These were the policies in which the Lutheran and Calvinist Churches most closely resembled Counter-Reformation Catholicism, which used different methods but for a similar end.[26]

In the case of Reformation studies, the return to a more critical theology in the 1960s cut off interest in a theology which required a high doctrine of biblical inspiration to become intellectually respectable, let alone persuasive. English scholarship, moreover, has not served Calvin very well. His sermons have not been translated; his letters are available only in an old and not entirely reliable version by D. Constable and M. Gilchrist (1858); his commentaries on the Old and New Testaments have fared better – for the New Testament there is a modern version edited by T. F. and D. W. Torrance – but these versions lack a full critical apparatus. No modern study of Calvinism has thrown much light on the nature of its socio-political decline in the seventeenth and eighteenth centuries. It hardly comes as a surprise to realize that little has been done to establish Calvin's intellectual relationship to his predecessors, whether in theology, philosophy, or mysticism. A few scholars have tackled the history of the development of Calvinist theology between Calvin's death and 1800: notably Brian Armstrong, *Calvinism and the Amyraut Heresy: Protestant Scholasticism and Heresy in Seventeenth-Century France* (1969); Olivier Fatio, *Méthode et Théologie, Lambert Daneau et les débats de la scholastique Réformée* (1976); and Richard Muller, *Christ and the Decree: Christology and Predestination in the developing soteriological Structure of Sixteenth-Century Reformed Theology* (1984).

Such subjects are something of an acquired taste. Secular historians, who increasingly dismiss the Reformation as a minor episode in Early Modern history, regard the subtle elaborations of later seventeenth-century Reformed theology as a minor, negative strand in the history of ideas; committed scholars, on the other hand, often disapprove of the Protestant return to a study of Aristotelian philosophy, because this allegedly meant a departure from the biblical basis of Calvin's theology. Protestant scholasticism, that is, lacked relevance to the modern Calvin-renascence. Lutheran theology after Luther has also been treated largely on confessional lines: the Formula and Book of Concord (1577, 1580) have been studied in terms of modern arguments about the nature of the Lutheran tradition and its contemporary application.

After so much talk of Calvinism as the theology of sovereignty it may seem paradoxical to find attributed to mid-sixteenth-century Calvinism (and not at all to Lutheranism) the origin of the modern ideology of revolution, the belief that the 'people' have an inherent right to resist a tyrannical government (among modern writers taking this view, see especially Michael Walzer, *The Revolution of the Saints*, 1965). This position has been rejected by Quentin Skinner, in *The Foundations of Modern Political Thought: The Age of the Reformation* (1978). Professor Skinner said that the traditional understanding of Luther as a political conservative who was willing to leave the kingdom of the earth to whoever chose to take it was incorrect, for when Luther had to face the political reality of what seemed an imminent Imperial armed attack on the Lutheran churches in 1530, both Luther and Melanchthon hastily constructed an intellectual defence of resistance, and therefore of revolution against one's admitted sovereign; in 1546 Lutheran theologians repeated and elaborated these arguments when Charles V attacked the Schmalkaldic League. Skinner also showed that similar ideas of the right of rebellion could be found in the medieval conciliar movement and that these had been developed in Catholic circles at the University of Paris by followers of Gerson and William of Ockham. Skinner accepted that most of the leading defenders of the right to revolution in the later sixteenth century in Holland and Scotland were Calvinists in practice, but said that the radical political theory was not itself distinctively Calvinist, nor was there, strictly speaking, a peculiarly Calvinist theory of revolution. Calvinist political writers in the 1550s drew on a tradition which had already existed in Catholic as well as Lutheran circles. The decisive factor on the Protestant side was not theological but political, because political events strained to breaking-point the theologically-based political passivity which had characterized the first phase of the Reformation. In the anti-liberal climate of the 1980s, of course, modern Calvinists may well prefer not to have primary responsibility for the theory of popular revolution.[27]

Martin Luther has never had as much influence on the British churches as Calvin, and it was unlikely that a theological renascence would be engendered by a fresh diffusion of his works, few of which had ever been translated into English. Luther, moreover, proved a difficult case for the committed historian to handle. For it was a question not of one Luther but of many, and of which Luther orthodox historians wanted to set up as the master of the Reformation.[28] At the beginning of the century Catholic scholarship had been given a new controversial vigour by H. Denifle, *Luther und Luthertum* (1904–1909), and H. Grisar, *Luther* (1911–12, ET 1914–1917): their books were published when the papal repression of Catholic Modernism was under way, and when Protestantism itself was being severely censured by Roman theologians as a source of modern heresy; Anglican orders had just been condemned as null and void by the Vatican in 1896. The discovery of Luther's pre-Reformation lectures on the *Epistle to the Romans*, lectures which permanently confused all theories of the great reformer's intellectual development by suggesting that his 'discovery' of the true nature of divine justification had occurred much earlier than at the crisis of the Reformation in 1517 (which he said had been the case, years later, as reported in the *Table-talk*), fuelled the controversy. These Catholic historians portrayed Luther as psychologically defective, an approach which was later borrowed by the French Catholic lay philosopher, Jacques Maritain, in a possibly more influential book, *Three Reformers* (1925), in which he dismissed Luther as a monk spiritually incapable of fulfilling the demands of the monastic system: Luther (Maritain suggested) confused his personal despair with the roots of Christianity, and what emerged theologically was a doctrine of grace without any concept of human freedom. Since the predestined man was sure of salvation, however, there was, paradoxically, no limit on the violence with which he might act in the interim.[29]

This version of Luther (essentially Denifle's) was important, because it shifted the historical emphasis from what Luther did to what Luther was like. Nineteenth-century Protestant historians had thought of him as the opponent of Catholic abuses, the hammer of the Vatican, and the reviver, theologically, of primitive Christianity. As far as they were concerned, the abuses were wrong, the papacy superfluous, and the theology scripturally accurate where it mattered, on the subject of justification by faith alone. As a person, therefore, Luther hardly counted, except that he was an ecclesiastical hero. His inner psychological make-up was left largely unexplored, because what stood out in Luther was not an identifiable personality, but an experience of grace. Now the Catholic post-Modernist attack on Luther; post-Modernist in the sense that it matched the hysterical attitude to Protestantism which dominated official Catholicism from Pius X until the Second World War, made the Reformation (as a disaster) result from Luther's disastrous inner being. Passionate and melancholy, his central doctrine mirrored his pessimistic temperament and spiritual experience. Strangely enough, but not so strangely when one remembers that this was to be the century of Vatican II, this 'Catholic' Luther gradually changed his character, becoming an anxious (but not unstable) monk whose search for personal deliverance, for certainty of salvation, was itself essentially Catholic, a spiritual questioning which a Catholicism true to itself would have instantly recognized and healed.[30]

It is on this basis that one returns to Jean Delumeau's understanding of the Reformation as essentially a series of events within Catholicism itself. At the time of the Pre-Reformation, he said, Western Christianity was living through a profound change. 'It opened itself to personal piety. It hungered for God. Becoming aware of its excessive ignorance, it demanded the Word of Life.' The case of the existential Luther, the Luther borrowed from Sören Kierkegaard, was now extended into a 'collective mentality' and bestowed on a whole culture. Luther stood out as one of a mass of anxious souls for whom a church which had temporarily fallen into the hands of a corrupt government could not provide – to this extent Delumeau, like Lortz, and Jedin before him in Germany, incorporated part of the older Protestant argument about 'abuses'. 'In fact, it needed the shock of the Protestant secession to compel the hierarchy to reform.'[31]

Delumeau saw himself as offering a complete re-reading of Western religious history, one which would at the same time put seventeenth-century Catholic history into a more favourable light, abolishing the concept of the 'Counter-Reformation' with its retaliatory, repressive, baroque and undeniably political aspects, and replacing it with a religious movement of vast duration, stretching from the Middle Ages to the middle of the eighteenth century, a movement for which no suitable name has been suggested, but any acceptable name for which would have to express the creativeness of a Christian (because also Protestant) and Catholic revival, 'Catholic' because this had to remain the true centre of the Christian tradition – one could not really allow that Protestantism had at a critical moment taken over the task of representing the gospel.[32] He reinforced his argument by examining the history of Catholic missions outside Europe in the Counter-Reformation period, which had been either ignored or depreciated by other students of the period: see for example, in English, H. O. Evenett, *The Spirit of the Counter-Reformation* (1968), and A. G. Dickens, *The Counter-Reformation* (1968).

There was a point, therefore, at which the secular and religious interpretations of Early Modern European history began to flow in a similar direction. Delumeau, for example, was distinguishing between 'superstition' – thought of as a kind of non-Christian state of the medieval mind – and a 'sacramental' religion, Catholicism in essence, which was inherently superior because divinely prompted. Peter Burke, on the other hand, and other historians closer to the *Annales*-Febvre *mentalité*, seemed to be repeating a late nineteenth-century distinction between 'popular culture' ('superstition' more widely defined to include much of what Delumeau was defending on the religious level), and 'civilization', an élitist ideology with a strongly rational, scientific content. The élites involved in the second case seemed to consist of intellectuals and members of the ruling groups. Both approaches replaced the Marxist concept of a conflict of classes, in which the poorer groups were the victims of the wealthier ruling groups, with a system in which the poorer groups were the beneficiaries of élite interference. Between the committed historians of theology for whom Protestantism seems to mean the puzzle of never being quite able to decide what Luther said, or exactly when he said it;[33] the secular historians for whom Protestantism operates as a vehicle for increasing the rationality of society; and the Catholic historians for whom Protestantism acted as a trigger mechanism which released the Catholic renewal movement, Protestantism as a series of historical events with an inner logic of its own hardly seemed to have occurred at all.

The present state of the study of sixteenth-century religious history reflects a balance of late twentieth-century interests. The collapse of the social and intellectual authority of Christian theology has left Reformation theology and its Catholic equivalent abandoned like whales on a beach. Ecumenism, which fostered the study of the sixteenth century in the years between 1920 and 1960, has also faded, or transferred to non-theological lines. As far as most committed historians are concerned, what stirs most interest in the Reformation is 'dechristianization', the decline of Western Christianity since the eighteenth century. Scholars have tried to put this observation of decline into perspective by examining the sixteenth century, and they tend to argue that neither the Reformation nor the Counter-Reformation achieved as much as was claimed in the past. This is a comforting discovery for the committed historians, because it reduces the significance of talk about Christian decline. Delumeau added to this the assertion that sixteenth- and seventeenth-century evangelization relied so much on the use of social power and the emotion of fear that when Christian institutions lost their political authority and Western society ceased to respond to the pressure of religious terror, some kind of dechristianization became inevitable.

The secular social historian of the sixteenth century is also deeply influenced by his contemporary situation. The American historian, Richard Trexler, for example, said that for the historian 'religion' existed only as behaviour, especially collective behaviour, the ceremonial and ritual of communities like Renaissance Florence, Trexler's principal field of research. The historian, he said, should not make estimates of the inner quality of alleged religious experience, but should attempt to grasp the pattern and purpose of communal rituals. He thought that one source of the Reformation was what seemed to be a wave of excessive ceremony and ritual in the late fifteenth to early sixteenth century, against which the Reformers reacted passionately, constructing new devotional communities which suited them better. Once they had broken the bonds which held them to Catholic society, they had to form the bonds of new societies; theological definition was a way of shaping these bonds and making them more permanent. Trexler really denied that 'christianization', in either Peter Burke's sense or Jean Delumeau's, occurred at all: there was no need for such a phenomenon. In the religious sub-culture which existed in 1500 (and which was not, I think, conterminous with the whole Western society, with all respect to Lucien Febvre) some religious institutions lost their grip on particular communities, and new religious institutions formed to take their place. Not all these new groups survived, and the survival of others depended on many factors which were not in themselves religious. The amount of 'religion', or of 'christianity', did not necessarily change much at all; instead, there was 'a search for group-identifying sets of behaviour permitting religious experience'.[34] This was an ugly way of putting it, but seemed to keep very close to the texture of events.

A society without important religious bonds – and Western societies are no longer held together by a popular culture in which religion plays a major role – still needs bonds of some kind which will generate the kind of communal emotions which sustain the existence of a nation. American intellectuals have become keenly aware of this in the period of right-wing reaction which has followed American defeat in the Vietnam War. They stand in a similar relationship to their own post-war society as Durkheim did to the French Third Republic at the beginning of the twentieth century. Like him, they want to recover the kind of community which can evoke a common loyalty and social morality; they believe that such communities existed in the past, before, as they believe, the social, industrial and religious revolutions of the nineteenth century destroyed their broader base. (By 'religious revolution' I mean the phenomena of 'dechristianization' and its twin, 'secularization'.) Unfortunately, one of the institutions which developed in the Early Modern period was the 'modern state', which, Trexler argued, now controls public ritual, and has destroyed the possibility of a creative common culture in much the same way as the Medicis did when they finally took control of Florence in 1529 and converted the city from a Republic to a petty princedom. The modern state does not care what its subjects believe in private as long as they join the public liturgical functions or demonstrations provided by the state. In theory, this guarantees a public ritual which cannot harm the modern state itself, that is, the élite which controls government; in practice, these state-devised rituals and demonstrations fail to strengthen the state, to give it the social unity and general acceptance of a moral code which animate and inspire. Social historians of the Early Modern period are motivated by a desire to understand what forms communities, and what corrupts them, and they are tempted to find in the past the society which they seek in the present. They usually interpret both Protestantism and Catholicism as kinds of would-be spiritual totalitarianism, but they also know that social order does not evolve spontaneously out of chaos. And chaos is what they are afraid of.

Perhaps both the committed and the secular historian need to come closer to the material they study. The most important book on sixteenth-century Protestantism written in recent years was Gerald Strauss's *Luther's House of Learning*, to which I have already referred. His conclusion was devastating to the traditional pious history of a heroic age:

> A century of Protestantism had brought about little or no change in the common religious conscience and in the ways in which ordinary men and women conducted their lives. Given people's nebulous grasp of the substance of their faith, no meaningful distinction could have existed between Protestants and Catholics – a distinction arising from articulated belief, conscious attachment and self-perception . . . One hesitates to think that the buoyant spirit in which urban circles had received or joined the Reformation in the 1520s and 1530s should have been so stifled by its subsequent routinization. But it is one thing to be

> carried along by the surge of a young cause in its heroic phase, and quite another to champion a creaking orthodoxy.[35]

Strauss's picture has been challenged, and no doubt the difficulty of interpreting the visitation records will be used to defend the older view. But Strauss's results suggest that modern historians, as well as folk-tradition, romanticized the depth of the religious movements of the sixteenth and seventeenth centuries. Perhaps even more damaging was Strauss's description of the kind of person which the Lutheran educational system set out to form:

> their model Christian was an essentially passive being prepared to acquiesce rather than struggle, distrustful of his own inclinations and reluctant to act on them; diffident, ready to yield when his personal wishes clashed with approved norms, unsure of his private judgement, hesitant to proceed when no one guided him, certain only of his own weakness as a creature and of the mortal peril of his condition as a sinner . . .[36]

It is not a winning image, and it reflected the confusion in Lutheranism between the conviction that only God could change the sinful heart of man, and the idea of using education as a means of facilitating the divine action. Even if the Reformers had 'succeeded', however, the value of this success would have been dubious. Less convincingly, Strauss was prepared to assume that left to itself by the Lutheran missioners and educators, the rural sub-culture functioned as 'a rich blend of intuitions and observations affording the devotee a satisfying and, one supposes, useful integration of nature and individual life'.[37] One may share his critical attitude to the 'urban academic's ingrained contempt for peasants and rural life', but also prefer Le Roy-Ladurie's judgment that the peasant sub-culture survived as 'a lively reaction of the peasant consciousness disillusioned with ideologies of urban origin, brutalized after 1560 by war, and haunted by the spectres of misery and death – and often by fear of sexual failure'.[38]

There is a coda to all this: Pietism. This is the proper name for the Protestant reform movement which is often dated from the publication of *Pia Desideria, or Heartfelt Desires for a God-pleasing improvement of the true Protestant Church*, by Philipp Jakob Spener

(1633–1705) at Frankfort in 1675. Pietism centred on the pursuit by small, essentially lay groups of believers of a direct experience of God as transforming power in the life of the individual. It could be said, and it was already said in the late seventeenth century, that Spener in his passion for holiness in the present, broke with the core of Luther's teaching, according to which the individual remains *simul justus et peccator* (justified but sinful), but Spener, appalled at the apparently slight affect of religious belief on behaviour, wanted the mystical union with Christ which, in Lutheran scholasticism, theoretically followed on from justification, to produce personal renewal and sanctification. Pietism did not simply mean seeking an inner, psychologically mediated experience of God (though this was what it easily became), but concentrated on the need to allow the Holy Spirit to change one's behaviour. Pietism sprang from near despair at the practical results of the Reformation and Counter-Reformation. It is therefore not surprising that what I have called the Georgian 'civic religion' and Pietism had in common the conviction that behaviour mattered more than right belief; they parted, however, on the question of the possibility of any direct divine illumination of the individual. Pietism spread from Germany to all other Lutheran Churches to North America, and to Britain where it deeply influenced early Wesleyanism.[39]

It is still true, I think, that historians have taken too little account of Pietism. There is now, however, a valuable volume of selected writings in translation, *Pietists*, edited by a Canadian scholar, Peter C. Erb (1983). Most of the study of Pietism has been by committed historians, and by German scholars who have specialized in its theological history. More recently the development, in the shadow of the Reagan Presidency, of a new phase of American Evangelicalism, anxious and organized to obtain political and social power, has stimulated further interest in the history of European Pietism, with which American Evangelicalism has obvious affinities. Peter Erb's critical comments on the later American history of the movement brings us close to Gerald Strauss again:

Among Pietism's North American descendants the emphasis on

> subjective individual experience, initially directed against an arid scholastic concern with a 'pure' doctrine, soon forced a peculiar semantic shift within the language of piety. By this shift, 'knowledge' of God was reduced to 'an emotional experience' undergone at conversion and in devotion, and the emphasis on faith soon turned that gift into a near-pelagian work. Pietism's radical division of head and heart would in time support anti-intellectualism. The movement's love-ethic, originally committed to a social gospel, shifted to attention on caring and duty, and may well have played a role in the development of totalitarian attitudes on both sides of the Atlantic. Confidence in salvation moved by way of Wesleyan assurance to certainty, and the conventicles, once formed for mutual encouragement, became the basis for an intolerant division of true against false Christians and Christianity.[40]

Anyone acquainted with Evangelicalism will recognize the substantial truth of this sketch. The founders of Pietism made considerable claims – which are often repeated in altered conditions in the late twentieth century – for the possibility of a direct relationship between the individual and God in the Holy Spirit. The committed historian, like Peter Erb, will want to say that 'Pietism must not be judged by its offspring'. The secular historian, however, should avoid the fallacy of the ideal type, should stick to behaviour. The best British instance of the approach of the social historian to Pietism is to be found in *Piety and Politics: Religion and the Rise of Absolutism in England, Württemberg and Prussia* (1983), by Mary Fulbrook, who used the concept of 'precisionist movements' to enable her to compare Puritanism in seventeenth-century England with Pietism in Germany in the late seventeenth and eighteenth centuries. She showed that in Württemberg between 1680 and 1780 Pietism was anti-absolutist but politically passive, whereas in Prussia between 1690 and 1740 Pietism was both politically active and pro-absolutist. The point about the English Puritans was that they were both politically active and anti-absolutist. The evidence, in other words, did not seem to justify making absolute claims about the political consequences of Pietism as far as the growth of the modern state was concerned; but Dr

Fulbrook argued that in fact there was a significant variable – the extent to which Pietism was either tolerated or opposed by the state administration. This was a fascinating study, but Dr Fulbrook's interest lay less in Pietism than in the relationship between ideas and events in politics, and the extent to which the formation of the modern state could be said to have been influenced by religious movements. There is a tragic irony in Spener's original hope for a generation of model Christians prepared for the Second Advent, when one compares it with the repeated tendency of Pietist groups to associate themselves with the holders of political power when the chance arose. What was apparently the deepest-rooted Protestant dissent from the secular in the seventeenth and eighteenth centuries was as easily attracted by the possession of power as were the contemporary leaders of the Catholic Renewal as Jean Delumeau describes them.

Mary Fulbrook's use of Puritanism as a variety of Pietism should not necessarily be accepted. The standard German work on Pietism and politics is *Preussentum und Pietismus* (1971) by Carl Hinrichs. In English, there is also *The Politics of German Protestantism: The Rise of the German Church Elite in Prussia 1816–48* (1972) by Robert M. Bigler, which traced the consolidation of the later alliance between the newly expanded Prussia and conservative Lutheranism.

A different view of the relationship between Lutheranism and the state in eighteenth-century Germany can be found in John Stroup's *The Struggle for Identity in the Clerical State: North-West German Opposition to the Absolute Policy in the Eighteenth Century* (1984). Stroup examined the long-established judgment that once the Enlightenment had weakened the confidence of the Lutheran clergy in the divine authority of orthodox doctrine they had no basis on which to challenge the demands of absolutist policy. He investigated the attitudes of the more articulate clergy in Electoral Hannover and Braunschweig-Wölfenbuttel and concluded that many of the clergy did fight for the independence of the church, and in doing so prepared the ground for the eighteenth-century effort to establish the ecclesia upon more than utilitarian (rational) grounds.

Why then, Stroup asked, had historians usually portrayed the Protestant churchmen and theologians of the Enlightenment as the passive tools of temporal government? Such a view, he answered, suited both the committed and the secular historian, because one of their premisses was that the German preference for the ideas of 1914 over the ideas of 1789 could be largely explained by the public passivity which characterized the Lutheran clergy from Luther to the twentieth century. German nationalist historians saw particularism as a brake on German progress towards liberalism. As for the committed historians:

> any evidence that rationalist theologians might have been able to defend (or even perceive) the interests of the Church or the unique raison d'etre of the clergy would have been taken as disconfirming the post-Enlightenment claim that such interests and professional purpose could be defended only by those who had overcome the claims of human reason.[41]

Twentieth-century ecclesiastical writers had persevered with this negative view of the Enlightenment churchmen. Above all, Stroup said, the situation had not changed: the difficulty of defining the nature and necessity of the Christian system, the search for ways of insulating the clergy from forces which would enrol them in the service of secular powers – these problems had not been solved since the eighteenth century. By depreciating the solutions of the Lutheran clergy of the Enlightenment, however, modern committed historians and theologians sought to commend their own.

Stroup's analysis was very important. There was never much to be said for the theory that one could explain the peculiarities of modern German history by referring to the alleged grip of Luther's political theology on the German imagination. What needed theological analysis and criticism was the hold of nationalism on far more than the German imagination, but twentieth-century theologians have consistently avoided the issue. In the German case, it looks as though Lutheran passivity served as a convenient religious pretext for the nationalist preference both in the nineteenth and the present century.[42]

3

Early Modern England: Was there Anything like the English Reformation?

How have recent historians dealt with 'the Church of England' in the sixteenth century? The neatest comment on this question was Christopher Haigh's, that 'while American, British and German scholars working on the German Reformation were trying to establish why their Reformation was as it was, specialists in the English Reformation still had not decided what their Reformation was actually like'.[1] Haigh suggested that a 'whig' interpretation of the English Reformation, one written from the point of view of the longer-term victory of Protestantism, was giving way slowly but inexorably to a better-grounded picture of the English Reformation as above all a struggle, of which the Protestant outcome was no more inevitable than the final Catholic defeat. He saw this as the paradoxical result of twenty years of historical writing which had been dominated by the publication in 1964 of A. G. Dickens' *The English Reformation*, which had itself transformed the classical Protestant view, best represented by Geoffrey Elton's *England under the Tudors* (1955), according to which what happened to the English church in the course of the sixteenth century was essentially the result of the action of strong central government operating on a passive people. Dickens made much greater use than his predecessors of diocesan archives, and argued that, irrespective of his difficulties with the papacy over his marriage problems, Henry VIII, would not have been able to maintain the English religious situation as it was about 1530. England had no Luther, but nevertheless in the opening years of the sixteenth century, a change of religious attitudes was taking place, parallel to what was occurring in the rest of Europe. Dickens broke with Elton's picture of a political revolution which involved religious (and as it happened Protestant) reform; he preferred to subordinate the political to the religious, and to see Protestantism as developing spontaneously from below.

One might categorize Dickens, therefore, as anxious to establish the credentials of 'Anglicanism' in a sixteenth-century indigenous Protestant movement which was satisfied with the church of the Elizabethan Settlement, and rejected the extremism of the late sixteenth-century separatists. Geoffrey Elton had been less concerned about the footing on which Anglicanism faced its Catholic critics, more devoted to exploring the political changes which transformed the constitutional position of both crown and church. It is true that he somewhat modified his earlier political analysis of the period, so that in *Policy and Police, The Enforcement of the Reformation in the Age of Thomas Cromwell* (1976), and *Reform and Reformation, England 1509–1558* (1977), for example, he portrayed a highly troubled society, in which dislike of religious change produced disaffection and conflict, and in which Cromwell had added to his perception of the need for powerful royal action from the centre an additional awareness of the importance of Protestant reform to the policy he was formulating. Elton, however, always insisted on the priority of politics, by which he seemed to mean the priority of the struggle for power. This can be seen in a late but characteristically vigorous article, 'Politics and the Pilgrimage of Grace' (in *After the Reformation*, edited by Barbara Malament, 1980), in which he totally rejected the Catholic historian, J. J. Scarisbrick's, interpretation of the 1536 Pilgrimage of Grace as 'a large-scale, spontaneous, authentic indictment of all that Henry most obviously stood for, and it passed judgement against him as surely and comprehensively as Magna Carta condemned John or the Grand Remonstrance the government of Charles I'. Elton was quoting from Scarisbrick's *Henry VIII*,[2] where Scarisbrick interpreted the rising as essentially a Catholic protest against unpopular religious policies. Elton's contrary conclusion, which ran against the currently fashionable way of understanding the situation in the 1530s, was quite different. The riot was at bottom the work of a defeated court political faction which used the social, economic and religious grievances which were to be found in the north of England, grievances which Elton linked not to popular unrest but to the distrust which the regional gentry had begun to feel towards central government and Thomas Cromwell in particular. Elton subordinated the religious element in the Pilgrimage of Grace to the political, and transferred the centre of the *political* upheaval from the country to the court. Looked at in this way, he said, the rising was not the protest of an outraged 'medievalism', but the first example of British 'modern' politics as they would be carried on down to the nineteenth century. It was always possible that religion had served as the ideology needed to turn conventional riots into a major rebellion, but Elton thought that the ideology was only superficial, not an authentic expression of the attitudes of the majority.

Elton and Dickens therefore represented a substantial commitment to Anglicanism as being historically, and therefore religiously and theologically, justifiable, as more than an institution got up to serve a limited purpose which died long ago; there was no suggestion here that the Church of England was no more than an institution imposed by force against the wishes, though perhaps not the will, of the majority of people. Only Dickens's search for links between Wycliffe, the Lollards and the English sixteenth-century Reformers seems to have broken down: modern research has widened rather than closed the gap, and has suggested that however remarkable a lay movement the Lollards organized in the fifteenth century, they barely survived the Lancastrian victory in the civil war, and had little to offer to the Henrician reformation.[3]

As far as Dickens and Elton were concerned, it could hardly be said that they had not decided what their Reformation was actually like. They saw the English Reformation as having taken place quite swiftly in the first half of the sixteenth century, partly no doubt because the Tudor governments acted steadily in a Protestant direction which Mary's reign was too brief to reverse, but also because a majority of English people changed willingly from Catholicism to Protestantism, a change which could be made in many different ways, with many different degrees of existential commitment. Keith Thomas, in his monumental *Religion and the Decline of Magic, Studies in Popular Belief in Sixteenth and Seventeenth-*

Century England (1971), reinforced this approach. Having first shown how the medieval church in England combined religion and magic, he said that the main thrust of Protestantism depended on a widespread rejection of this traditional set of religio-magical practices. 'The decline of the old Catholic beliefs was not the result of persecution', he wrote, 'it reflected a change in the popular conception of religion . . . Protestantism presented itself as a deliberate attempt to take the magical elements out of religion, to eliminate the idea that the rituals of the Church had about them a mechanical efficiency, and to abandon the effort to endow physical objects with supernatural qualities by special formulae of consecration and exorcism.'[4] Although one paradoxical effect of this side of Protestantism – perhaps one should call it the Erasmian side – was to give magic a temporary increase of popularity in certain quarters, Keith Thomas himself considered that by the early eighteenth century both magical and Christian beliefs were losing their hold on English society.[5]

Thomas's argument should be compared with Richard Trexler's[6] that modern historians of the sixteenth century were imposing their own academic rationalism on the past and therefore misunderstanding what happened in the Reformation. Of course, many historians, Protestant as well as Catholic, have regarded Erasmus as less than a respectable figure. The *Colloquies* (see the excellent modern translation by D. F. S. Thomson, 1965) still offend some readers. *The Pilgrimage of True Devotion* (1526), for example, which described Erasmus' visits to Becket's shrine at Canterbury and the Marian shrine at Walsingham, provoked A. J. Krailsheimer to indignation.

> Erasmus paints an unattractive picture of somewhat seedy piety, with the rapacity of the guardians and implausibility of the relics duly highlighted. Calvin and Voltaire adopt almost the same arguments and the same tone for their very different reasons in attacking Catholic credulity and abuses, but the timing of Erasmus' attack distinguishes it from any subsequent one. Such irony and scepticism were weapons of which anti-Catholics were not slow to avail themselves, and if Erasmus died protesting his orthodoxy, he cannot avoid the responsibility

> (or credit, depending on one's point of view) for forging such arms . . . he had started a fashion and set an example.[7]

Depreciation of Erasmus serves only to obscure the presence of many other people in the early sixteenth century who shared his religious attitudes at least on the negative side, though they were less easily persuaded by his plea that true Christianity led to charity, peacefulness, toleration and simplicity.

We must turn aside here for a moment to look again at the question from which we started this section: what was 'the Reformation' actually like? The traditional church historian was apt to define the 'Reformation' in terms of his favoured theological tradition: the 'true' Reformation was rarely, if ever, Baptist, Socinian or Erasmian. It was Lutheran, or Calvinist, Zwinglian or even 'Anglican'. Historically, the 'Reformation' as a mixture of all the events suggested by these labels would have to be defined more widely, and one may sometimes feel that the most obvious result of reforming activity, not only in England but also in many parts of Europe, was not so much theological or ecclesiastical, as it was warfare, persecution and iconoclasm – the destruction of physical objects of a religious nature or connection. As John Phillips put it,

> the reformation of images in England entailed the beating down of walls and church fittings, the smashing of stained glass and sculpture, the ripping and tearing of paintings and tapestries; it included the destruction of objects whose only offence was that they were ornamental and decorative.[8]

And this process, which in England began with the dissolution of the monasteries in the 1530s, did not end until the restoration of Charles II. This assault was not invented by modern historians; it altered the external religious appearance and spiritual ethos of England decisively, and it was the cumulative work of many people over many years. John Phillips argued that the medieval image of Christ and his saints was inextricably part of the philosophical fabric of the social and political order, so that to destroy a sacred object was inevitably an attempt to damage the fabric of the state. In such a world, he said, 'the breaking of these images was an expression of a highly developed order of philosophical daring violence'; it led to the break-up of the fundamental intellectual presuppositions of the political and religious organizations of the time, and deeply affected religious devotion and artistic method. Phillips said that Henry VIII, anxious to magnify the crown, broke the symbolic links between royal power and Rome; the royal arms replaced the crucifix and other distinctly Roman images in the parish churches; Elizabeth I's portraits acted as the equivalent of older divine images and she had many of the Virgin Mary's symbols applied to her. In the long run, Calvinism revolted against the political and ecclesiastical power of the crown, and 'iconoclasm became an essential element in the Protestantization of England that, in part, resulted in the revolution of 1642'. Art secularized itself in deference to the patronage of the nobility and gentry. 'The net result was the development of new modes of human experience and thought.'[9]

In the long run English iconoclasm ended in the eighteenth-century dearth of images: the Ten Commandments painted in gold leaf on a black board on the wall of the parish church was no more than a magnified page of a book. England, of course, had not been the only scene of Protestant and Catholic violence and image-breaking in the sixteenth and seventeenth centuries, and various explanations have been offered of what happened. Older committed church historians concentrated on the wickedness of either the blasphemous Protestant iconoclasts or the murderously enraged Catholics. Some modern accounts (e.g. Phillips) have pointed out the weaknesses in the Catholic and Protestant theological cases for and against the use of images, and minimized the importance of Calvin's insistence that art had no place in worship. Instead, they stressed the political and economic origins of disturbances like the wave of iconoclasm which spread through almost the whole of Flanders in the second half of August, 1566. In such commentaries (e.g. Trexler), the destruction of images was largely interpreted as a blow against the power of those who employed them; there was also the recognition that the destruction of a régime required the clearing away of the political and religious symbols of the régime's power. In our own time, for example,

Stalin's death was followed by the laborious tearing down of his statues through most of Communist Europe.

This kind of general, secularized explanation was sensibly criticized by Phyllis Mack Smith in *Calvinist Preaching and Iconoclasm in the Netherlands 1544–69* (1978). She thought that although economic grievances and hostility to the priesthood as a privileged group contributed to the emotional storm which raged through the Flanders iconoclasm, its principal aim was to attack the authority of the Catholic Church. Nevertheless, she said, 'given the fact that religious violence was of immense significance to so many different people – for so many reasons – why was there so little of it?' Whether one described iconoclasm as an act of magic (challenging and defeating the supernatural power latent in the images of Christ, Mary and the saints), or as a gesture of religious outrage especially against the priests, or as a symptom of social revolution, in which case the act of iconoclasm would be almost one of despair, the behaviour of the majority of people, who remained passive throughout, who neither smashed images nor defended the Catholic establishment, was left unexplained.[10] This conclusion seems to me to be applicable to many essentially untestable assertions advanced by social and sociologically-minded historians in the guise of explanation. Where general explanations do not correspond to widespread behaviour of the type suggested (as in the suggestion that widespread economic distress, and not some kind of religious feeling, was the chief cause of the iconoclasm in Flanders), the argument needs refinement and additional support before it can be regarded as significant – evidence about economic distress is evidence only about economic distress, and does not in itself point to any inevitable kind of action at all. This criticism would also apply to Janine Estèbe, *Tocsin pour un massacre, La Saison des Saint-Barthélémy* (1968), who said that both Catholic and Protestants felt the other, rival group as a source of pollution in the community, pollution which could be removed only by violence, so that in France the Calvinists destroyed Catholic statues, relics and eucharistic wafers, while Catholics, denied a simple symbolic focus of reprisal, sometimes killed Catholics. This view was elaborated by Natalie Zemon Davis, in *Society and Culture in Early Modern France* (1975), who conveyed vividly the horror which each group felt at the religious behaviour of the other. Similar horror and hostility accumulated more slowly in England after the 1560s, because the two communities were no longer so constantly in sight of one another, but its deeper, venomous presence helps to explain the savagery of the Civil War and the cruelty which could be released even late in the seventeenth century by the Titus Oates affair.[11]

Committed church historians avoid the conclusion that the most far-reaching, because secularizing, outcome of the Reformation and Counter-Reformation (for here one must certainly take them together as part of a total phenomenon) was outburst after outburst of iconoclasm, civil and national war, and the torture and execution of religious opponents on the ground that their opinions were dangerous to society. This was the unacceptable face of Christianity, and historians have therefore tried hard to disconnect the violence from Christianity. Some have explained what happened as the re-emergence of a frustrated primitive paranoia from the collective unconscious of the people. Others have attributed the apparently religious violence to the pathological results of certain kinds of child-rearing, of economic deprivation (as above) or loss of social status. The history of the twentieth century suggests that violent, cruel behaviour has a very powerful attraction for human beings. Natalie Davis, however, said that religious violence 'is explained not in terms of how crazy, hungry or sexually frustrated the violent people are (though they may sometimes have such characteristics) but in terms of the goals of their actions and in terms of roles and patterns of behaviour allowed by their culture. Religious violence is related here less to the pathological than to the normal.'[12] Human beings are violent, and their violence serves religious ends as it serves others. And even before the end of the sixteenth century Montaigne was saying that cruelty was the worst of our ordinary vices.

If, then, we ask, what was the Reformation period like? we have to accept, I think, that 'religion' released violence and cruelty. The intensification of religious feeling and belief which allegedly was part of both the Reformation and the Counter-Reformation did not prevent this. Can we identify this 'religious emotion' more accurately? 'In 1566,' wrote Phyllis Mack Crew, 'an image-breaker at Ypres was approached by a Catholic who told him to spare the organ: "No, no", the man answered, "It must all be broken. We have had too much to do with idolatry." '[13] Iconoclasm seemed to express a wave of impatience with a whole way of being religious. In the English instance, one cannot attach primary blame to Calvinism or to the Puritans: the uprooting of monasticism as an institution, which included the destruction of the great centres of pilgrimage like Canterbury and Walsingham as well as the gutting of two-thirds of the monastic churches, was no doubt influenced by the writings of Luther, Tyndale and others, but the positive religious emotion (as distinct from the local forces of greed and naive vandalism) was the emergence, as John Phillips suggested, of a profoundly new attitude to salvation.

> With the growing emphasis on Christ as sole mediator between God and man, English piety would in time cease to be expressed through the Virgin Mary and the saints, in tangible signs and ceremonies . . . biblical stories would replace the legends of saints and their images.[14]

This, in a limited sense, was true enough, but it was not the profoundest meaning of what took place. On the one hand, Protestant despoilers had invaded sacred space with hammers and crowbars; they had burned famous images of the Virgin Mary and the saints and had obliterated their relics; they had wrecked altars; they had dispersed monks and nuns as superfluous people. They had done this and much more and neither Christ nor the Virgin nor the saints had intervened, there had been no over-whelming evidence of supernatural retribution. Natalie Davis illustrated the crisis of faith in the following story:

> A Protestant crowd corners a baker guarding the holy-wafer box in St Médard's Church in Paris in 1561. 'Messieurs,' he pleads, 'do not touch it for the honour of Him who dwells here.' 'Does your god of paste protect you now from the pains of death?,' was the Protestant answer before they killed him.[15]

On the other hand, divine protection had failed the Protestants as well. In England, no supernatural agency had saved them from Mary's persecution. To quote from Natalie Davis again:

> Even the dead were made to speak in Normandy and Provence, where leaves of the Protestant Bible were stuffed into the mouths and wounds of corpses. 'They preached the truth of their God. Let them call him to their aid.'[16]

If there was a new attitude to salvation, it was partly because Catholics and Protestants had combined to empty the traditional Western religious system of much of its popular content, whether one describes this as magic, superstition, or providential faith. The Christian religion lost its firm grip on the external world; piety turned increasingly inward because it had nowhere else to go; that the long-term effect on Catholicism was the same as it was on Protestantism is clear when one considers the Catholic Enlightenment in the eighteenth century and the dechristianization crisis in France. Whatever Reformers and reforming Counter-Reformers did together for the evangelization of Western Europe was nothing compared to their joint contribution to the gradual secularization of the culture. It was a question of conflict (between Catholic and Protestant) which developed a ferocity out of any proportion to the apparent religious differences involved; this ferocity revealed a mutual heartlessness within the religious emotion itself, and this lack, an inner religious failure, generated a corresponding indifference to religion in others. As a result, much of the history of Western religion in the nineteenth century was the story of an attempt to recover the Christian grip on the external world which had been lost, to restore, in England as elsewhere, the religious sub-culture which employed images, pilgrimages and relics, fostered miraculous healings and supernatural visions, and gave a central place to religious orders.

I began this section by referring to Christopher Haigh's view that scholars of the English Reformation were shifting from the 'whig' approach of Dickens and Elton to an interpretation which emphasized, *per contra*, the contingent nature of the process, and therefore the possibility that Catholicism in England might, as in France, have finally beaten off the Protestant bid to dominate the religious culture. In some ways this meant a reversion to the older Catholic perspective which may be traced through the books of Phillip Hughes. In *A Popular History of the Church* (1939) he said that at the start of Elizabeth I's reign 'all the bishops were deposed and a new self-consecrated hierarchy of heretics took their place'; in *Rome and the Counter-Reformation* (1942) he modified this to the statement that the Elizabethan Church Settlement was the work of a minority who forced their system on a reluctant majority who would probably have preferred Catholicism (a judgment not entirely absent from more recent books). Finally, in *The English Reformation* (3 vols, 1950–54) he presented an interpretation of the English Reformation in which he agreed that the whole affair showed the disastrous outcome of bad Catholicism, but not that Catholicism was wrong in principle as the leading Reformers had maintained. Hughes's emphasis on the Elizabethan persecution of Catholics annoyed his Anglican reviewers, who were accustomed to assume that whatever Elizabeth did was cancelled out by the actions of the Marian regime. Hughes did not really have any doubts about what the Reformation in England was like: it had been a disaster, both for the Catholic Church, and for the country. Similar feelings seemed to lie behind *The Religious Orders in England* (3 vols, 1950–59) by M. D. Knowles, who began his career as a Benedictine and ended it as Professor of Modern History at Cambridge (despite being perhaps the most distinguished medieval scholar of his time). Knowles's concept of monasticism became so austere that he despaired of the system in his own time and said that his knowledge of it helped him to understand what had gone wrong in the sixteenth century.

The mediating Anglo-Catholic understanding of the period, that Elizabeth's church settlement was intended to revive a 'Catholic Anglicanism' which had its origins in the reign of Henry VIII (see, for example, the American scholar, P. M. Dawley's *John Whitgift and the Reformation*, 1955, and the much earlier Maynard Smith's *Pre-Reformation England*, 1938, according to which the real, 'Catholic' reformation was Henry VIII's, whereas 'Protestantism' was of alien origin and 'not in accord with the national temper') fitted well with Hughes's model, because it dismissed the 'Protestant' position as not 'Anglican' and looked cautiously towards a future reconciliation of the Church of England with the Church of Rome. This was not simply committed history, but a highly-charged denominational reading of the past, and this was what

Elton was objecting to when he said that although it was usual to call the Elizabethan Settlement a compromise,

> contemporaries did not think that the Established Church rested halfway between the rival denominations: they thought this was a Protestant Church . . . It was only the further development of Puritanism . . . as well as Elizabeth's diplomatic suggestions to a number of deliberately blind Spanish and French emissaries that her protestantism was after all quite like catholicism that disguised the nature of the settlement.[17]

The revisionism to which Christopher Haigh referred – and which may reasonably be called Catholic revision with a Catholic tendency – introduced a revised version of the Hughes position; that is, it started from a rejection of the claim of Elton and Dickens that the English Catholic Church in 1500 had lost much of its popular support and that Protestantism spread spontaneously and rapidly from below quite apart from monarchical prompting. Alan Kreider, for example, in *English Chantries and the Dissolution* (1979) pointed out the popularity of the chantry-system right down to the 1530s; pilgrimages continued (though these had many attractions not strictly religious, they were also the package-tours of their time); and although the last recorded miracle at Beckett's shrine seems to have occurred in 1474, there were about three hundred at Windsor (Henry VI's shrine) in the last decades of the fifteenth century. *The Cardinal's Court* (1977), by J. A. Guy, and J. J. Scarisbrick's work on Wolsey both suggest a movement of Catholic reform in England in the 1520s, which came too late to forestall the demands for radical change, but also implied that Catholic institutions were not entirely moribund. Haigh himself argued that Protestantism prospered in many towns, but advanced much more slowly in the less literate countryside, where traditional rituals which reflected the agricultural year and provided at least psychological protection from the dangers of rural life, were not given up easily. As England was largely rural, this would imply some kind of Catholic majority for at least a generation after 1530. In fact, the argument goes, it was only in Elizabeth's reign, the way having been paved by the repression of dissent under Henry

VIII and Edward VI (and indirectly by the brevity of Mary's reign) that Protestantism had a significant effect on the countryside.

Once again, it is not so much that some historians cannot decide what the English Reformation was like, as that they do not like the kind of Reformation which they have been asked to see. One is reminded of a general comment by John Bossy on the Reformation as a whole: 'I am not sure that it liberated people from the past in any way that one would want to be liberated from it.'[18] He himself, nevertheless, regarded the Reformation as a 'drastic reconstruction of Christianity', and said that its first visible sign was the casting-off of the saints:

> It took the form of a systematic vandalising of their images in canvas, wood and stone, by a public authority, a mob to which reformed Christianity had been preached, or a combination of both', and this represented, he said, a protest *against* the humanization of the social universe which had previously been affected in traditional Catholic belief by the reconciliation of man and God.[19]

This was a negative judgment on the Protestant movement, but Bossy was not repeating the ecumenical view that Catholic and Protestant were divided by misunderstanding, not by any important underlying principle. He seemed to be thinking of Luther and Calvin as having expressed an idea of the sinner's faith-relationship with Christ which excluded the possibility of human penitential or compensatory behaviour, and which left the sinner depending on a single channel of divine reconciliation: from the Protestant religious consciousness there faded out Mary, the Holy Family, the saints, and the idea of god-parents. In England, iconoclasm certainly followed, and the devastation spread through the countryside as well as through the towns in the 1530s and 1540s. If one offers broad socio-historical explanations of what happened, as John Bossy did in the passage just referred to, one has at the same time to accept that such a violent shattering of what religion had been (whether one calls it 'élite' or 'popular' religion hardly matters) must have corresponded to an inner cultural upheaval of no mean dimensions – a conclusion which really suggests that Catholic historians may exaggerate the contingent character of the English Reformation, and the extent to which it had to be imposed from above. To judge the whole period as an undesirable 'liberation from the past' – as John Bossy did – is perhaps to make a confessional statement rather than a historical judgment on the past. Bossy, however, like other British historians of the Early Modern period, was rejecting the French view of Early Modern Europe.

> Among disfigurements of this piece of the past I count the idea that medieval Christianity was a burden which most of the population of the West was delighted to shake off; or that there was something you can call 'popular culture' and distinguish radically from something called 'elite culture', especially when that popular culture is held by axiom to be non-Christian; or that Christianity was brought to the people during or after the sixteenth century.[20]

No simple summing-up is possible here, because two kinds of committed Catholicism, conservative and radical, dominated the suggested perspectives. Bossy, the more conservative historian, saw the Reformation as a process of disintegration: if the achievement of medieval Christianity at its best had been to maintain the parish church and churchyard as a place of public holiness where the parish could assemble together to combine sociability with the worship of God, what triumphed through the Reformation was the dissolution of that corporate act into what Bossy called 'the private eucharist of an asocial mysticism', whose aim was the peace of the individual. Bossy (like Richard Trexler) deplored this shift from a public to a private spirituality, a process which could be seen at work already in the fifteenth century. As far as England is concerned, Bossy's position has the virtue of preserving the idea of Protestantism as an attack on something (Catholicism) already there. Rejection of the Protestant 'whig' interpretation, however, ends in the unsatisfactory situation of historians discussing at length what might have happened: this makes for good journalism rather than for history.

From the Anglican point of view, however, what has confused the issue is the long Anglo-Catholic campaign to convince the Church of England that everything which disappeared from

Anglican usage in the sixteenth and seventeenth centuries, and everything in the way of 'Catholic' usage that John Henry Newman demanded in Tract Ninety, was *really Anglican*, and had only slipped into abeyance because of the temporary ascendancy of sub-Christian liberals and evangelicals in the eighteenth century. If the eighteenth century was regarded as not part of the true history of the Church of England, Laud and Keble could be linked. In this school of thought 'development' meant 'Catholic' development (as in Newman): Protestant 'development' meant degeneration. For Newman, Catholic development meant the Roman Church becoming more Marian (and this was the general direction of Roman Catholic change in the nineteenth century); for the residual Anglo-Catholics development had to mean the Church of England becoming more 'Catholic'. This historical agreement reached a critical point after 1870, because the dogma of papal infallibility, together with the later proclamation of the Bodily Assumption of the Virgin Mary, showed that modern Roman Catholicism differed from Protestantism in ways which could not be accounted for by appealing to religious concepts of public and private piety, or to social distinctions between medieval solidarity and modern civility. The problem, to revert to Christopher Haigh's formulation, is not that historians cannot make up their mind what the English Reformation was like, but that historically there never was a completed and agreed English Reformation to like or dislike. Even Elton's bland statement that in Elizabeth's reign everyone knew that the English church was Protestant begs the question: what everyone knew turned out not to have settled the question.

4

Baroque to Secular: Religion in England

The Seventeenth Century

The study of the history of the Church of England raises acute problems of historical identity. Its basic institutions – parishes, sees and so forth – have a social and economic life of their own which can be, and often is, treated historically from a purely secular point of view, but as soon as one turns to their religious purposes and to their relation to the state, both of which were altered drastically in the sixteenth century, one faces competing claims as to what the history is about, and as to what constitutes 'Anglicanism'. Although there is legal continuity, and although a mild degree of establishment has lingered into the late twentieth century, there is no question of any other continuous identity except in the eyes of particular schools of interpretation. These differences of interpretation are more than academic: they have been institutionalized into opposing parties.

All this has had a profound effect on the ways in which the ecclesiastical history of the Church of England has been written. That history may be summed up in terms of two major conflicts. First, the conflict between the crown, or politicians using the authority of the crown, on the one hand, and groups of clergy and laity on the other, for institutional control of the church and the advantages which this might be expected to bring at a specific historical juncture. Second, a more internal conflict between groups committed to mutually hostile interpretations of the nature of 'the Church of England', conflict which had its roots in the ambiguity of the Protestant Reformation in the sixteenth century, and therefore in the social divisions which helped to produce and limit that Reformation. Modern Anglican ecclesiastical historians have usually derived their understanding of the Church of England's past from one or other of these competing ideologies: Puritan, High Church, Evangelical, Latitudinarian, Anglo-Catholic, Liberal and so forth. These ecclesiastical views have influenced secular historians, who have manipulated terms like 'Puritan' and 'Evangelical' with excessive freedom, as though it was easy to define and identify them both theoretically and socially. In addition, ecclesiastical historians have sometimes offered their own reconciling version of Anglican history, in which the forces which constantly struggled for power within the institutionalized framework of the Church of England were seen as somehow (no doubt Providence was the key) working together for good. What was meant by 'good' here remained obscure, but the reference seemed to be to the survival of the church itself.

The Church of England has also to be studied as part of the history of the total national religious culture, of which the Christian tradition formed the largest but not always the only constituent. In the sixteenth century this national religious culture was still largely coextensive with society in general, but in the following century a secular culture began to define itself with increasing clarity. From the middle of the sixteenth century, moreover, the 'Christian culture' was itself divided, because the English Roman Catholic community survived the Reformation; and a second, Protestant and separatist sub-culture grew apart from the Establishment from the 1590s. This meant that throughout the seventeenth century the Church of England was subject to repeated attempts at redefinition: it did not so much exist as find itself invoked as part of political and social programmes. British society suffered from deep internal conflicts, which were reflected in the religious sub-culture. Both Puritanism, at the start of the century, and High Anglicanism from the 1660s, may be interpreted as attempts to seize the Establishment from within and to use its resources to promote a particular socio-religious point of view. Puritanism as a movement was defeated, and later Anglican historians sometimes labelled Puritanism 'non-Anglican', identifying it with the various critical groups which merged to make the Parliamentary side in the Civil War. In the wake of its defeat in the field, as well as in the context of the execution of Charles I, 'Puritanism' was excluded from 'Anglicanism' by definition. The field was then free for its redevelopment on the theoretical plane as the ideology of a new class emerging from the wreckage of feudalism (see Christopher Hill, for example, in *Society and Puritanism in Pre-Revolutionary England*, 1964) or as the *weltanschauung* of men and women alienated from the social and ecclesiastical society which they knew (see Michael Walzer, *The Revolution of the Saints*, 1965).

The failure of the High Church Party, which culminated in the trial in 1723 of Bishop Atterbury, the aging High Church leader who had taken part in a Jacobite conspiracy aiming at the invasion of England, was much more important from the point of view of the church historian. 'Puritanism' is still remembered as a movement which wanted to use political power to impose its moral and religious system on the nation at large. What is often forgotten is that Restoration High Anglicanism was a more clearly defined movement with similar aspirations, and that Archbishop Sancroft ended his life as a Nonjuror only because the Stuart monarchy finally refused to impose High Anglicanism as an absolute system. G. V. Bennett said of Atterbury:

> His real loyalty was not to the Stuarts but to an old-fashioned vision of the alliance of Church and State given to him by an education in Restoration Oxford. It was a uniquely English version of the union of a national church and a régime of absolute monarchy, deriving from Archbishop Laud and developed under Sheldon and Sancroft in the era after 1660. In it the Church of England, with its ordered worship and a conservative theology rooted in patristic learning, received from the civil power continual support and comfort in its role as the guardian of the morals and religious duties of the nation. And in return the Church fostered loyalty and obedience with all the ideological resources at its command: in the education of the young, in the elaboration of social and political theory, and by its influence as a major landowner. This vision of the cooperation of a loyalist church and a pious Anglican ruler could hardly survive King

> James II and the onset of the 'Age of Reason', and it foundered utterly after 1714.[1]

Atterbury, given the chance, one feels, would have reduced both Dissent and Roman Catholicism to a barely tolerated minimum. His High Church policy failed at least in part because the Stuart experience had appreciably weakened the hold of the Christian sub-culture on British society. The Whig Anglican rationalists who superseded Atterbury had fewer illusions about what was still politically possible for ecclesiastical influence, and they reinterpreted 'Anglicanism' as a much more relaxed kind of civil religion, of which Benjamin Hoadly was the expert advocate.[2]

Atterbury can also be seen as representing the English equivalent of that fusion of the Counter-Reformation with Baroque absolutism which characterized Louis XIV's vicious religious persecutions in the late seventeenth century, and Habsburg religious policy for much of the eighteenth century. In Hungary, for example,

> the archbishop of Esztergom was commissioned in 1763 to draft a project on the propagation of the Catholic faith. The document he prepared became the mainstay of Maria Theresa's anti-Protestant acts. It included a ban on 'heretical' (i.e. Protestant) publications, a ban on those educated abroad from entering holy orders, a requirement that Protestants attend Catholic services before going to their own, the deportation of Protestant ministers who challenged Catholic doctrine, the enforcement of earlier decrees restricting Protestant worship to the articular places . . . and a declaration that all the Protestants' remaining rights were to be considered valid only *ad hoc* (sic). It contained a long list of Protestant disabilities, all of them invidious, some of them affronting. These abstruse restrictions on freedom of conscience were being introduced in Hungary as the ideas of the Enlightenment were burgeoning in the west.[3]

One should probably go further, and say that one of the more significant reasons for the growth of Enlightenment attitudes, in England as well as in Hungary, was the spectacle of Baroque religious absolutism itself. Hoadly was no model of Christian perfection, but he reflected accurately enough a feeling that the Baroque alliance between church and state had encouraged various forms of Christianity to exaggerate both the political claims of the church and the intellectual claims of its theologians.

It is an example of the power of the High Church ideology, however, that Dr Bennett did not regard this outcome, the failure of Baroque Christianity, as having been inevitable. No doubt, he said, in the political and intellectual conditions of the eighteenth century religious affairs were destined to recede from the centre of the political stage: but before 1714 it was by no means obvious that this had to be the case. 'Anglican Toryism, with its vision of a stable society, built on religious assumptions and compacted into a moral order, was a faith which certainly the majority of Englishmen embraced in 1688; and it was to take a veritable shaking of the foundations before it appeared as obsolete as it did in 1730.'[4]

Such a view reduces James II's Catholicism to a historical accident, whereas James acted in the context of the Roman Catholic community which had survived the Reformation and which had not completely surrendered to the idea that 'Anglicanism' was the natural religion of the English people. A struggle for ecclesiastical power was still going on. Bennett, however, resting his narrative on Atterbury's career, gave no positive account of Roman Catholicism because the Anglican point of view did not require one; instead, he treated Catholicism either as an obsession in the mind of the Old Pretender, or as a trap which closed on individual members of the High Church party as they lived in exile. Bennett's text implied the standard modern view, common to High Anglican, Wesleyan and Anglican-Evangelical sources, that in the Hanoverian period the Church of England was not really 'Anglican', but was corrupted by 'the vogue for an extreme rationalism in religion, when any appeal to the tradition of the past was equated with mere superstition and the Deist challenge to orthodox Christianity was regarded as unanswerable.'[5] On the one hand, then, there was true 'Anglicanism' – even if there were rival claims to represent it, for original Wesleyanism also presented itself as a kind of 'reforming Anglicanism' – and on the other there was a mischievous vogue for extreme rationalism in religion.

This is surely no longer a satisfactory image of eighteenth-century English religion. It pays insufficient attention to the general European shift towards a new market economy which was affecting all religious attitudes. It also minimizes the extent to which all forms of Christian orthodoxy had lost prestige because of the part the churches had taken in the sanguinary politics of the sixteenth and seventeenth centuries; this was part of the explanation of the sharp reaction against the religious fanaticism of the Sacheverell years. Extreme rationalism was more than a vogue, it was the deeply-felt conclusion of a long European experience, and it was not to be easily reversed. Rationalism made toleration possible, and for the moment tolerant attitudes seemed more useful than religious ones. The situation may be compared with that of later twentieth-century politics, in which a fusion of Western political and religious values into an anti-Marxist, anti-Russian ideology has been a thoroughly unhealthy and unhelpful process, which is making a third world war more probable.

Like most ecclesiastical historians, Dr Bennett assumed the ontological primacy of ideas over the social and political movements of history: he therefore largely accepted the High Church Tory view of what the High Church Tories were doing, that is, fighting to maintain one kind of 'Anglican' hegemony in British society, and (one may add) their own interests in the profits of the Establishment. His approach can hardly offer more than a description of the party's ideas and of the extent to which they imposed their ideological system on others. High Church Toryism collapsed politically, but its language-system survived to torment those who had committed their lives to it; those who, like Atterbury, ended as Jacobite conspirators, seem more out of touch with political reality than those who switched to Roman Catholicism. Although John Keble and his Anglo-Catholic friends revived much of the vocabulary in the 1830s, they could not acquire the political power with which to impose their language on the wider social and political systems of the time; this did not prevent them from talking as though victory were possible, or from sometimes indulging in a self-indulgent cult of 'Charles the Martyr'. They found that the revised version of the older language worked only within the borders of the Church of England itself, where a considerable number of the clergy were able to use it to express their grievances and to organize themselves in pursuit of the ecclesiastical power needed to change the situation.

By the 1840s, in fact, the struggle for control of the Church of England was institutionalizing itself in the form of the Anglican-Evangelical and Anglo-Catholic sub-cultures (or parties, as they have usually been called). The total defeat of Jacobitism, made obvious in the '45, left eighteenth-century High Churchmen stranded, and their role in relation to the state was taken over by the Latitudinarians, the upholders of the Georgian civic religion. This High Church withdrawal into parochial obscurity made it more rather than less difficult to define what 'Anglicanism' meant. And if one allows that Wesleyanism developed at least on the fringes of the Establishment, one has to interpret the Wesleyan societies between 1740 and about 1770 as an attempt to capture the Church of England and reform it from below, an attempt not likely to succeed in the social conditions of the period. John Wesley's occasional banging of a High Church drum – as when he resuscitated the doctrine of political obedience at the time of the American War of Independence – should not conceal the fact that his followers themselves were not 'High Churchmen' at all, but part of a general European, late seventeenth century Pietist reaction away from dogma in pursuit of an inner psychological illumination which would lead to the believer's conversion and final sanctification. Historically, the Wesleyan societies had ceased to be an organic part of the Establishment by the 1770s; they moved off in the direction of the anti-Anglican Protestant sub-culture, which did not welcome them, and of which, socially, they did not want to be a part. Anglican Evangelicalism – at first a clerical movement – originally filled the same social gap in the Church of England. The rise of an extreme anti-Christian and populist politics in France in the 1790s in the brief crisis of 'dechristianization' alarmed the British ruling groups and gave the Anglican Evangelicals, who were entirely committed to the political status quo of the *ancien régime*, a chance to attain respectability and influence, but the revival of the High Church vocabulary in the 1830s suggests an enduring social antipathy between two sizeable groups of people who both thought of themselves as

'Anglican'. One cannot, I feel, give total priority to the pressure of ideas: there was a social cleavage which cried out for linguistic expression which, in its turn, accentuated the conflict. As Karl Marx said in 'The Eighteenth Brumaire of Louis Napoleon', 'men make their own history, but they do not make it just as they please; they do not make it in circumstances chosen by themselves, but under circumstances directly encountered, given and transmitted from the past'. Tension between the two Anglican sub-cultures was acute enough to delay the further modernization of the Church of England during the Victorian period, minor adjustments apart. The seventeenth-century divisions had involved rival concepts of political society and had reached a climax in civil war; in the nineteenth century, however, the collision between Anglican Evangelical and Anglo-Catholic gradually receded from the public consciousness, never threatening to set society on fire. Much more political excitement was generated by the persistent campaign of the Nonconformists for the disestablishment of the Church of England (in the 1830s and the 1870s especially), and for the removal of the restrictions on the civil rights of Dissenters, some of which went back to the seventeenth century. The Anglican myth, however, as formulated in the Victorian period, did not attach much significance to Dissent's separate identity, but presented 'Dissent' as a lack of something which 'Anglicanism' possessed.

In the present century a revived Roman Catholic community has entered the arena and has competed for primacy in the total Christian sub-culture, now itself much smaller than it used to be, and more evenly balanced by a religious sub-culture which is not Christian. As a reflection of this, historians can already see signs of the emergence of a 'Catholic' version of 'Anglican' history. A new school of ecclesiastical historians is rewriting the overall history of both the religious and the Christian sub-cultures in Catholic terms, making use of changes of interpretation which have already been applied to the problems of the Continental Reformation. The European Reformation, we are now sometimes told, was a regrettable series of erratic developments which divided a church which need not have been divided. A similar convention is forming that the English Reformation was no more than an affair of institutions which should be looked at institutionally; that English Protestantism should be defined in 'Anglican' language as a group of relatively minor theological and ecclesiastical readjustments to the state of the English medieval ecclesia; and that separatists, radicals and puritans were outsiders. We may soon be told that 'Catholicism' has always been the real content of Christian culture in England, and that 'Anglicanism' was an erratic, temporary, half-regrettable and wholly dispensable Anglo-Saxon variety of Catholicism proper which can now find its full expression in a quiet return to Rome. Since the mid-nineteenth century a steady campaign has continued to set up a Catholic version of English religious history since the Reformation in which the central figures have been Thomas More, Oliver Plunket and, more recently, John Henry Newman. After 1850 the re-established Catholic hierarchy encouraged the hope of a future Catholic reconversion of England, an idea which has not been seriously challenged by Professor John Bossy's proposal to relate the history of English Catholicism to that of English Nonconformity rather than to that of the Church of England (see *The English Catholic Community 1570–1850*, 1975).

Sub-Cultures of the Church of England

In Anglican historiography, however, the eighteenth century remains a century of sober decline. In that period, the Church of England, as the established church, remained faithful to the Hanoverian state, but lost effectiveness partly because of the intellectual pressure of the Enlightenment, partly because the ecclesiastical system was socially exploited by members of a corrupt governing-class, and partly because of the church's essentially still unmodernized institutions. In contrast, the nineteenth century stands out as a century of recovery – an interpretation which underlay, for example, *The Victorian Church* (2 vols, 1966, 1970) by Owen Chadwick. In its vaguer form the argument may be found in the Preface to David Edwards's *Christian England* (vol. 3, 1984), where he said that

> this book tells the story of how the Evangelical Revival brought

> a new power to personal religion for many of the English including the Methodists and the other Nonconformists. It was followed by a Catholic revival both in the Church of England and in the enlarged Roman Catholic community, together with a new determination to respond to the needs of a larger population in the world's first industrial nation. Such revivals made Victorian England as religious as it was, with a faith which sustained poets from Wordsworth to Hopkins and much philanthropy – and which spread (like the connected British Empire and commerce) into all continents. Even this mere sketch of the Victorian age brings together many outstanding men and women. For all its faults it was an age full of courage and creativity, one of the peaks of Christian civilisation; only people not fit to be compared with the Victorians will sneer at them.[6]

The more sophisticated version of this theory of an Anglican and Christian recovery combines the effect of three forces: first, Anglican Evangelicalism; second, Anglo-Catholicism; and third, a long-running search for institutional modernization, which culminated in the setting-up of the Church Assembly in 1919.[7] The feeling that so much effort cannot have been for nothing might be said to be the hall-mark of the traditional ecclesiastical historian, and one finds this clearly brought out by another Anglican historian, Paul Welsby:

> The picture since 1945 is a mixed one. Certain new housing areas and downtown parishes have lacked the resources for mission and care . . . Congregations elsewhere have been mostly middle-aged or elderly, . . . A number of clergy have feared to share their minstry with the laity . . . Too often worship has been formal and uninspired and the stranger rejected or ignored. Yet one of the most remarkable features of our period has been the way in which life in so many parishes has flourished in contrast with the disillusionment experienced in the national life of the Church . . . The loss of the sense of God has posed new problems for evangelism, because those for whom God is dead, irrelevant or insignificant see no need to acknowledge and worship Him. Yet in spite of this, and although it has not grown

in numbers, the Church has improved in many ways and has produced congregations which are lively and vigorous.[8]

The Anglican Evangelical contribution to the myth was made in the eighteenth and the first half of the nineteenth centuries. The early stages of the movement are interpreted as the religious reply of the Establishment to the scepticism of the Enlightenment; in the nineteenth century it is celebrated as the conqueror of slavery, the protector of child labour, the inspiration of a hundred different societies for doing good. After the victory over the West Indian planters in 1833, however, the Anglican Evangelicals gradually faded from public notice and therefore from the secular historian's attention. In the Anglican Evangelical version of Anglican history the evangelical campaign to save the true Protestant Anglican tradition is constantly thwarted by Anglo-Catholicism; some Anglican historians, however, unduly minimize the significance of the opposition between the two groups. Instead, they tend to follow the lead of scholars like Geoffrey Best, for example, in his much-needed cool look at *Shaftesbury* (1964), who said that 'there was so much Evangelicalism of one kind or another about in early Victorian England that the historian cannot define it further than by noting what in general men who were ready to acknowledge themselves as Evangelicals believed, and by noticing how similar their reactions were to certain stimuli – Popery, Puseyism, Lord's Day Observance, Liberal theology, slavery, overseas missions, dancing and the theatre'.[9] Literary critics, like Elizabeth Jay, in her book about the Victorian novel, *The Religion of the Heart* (1979), have taken up and spread this notion of a diffuse but powerful 'Evangelicalism' which is represented as generating a specific Victorian mentality. Another literary critic, Valentine Cunningham, even defended this generalized Evangelicalism against one group of its Victorian critics: in *Everywhere Spoken Against, Dissent in the Victorian Novel* (1975) he vigorously defended Dissenting ministers against the unfavourable image which they were regularly given by novelists like Charles Dickens. The hypocritical priest is a stock character both of folk-lore and fiction, and the Anglican clergy did not come off better. Dickens was not writing as a historian, but he may have been reflecting a strain of anti-clericalism which had its immediate source in Rousseau's *vicaire savoyard*.

Cunningham's book had the merit of insisting that one should not confuse distinct sub-cultures, that all Dissenting 'evangelicalism' was not the same as all Anglican 'evangelicalism', that here as elsewhere one should resist the advance of the army of ideal types. However, the assumption of a widely-diffused and vaguely defined religious ethos has spread without ever being tested in a major examination of the field. There was a group of older books: G. R. Balleine's *History of the Evangelical Party in the Church of England*, first published in 1909 and extended by G. W. Bromiley in 1951; L. G. Elliott-Binns, *The Early Evangelicals* (1953); and J. S. Reynolds' *The Evangelicals at Oxford 1735–1971* (1953). J. C. Pollock's *A Cambridge Movement* (1953) was a history of the Student Christian Movement of the late nineteenth century, which began in the Evangelical sub-culture but was divided by the impact of liberal theology and High Church politics; Pollock also wrote *The Keswick Story* (1964), a study of the American Holiness movement as it finally made an impact on British Evangelicalism in the last quarter of the nineteenth century. In a brilliant and not altogether implausible flight of the imagination, the military historian, Correlli Barnett suggested that this diffused Evangelicalism impregnated the Victorian ruling-class with a sense of guilt which made it impossible for them to cope with the problems of possessing and defending the British Empire,[10] but the kind of committed writer we are discussing here was chiefly concerned to bring Evangelicalism into the foreground of the Victorian picture, to emphasize its theological loyalty to the Reformation of Luther and Calvin, to show positive social value, and to work out for the Anglican movement as distinguished a pedigree as that of Anglo-Catholicism (if one includes Charles the Martyr and John Henry Newman). This new Evangelical pedigree included John and Charles Wesley, who were not Anglican Evangelicals at all, despite the determination of writers like J. S. Reynolds to treat them as such; the two Henry Venns, of whom the nineteenth-century missionary leader emerged as much the more important and the less typically evangelical; Charles Simeon (1759–1836) – there was a bicentenary appraisal, *Charles Simeon*, edited by Michael Hennell, in 1959; and J. C. Ryle (1816–1900), the Etonian first bishop of Liverpool (from 1880 almost until his death) and the Evangelical conscience of the Church of England in his own opinion.

If this list is considered as the rough equivalent of John Keble, Edward Pusey and Charles Gore, it gives a measure of the undoubted decline of Anglican Evangelicalism in the later nineteenth century. Essentially, the Evangelicals as a clerical group were outmanoeuvred in the 1840s on their own favourite territory of doctrinal purity by the even fiercer dogmatic intransigence of the Anglo-Catholics, and then isolated still further in the 1880s when Gore persuaded the younger Anglo-Catholics to follow him in a subtle if impermanent theological combination which might be called Patristic Liberalism. The bicentenary volume on Simeon accepted Charles Smyth's judgment (in *Simeon and Church Order*, 1940) that Simeon ranked 'with Samuel Wilberforce, bishop of Oxford, the Remodeller of the Episcopate, as Burgess called him, as one of the founding fathers, or Remodellers of the Church of England in the nineteenth century', but if this were true the history of Anglican Evangelicalism after Simeon's death would have been very different. It is arguable, of course, that the episcopate was not remodelled by Samuel Wilberforce, who only made his fellow bishops feel obliged to work harder without changing the system within which they worked; and that what remodelling was done to the Church of England as a whole was brought about through the Church Commissioners (for whose history see Geoffrey Best, *Temporal Pillars*, 1964, and Olive Brose, *Church and Parliament, the Reshaping of the Church of England 1828–60*, 1959): but the Church Commissioners reformed rather than remodelled, they rescued the Establishment financially, but they did not innovate. Simeon was really the invention of committed historians in search of an ecclesiastical hero. Nothing in his writings (Arthur Pollard edited a short selection of his sermons called *His Master's Voice* in 1957) or his practical spirituality prepared anyone for the swift return of religious symbolism; he had no accurate vision of what was happening to the Anglican Church in the 1820s, though he lived in constant contact with young ordinands in Cambridge. In the closed Evangelical sub-culture which he dominated, religious revival still meant what it had meant in the eighteenth century:

justified earnestness, over against the Hanoverian civic religion. Nothing Simeon said or did helped men in a period when Evangelicalism had come to be rejected as formal, and when religious revival meant the passionate Anglo-Catholic return to the use of images. This was a far cry from the tradition which caused Simeon to say that 'all attempts to reform the Roman Catholic Church will be in vain and there must be an extermination of it as a church, and any conversion must be of individuals'. Although Peter Toon, in *Evangelical Theology: The Response to the Tractarians* (1979), tried to show that Evangelical Anglican theologians were capable of answering Pusey successfully by an appeal to the post-Reformation divinity of the Church of England, and through that to the Patristic authors, and were entitled to claim that Pusey was an innovator, not a restorer of the true Anglican past, Toon himself was still arguing as though the issues could be judged in terms of the theological limits which Simeon and his associates laid down. The sad truth was that writing when they did, and within the limits they chose, neither the Evangelical nor the Anglo-Catholic theologians were likely to stumble on anything of permanent value; they were appealing to absolute authorities which no longer had authority. Newman glimpsed this when he wrote Tract 90 to dissolve the Thirty-Nine Articles, but it was to be the 1860s before theological debate in England began to leave the shelter of the past.

We need a social history of Anglican Evangelicalism much more than an intellectual history. Doreen Rosman's *Evangelicals and Culture* (1984) used the evidence of periodical literature to show that between 1770 and 1833 Evangelicals shared the ideas and tastes of their contemporaries rather more than has been realized, but she has to admit that by the 1830s their tendency to withdraw into a biblically-defended, separatist, but not altogether convincingly otherworldly sub-culture was driving them closer and closer to a philistine abjuration of experience. And Michael Hennell thought that in the period down to 1870 Evangelicals showed an increasing strictness and rigidity towards the 'world', as practices allowed by earlier evangelicals were in turn rejected by their successors.[11] Anglican Evangelicalism did not take over Victorian society, but was gradually driven onto its margin, and Anglo-Catholicism, for all its bravura and its not dissimilar impulse to reject the 'world' – the bravura and the asceticism did not always combine too well – probably had less social impact outside the Church of England itself. To some extent this misreading of early Victorian society[12] mistook for the effects of Evangelical Pietism the mid-Victorian drive for 'respectability', a secular style which attracted many working-class as well as middle-class people. Respectability was not necessarily a religious value or goal, but a question of what clothes one wore, how one spoke, what kind of people one associated with, and what kind of people one dissociated oneself from. None of this required religious sanctions or the efforts of pressure-groups, but membership of a religious group offered support to one's claim to respectable status.

In the standard version of the Anglican myth, however, Anglo-Catholicism is made the principal agent of the nineteenth-century recovery. The implied claim that Anglo-Catholicism was a *natural* Anglican development, which summed up and even recovered what 'Anglicanism', itself a nineteenth-century word, implied, has obscured the study of why Anglo-Catholicism ever happened. For it may seem quite *un*natural that young self-styled Anglicans in the 1830s should have been advocating a celibate priesthood, aural confession, monasticism and the cult of saints and relics, together with a total scorn of anything which could be called 'Protestant'. Celibacy, the confessional, pilgrimages to shrines, and contempt for the Reformation, had not been typical of the Church of England from the end of the sixteenth down to the nineteenth century. Nevertheless, the guardians of the myth have accepted what happened in the 1830s as though it could be explained quite easily, and have perhaps betrayed a certain satisfaction that Anglo-Catholicism has limited the ecclesiastical influence of Anglican Evangelicalism without itself ever achieving complete mastery over the Anglican system.

Historically, the Anglo-Catholic movement is not much noticed by secular historians after its moment of crisis in 1845, when Newman departed for Roman Catholicism. Anglican apologists exaggerate the small-scale activity of Anglo-Catholic priests in late nineteenth-century poor parishes as evidence that the Establishment really cared for the working-classes, and that Anglo-Catholicism itself possessed a formula for their reconversion. One consequence of the absence of a conflict-view of nineteenth-century Anglican history is that historians in general fail to relate Anglo-Catholicism and Anglican Evangelicalism to one another after the brief encounters of the 1860s, whose unpleasant violence is attributed to popular ignorance. The Church of England is described as following a line of development which reconciled extremes into a coherent, creative tradition. It would be equally plausible, however, to argue that the nineteenth-century Church of England was still a set of institutions in search of an identity, and that the institutions failed to adapt adequately to changes in the nineteenth century because they had become the battleground of irreconcilable and fundamentally irresponsible opposing forces.

An example of how the accepted myth affects contemporary judgment can be found in a review by A. O. J. Cockshut of *Charles Lowder and the Ritualist Movement* (1982), by L. G. Ellsworth. Lowder was a Victorian Anglo-Catholic priest who spent much of his later career in London's dockland. Cockshut repeated the standard ecclesiastical judgment that Lowder's labours were heroic, and accepted the Anglo-Catholic version of his behaviour without hesitation. Of A. C. Tait, who as bishop of London tried to discipline Lowder, he said that he 'may be said to have fully earned his elevation to Canterbury by his waspish insistence on Protestant Erastianism at all costs, whatever the harm done to his clergy and to the religious life of the people'. The attitude of other bishops, equally critical of the Anglo-Catholic movement, would be inexplicable (Cockshut said) 'unless we are to be satisfied with the cynical explanation that they acted simply to further their own interests'. Such bishops preferred a dead Protestant parish to a flourishing ritualistic one; Protestants who never went to church might be virtuous enough in episcopal eyes, but an Anglo-Catholic was automatically suspect, if not actually a criminal. This is myth – Lowder as hero and martyr, Tait as a figure of contempt – a myth invented in the heat of action, but repeated without serious attempt at historical understanding. In the England of the 1980s the idea that there was no alternative to the extreme party-line had become fashionable again, and conflict-images of politics were popular. In such an atmosphere Anglo-Catholicism seemed justified by its partial success, and by its rejection of relativism.[13]

No revolutionary advances have been made in the study of Anglo-Catholicism, in the sense that the narrative line after 1845 is no clearer in 1985 than it was forty years ago, and that the most recent study of Anglo-Catholic ritualism, James Bentley's *Ritualism and Politics in Victorian Britain* (1978), the first detailed study of the failure of the Public Worship Regulation Act of 1874 to stop the spread of Anglo-Catholicism by putting legal limits on the freedon of the parish clergy to introduce liturgical changes, was uncritical of the Anglo-Catholic version of Anglican history, and set the scene too much in the world of Victorian 'high politics'. The nearest attempt at serious innovation was in Kenneth Thompson's underrated *Bureaucracy and Church Reform* (1970), which analysed the history of the nineteenth-century Church of England in the spirit of Weber, taking as a starting-point the assumption that changes in British society compelled the Anglican Church to face the option of rationalizing its structure and creating the kind of central bureaucracy which a 'modernized' ecclesia would have required. He showed how the embattled parties of the Establishment presented the emergence of a consensus about institutional reform throughout the Victorian era. As Thompson wrote, 'what was needed in the long run was a theory which could reconcile expediency in adapting norms (the concern of the reformers) with legitimation in terms of religious principles (the emphasis of the Oxford Movement)', but neither of the principal ecclesiastical groups was able to work out such a theory for itself, or to accept the proposals of its rival. 'Nothing deterred Newman', Thompson said, 'from leading a movement to fight the rationalistic pragmatism of the new middle class, under the name of the Church as the embodiment of transcendental values and supernatural qualities.' To put it more bluntly, reform was profane and resistance to institutional change was a virtue. This in no way prevented Newman from demanding changes on the dogmatic and liturgical plane – 'liturgical' not so much in terms of what the priest did or wore, as in terms of what he was understood to be doing, or intending to do.[14] If one interprets the situation of the Church of England in this way, both Anglo-Catholicism and Anglican Evangelicalism were at least as likely a cause of decay as of regeneration. Indeed, the Church Commissioners, who found little favour with either party, should be given some of the credit for the institutional recovery that took place. In any case, Kenneth Thompson produced an account which had the prime virtue of accepting a conflict-model of what happened, and of trying to explain what this conflict implied for the Establishment as such.

Another book which hoped to combine sociology and committed history was *A Social History of the Diocese of Newcastle* (1981), edited by W. S. F. Pickering, and intended to commemorate the centenary of the diocese's foundation in 1882. Here the contributors, one or two of whom were still bitter at the original hostility shown towards Anglo-Catholicism in the diocese, not least by one of its earlier bishops, failed to come to grips with their own statistics, which suggested that this diocese, started when the campaign to revitalize the Establishment in the industrial areas was at its height, never really succeeded, but actually declined, slowly at first, and then quickly from the mid-twentieth century. This was the basic event which should have controlled the perspective of the writers; without that perspective one is left with fascinating, but disorganized, information, and without confirmation of the importance attached to the Anglo-Catholic revival by tradition.

Such criticisms will not please church historians for whom the church, however visible and however visibly corrupt or in social decline, still retains the aura of a supernatural foundation. That was the mood in which the centenary of the Anglo-Catholic movement was greeted in 1933. Thus *The History of the Anglo-Catholic Revival from 1845* (1932) by W. J. Sparrow Simpson, at least concentrated on the period after Newman's secession but suffered from the author's conviction that the movement was and always had been an unmixed blessing. *The Development of Modern Catholicism* (1933) by W. L. Knox and A. R. Vidler was a theological essay which aimed to show that the Liberal Catholicism in which the writers ardently believed was the natural heir of Tractarianism, which had so far succeeded in restoring the life of the Church of England that it was possible by the late nineteenth century for the very Liberalism against which Tractarianism had originally protested to enter into a fruitful union with Catholicism itself. As I have already suggested, the absence of a sound basis in social history makes this positive interpretation of the Anglo-Catholic revival difficult to defend, all the more because Knox and Vidler published their book at the moment when Liberal theology was going into an abrupt decline, from which, as far as Anglo-Catholicism was conerned, it would never recover, because the logical conclusion of Vidler's position – Catholic Modernism – was unacceptable in Rome, the final court of dogma in Anglo-Catholic circles. This is not to say that they were wider of the mark than W. G. Peck, who said in *The Social Implications of the Oxford Movement* (1933) that

> the Oxford Movement was part of that wider revival of Catholic thought which has now become one of the most notable features of the intellectual situation at the very time when the exhaustion of the secular adventure has produced so inclusive a confusion. To learn the right use of the world, and the satisfying structure of society in that operation, men must now return to the principles of the sacramental fellowship from which they have strayed so far.[15]

In reality, not only Liberalism but also the Catholic revival was dying down in the 1930s, and the future did not demonstrate the exhaustion of the secular adventurers. As far as the sociology of religion was concerned, what lay ahead was the over-use of words like 'secularization', not 'sacramental fellowship'. In itself, Anglo-Catholicism would have to wait on the outcome of a conflict in the Roman Catholic Church which would surface in the second Vatican Council, but remain undecided in the 1980s.

I do not mean that these writers should have been able to foresee the course which Western institutional religion would take, but that what they said underlines the importance of the historian's not believing that he has perceived an underlying continuity in historical events, whether the alleged continuity is materialist or supernatural. When Sir Owen Chadwick gave his verdict on Anglo-Catholicism in *The Victorian Church* (1966), he was more cautious than the celebrants of 1933. He said that

> beneath popular disesteem and public weakness they strengthened the soul of the Church of England . . . No one did more to drive Anglican worshippers out of formalism, to give them a

> sense that Christianity had a history and a treasure not insular, and to enable sympathetic hearts to perceive the beauty and poetry of religion.[16]

This was safe enough, and both in his own anthology, *The Mind of the Oxford Movement* (1960), and in another, similar, reader *Anglo-Catholic Theology* (1965), edited by an American scholar, E. R. Fairweather, there was a tendency to suppress the controversial nature of Anglo-Catholicism, to leave the impression that its mind was traditional, lofty and dull.

At the time of the centenary in 1933, however, E. A. Knox, a former bishop of Manchester and a distinguished Evangelical, whose son, Ronald, had become a Roman Catholic, made a gallant attempt in a now forgotten book, *The Tractarian Movement 1833–45*, to place the movement with more precision, and to raise the question of its intellectual standing. He said that Tractarianism was part of a more general revival of religion in Europe in the second quarter of the nineteenth century. It was a tragically mistaken movement, however, because the Tractarians, impressed by the 'encircling gloom' of the 1830s, found the root of all evil in the rebellion against the divine authority of the church, by which they meant the romantic church of the Middle Ages, and thought that if this authority could be restored all would be well, whereas, Knox said, the real danger to Christianity lay in the liberal theology of Strauss and his successors, and to this the Oxford Theologians had no answer at all. 'For this attack', he wrote, 'the Oxford Divines had made no preparation. Of German theology they had studied nothing but the Roman Catholic Symbolic of Mohler. Scientific history they had despised and had done their best to discredit. While Thomas Arnold had studied the system of Niebuhr, they had regarded his doing so as another evidence of his heterodoxy. It was ludicrous, had it not been inexpressibly sad, that against the deluge of Strauss' *Life of Jesus* the great and brilliant Newman provided nothing better for his followers in the way of historical refuge than *The Lives of the Saints*.' Oxford, he said, had no 'rational defence against a deliberate onslaught on the foundations of the Catholic Church'.[17]

There was some truth in this, though it could have been said as accurately of Charles Simeon and the Evangelicals of the same period that they did not understand the kind of historical experience which lay behind Liberalism, and that both groups exaggerated the significance of the appeal to religious experience which became, in rather different forms, the core of their reply to the Liberal position. Knox ignored the sense in which Anglo-Catholicism developed as a defence against Evangelicalism itself. He was on better ground when he declared that the Anglo-Catholics failed at what for them was a crucial point – they failed to increase the authority of the clergy over the Anglican laity, who persisted in what he called 'the national refusal to be governed by the clergy even in things spiritual'.[18]

Knox was writing at the end of a long, embattled period which had reached its climax in the parliamentary débacle of the 1928 Prayer Book when the House of Commons, claiming, however perversely, to represent the 'Anglican laity', had blocked the liturgical changes which the Anglican episcopate had brought forward in the hope of reconciling the opposing wings of the Established Church. Anglo-Catholicism was never to seem so important again, and this is perhaps why it has not been studied extensively. Late Victorian ecclesiastical history is still often seen through overcommitted eyes, as when James Bentley said that when Anglo-Catholic priests successfully resisted the application of the Public Worship Act of 1874 they 'not only preserved the Anglican clergyman's ancient freedom; they also advanced the cause of toleration in Victorian Britain'.[19] The three-way struggle between moderate institutionalists like A. C. Tait, an Anglo-Catholic extremist like Pusey and an Evangelical extremist like J. C. Ryle was not about individual liberty and toleration but about the definition of 'Anglicanism', about the role of the laity, quite as much as of the priesthood, in the Established Church, and about the credibility of Christianity in a modernizing society.

Like most of the Victorian Anglican episcopate, Tait was unable to agree that there was good ground for regarding monasticism as 'Anglican'; he disapproved of life-vows, and he also found little or no religious value in the kind of opposition which the conventual life set up against the 'world'. Anglican historians have not discussed the subject at length. There is a not very critical biography of *Priscilla Sellon* (1950) by T. J. Williams; Pusey called her 'the restorer after three centuries of the Religious Life in the English Church'. P. F. Anson's *The Call of the Cloister* (1955) and A. M. Allchin's *The Silent Rebellion* (1958) both offered an approving narrative. In 1980 M. L. Smith edited a collection of essays about the ablest, if not always the most endearing, founder of Anglican monasticism, *Benson of Cowley:* Richard Meux Benson must have been one of the very few modern leaders of the Church of England to be suspected of Jansenism, in this case a code-word for Benson's pathological rejection of the creation as fallen. Only Michael Hill, in *The Religious Order* (1973), broke new ground by tackling the monastic movement in sociological terms.

The third constitutive element of the alleged Victorian Anglican recovery was the slow process of modernization which lasted from the setting-up of the Church Commissioners in the 1830s (see Geoffrey Best, *Temporal Pillars*, 1964) to the legislation which produced the Church Assembly at the end of the First World War. Anglican historians have not yet worked on this area very much, and when they do, they tend to assume the suitability of whatever changes occurred. In fact, the modernizing schemes have not worked well, for two main reasons. In the first place, the reformers never achieved an effective centralization of the Establishment, with some sort of 'cabinet', episcopal or otherwise; they encountered desperate resistance to the committee-system, or bureaucratization, which was essential if their plans were to succeed. (See K. Thompson, *Bureaucracy and Church Reform 1800–1965*, 1970.) In the second place, there was no fundamental reconsideration of the parish-basis of the historic Church of England. Anglican history has been written on the principle – it is far more than an assumption – that the parochial system is the ideal-type of the ecclesia; this belief is deeply rooted in the institutions as they are, and has been transmitted to generation after generation of priests. Proposals for a more flexible system were advanced in the mid-Victorian period, but they were virtually ignored, and the history-books have been written on the assumption that the defenders of the parochial system won the argument. There has been no general acceptance of Kenneth Thompson's view that the Anglican Evangelical and Anglo-Catholic parties contributed to the comparatively slow rate of administrative reform (and therefore to the equally important failure to sustain a religious reformation) because they did not want 'modernization' to be successful, did not want to see the parish system modified, and put the growth of their own organizations before any other kind of centralizing ecclesiastical development, which might make it easier for the episcopate to discipline the clergy.

The obvious criticism of the most common, and even semi-official, interpretation of the history of the nineteenth-century Church of England, is that it fails to cope with the apparent record of the Victorian Establishment as weakeningly divided, above all where the clergy were concerned, into three unequal and conflicting interest-groups: a large centre-party of uncertain leanings, and two smaller, but tougher wings. The Anglican Evangelicals were numerous, well-organized locally, but as the century advanced they suffered because they were committed against the direction in which change was moving. The Anglo-Catholics were perhaps fewer in number at the clerical level, but had a firm commitment to innovation on dogmatic principles. The soft-centre, as one may call it, was never much organized, and therefore was never able to use its superficial majority to limit the damage done by the conflict between the two 'undeclared sects', or rival religious sub-cultures, or pressure-groups. The soft-centre did not form a third party, sect or pressure-group, least of all a liberal pressure-group; the theological liberals among the clergy never controlled the centre.[20] The struggle between Anglican Evangelical and Anglo-Catholic does not seem to have been creative, but in Anglican mythology the combined efforts of the two groups are said to have animated a body which was otherwise in danger of finding that it had no soul. The secular historian is bound to doubt this picture of a nineteenth-century Anglican recovery, if only because the Church of England has been in overall decline for most of the twentieth century, an event which does not suggest that the measures taken in the Victorian period succeeded.

Some Anglican writers, including the committed church historian Edward Norman, and the political theorist Maurice Cowling, in *Religion and Public Doctrine in Modern England* (1980), blamed this decline not on the Anglo-Catholics and Anglican

Evangelicals, but on the clerical leadership of the Establishment, a group to which they attributed a distinct social personality. They argued that this combination of bishops and professional theologians was socially vulnerable to the ideas of its secular class-equivalent and therefore easily corrupted by the shift to centre-left or liberal humanist policies and opinions which began in the later nineteenth century and which expressed itself in the church as notions of 'liberal' or 'radical' theology, as the belief that 'Christian socialism' was the natural political programme for the ecclesia, and as unwanted and even illiterate proposals for 'liturgical reform', which boiled down to an aesthetically and spiritually destructive 'modernization' of the language of the *Book of Common Prayer*. These views could also be found in the work of the Anglican sociologist of religion, David Martin (*A General Theory of Secularization*, 1978, and *The Breaking of the Image*, 1980): he shared the same conviction that the history of the Church of England had become a story of self-betrayal, of clerics who imagined that they were freeing Anglicanism from secularization when they were actually capitulating to it.

Maurice Cowling advocated a Christian conservatism, a way of thinking which he described as 'a reaction to the realization that a post- or anti-christian doctrine not only exists but has gained ascendancy, at the same time that universal suffrage and universal education had transformed its area of operation'. The primary form of a Christian conservatism, Cowling said, was dissent, 'a Jacobitism of the mind which can do little more than protest its conviction that the modern mind is corrupt'. 'Jacobitism' had a ring of its own: to have said 'a Stuart mentality' would have given too much away, perhaps, but 'Jacobite' had the romantic sound of the lost cause, though what Cowling suffers from (in historical terms) is surely Jansenism, not Jacobitism.

Cowling's notion of the modern mind's corruption seemed to start from its rejection of Christianity, whose institution he saw as having lost all authority in modern politics, to the great detriment of public policy-making. He interpreted the rejection of Christianity as the rejection of the transcendent power of God, and of the Christian understanding of man as fallen – so fallen that whatever he might do only reproduced that fallenness, and that he could pursue holiness only by the most rigorous dissent from being human in any liberal humanist way. Cowling did not really believe in the possibility of an innocent rejection of Christianity, at least on an intellectual level; the educated Westerner should know better than to capitulate to liberal humanism. It was part of his indictment of ecclesiastical politicians that when they asserted a role in public policy-making it was only to support liberal humanist ideas about equality, education and ethics.

Rigour apart, Cowling's position was not original, and it could lead him on to dangerous ground, as when he patronized Enoch Powell as a politician: but Cowling declared that one needed a certain bloody-mindedness to extract oneself from the liberal trap, and that Powell was aware of this. Nevertheless, his position enabled him to make an interesting critique of the leading British church historian, Owen Chadwick. In *The Victorian Church*, Cowling said, Chadwick had argued that Christianity had nothing to fear from historical or scientific truth, that Victorian churchmen had done well to disengage themselves from conflict with science, and that biblical scholarship had strengthened orthodox understanding of the Bible far more than had been expected. Cowling continued:

> Chadwick assumes, as it seems mistakenly, that the period between 1840 and 1900 was crucial. He believes that a via media was open and that, under Tait's leadership, obscurantism was avoided. Though dangers arose on the way, he assumes that the nation's mind was not alienated, and that the christian intelligence gained from the challenges that it faced.[21]

Cowling thought that Chadwick had misread the historical evidence completely. It was significant, he said, that Chadwick had written virtually nothing on the twentieth century, yet it was the twentieth century which had seen the culmination of the Victorian process in the political domination of secular creeds and in a positive indifference to Christianity which was unlike what had happened in previous centuries. Chadwick, on the other hand, wrote as though secularization had fallen back in the late nineteenth century, not just because there had been a reaction against science and positivism, but also because the Christian churches had preserved a viable position. He left the impression that 'decency, simplicity and religion can prevail'.[22] Cowling, however, while no doubt believing that religion could survive, thought that too much of the religion had been sacrificed to make Anglicanism simple and decent.

Theories of Methodism and Nonconformity

The modern study of eighteenth-century Anglican church history still depends to some extent on the work of Norman Sykes, whose biography of Edmund Gibson, the Bishop of London from 1723 to his death in 1748, appeared as far back as 1926. Sykes's reputation was established by *Church and State in England in the Eighteenth Century* (1934); his one serious failure was a lengthy biography of the early eighteenth-century Archbishop of Canterbury, *William Wake*, which came out in 1957.

Sykes tried to combine a detailed apologia for the seventeenth- and eighteenth-century Church of England with an aggressive reinterpretation of its history from the point of view of the twentieth-century Anglican soft-centre where neither Evangelical nor Anglo-Catholic has the last word. He was so far successful that G. V. Bennett wrote of *Edmund Gibson* and *Church and State* that 'taken together, they made possible a reassessment of the eighteenth-century Church of England, revealing indeed its immobility and involvement in the world of patronage and politics but showing that in pastoral matters its record was not one of unrelieved torpor and neglect as had so often been asserted'.[23] Bennett was referring to the steady denigration of the Hanoverian clergy in both the Methodist and the Anglo-Catholic tradition. When *Church and State* was published, however, Sykes had been criticized on the ground that his book was special pleading. Special pleading was exactly what Sykes had demonstrated in earlier versions of the history of the eighteenth-century Establishment – for despite his book's wide title he said little about either Methodism or Dissent. An excellent example of how Sykes attacked the dominant version of the Anglicanism of the *ancien régime* was his criticism of an essay which S. L. Ollard had written on the controversial subject of confirmation (in 1926). Sykes took the chance to defend the episcopate of the eighteenth century:

> In their endeavours to grapple with the many obstacles to pastoral oversight and to the discharge of the spiritual administration of their office, the 18th-century episcopate merit a juster measure of appreciation than has been their lot at the hands of subsequent historians. The Georgian bench indeed has been pilloried as a byword of sloth, inefficiency and neglect. Apologists have shown a marked capacity for differentiation between the same characteristics when present in bishops of the Caroline age and in those of its successor. The biographer of Lancelot Andrewes (seventeenth century) allows that 'we know little of his distinctively episcopal work, his few extant letters making no special mention of pastoral duties'; but he is careful to add 'that the standard by which a bishop's work was measured in those days was not that of our own time'. The nicest degree of discrimination between prelates of the High and Low-church traditions is shown by Canon Ollard in his survey of confirmations. Although referring to the enquiries of Barlow of Lincoln (High Church) concerning confirmation, he makes no mention of that bishop's complete and protracted neglect of his diocese, whereas he is at pains to note of Hoadly (Low) that 'he never visited his diocese of Bangor, nor apparently Hereford.' . . . The restriction by Bishop Bull (High-Church) of confirmations to the place near his residence, owing to his inability to visit his diocese in person and to travel through its territory to confirm, is applauded as 'an advance upon the practice which confined confirmation to the bishop's visitation'; whilst of Gilbert Burnet (Low) it is stated that in his *Discourse of the Pastoral Care* 'confirmation is not mentioned under a bishop's duties', although that prelate is allowed the credit of having been 'active in administering confirmation and in twenty years had confirmed in 265 churches in his diocese'. Finally, following a summary of the confirmation tours of Archbishop Drummond of York, who died in 1771, and without any later reference save a reference to confirmations in the diocese of Ely in 1829 and 1833, Ollard affirms that 'the evidence for the later years of the

> eighteenth century and for the earlier years of the nineteenth, points to the conclusion that carelessness and infrequency in administering confirmation were reaching their lowest level, comparable only to the period of neglect when Calvinism was at its height two hundred years before'. Before such a tribunal the 18th-century episcopate may well decline to plead its defence.[24]

Sykes was not offering an unbiased version of Anglican history, but he showed that it was possible to argue plausibly that eighteenth-century Anglicanism, the lost century of Anglican tradition, ought not to be singled out for adverse criticism; that many of its clergy, though neither Wesleyan nor Anglo-Catholic, had quietly devoted their lives to their parishes; that the bishops should not be judged in terms of the ambitious, theological rationalist Hoadly, but Hoadly himself in terms of his betters – men who struggled to cope with their ramshackle, rambling dioceses and who had neither the railway nor the motor-car to lessen the strain. In later years Sykes over-identified himself with the sufferings of an allegedly unfairly harassed episcopate, and in his contribution to *The Interim Statement on the Conversations between the Church of England and the Methodist Church* (1958) even said that 'it was not the case that the spread of Methodism was frustrated or hindered by episcopal action . . . instead a juster charge against the episcopate would be that no steps were taken to establish a corporate policy'. It was a rather desperate defence of the eighteenth-century hierarchy's reaction to Wesleyanism to say that the bishops did not actually do anything to hinder it, and such a categorical assertion depended on how one defined 'hindrance'. Sykes, however, took little interest in the Evangelical side of the eighteenth century; his vision of the establishment hardly allowed for its existence; John Wesley figured most vividly in *Church and State* as a critic whose hysterical condemnation of the Anglican priesthood could be (and rightly) rejected. Nevertheless, what Sykes was doing in 1958, or what he may have hoped that he was doing, was helping to speed the work of an Anglican-Methodist reconciliation.

This concentration on the church as an ecclesiastical institution (Sykes produced little in the way of an economic or sociological study of the church of the Enlightenment) suited the mood of a clerical sub-culture deeply involved in efforts to unite the institutional world-ecclesia. In *Old Priest and New Presbyter* (1956), which was an extension of an earlier essay, *The Church of England and Non-Episcopal Churches in the Sixteenth and Seventeenth Centuries* (1948), Sykes tried to influence the ecclesiastical politics of his time by using the historical method as he understood it to settle the long controversy over the Anglican attitude to episcopacy, presbyterianism and papacy since the Reformation. This was very much an ecclesiastical subject: what was at stake was the Anglo-Catholic interpretation of the Anglican past. Myth and event were hopelessly entangled, but Sykes thought that it was possible to clear the ground.

He sought to show that between the Reformation and the nineteenth century there had been a general refusal by Anglicans of many different shades of opinion to regard episcopacy as of the essence of the church's being: most Anglican had recognized that 'in cases of necessity' it might be dispensed with. Moreover, not only was it agreed in theory that the 'cases of necessity' argument applied to many of the Continental reformed churches, but in practice these churches had not commonly been refused 'the true nature and essence of a church', however short they might fall of 'the integrity and perfection of a church'. Sykes worked out in detail such examples as the regular employment in eighteenth-century India by the Anglican authorities of Lutheran ordained missionaries, a practice which had certainly involved recognition of their ministerial orders. Having established the existence in the sixteenth, seventeenth and eighteenth centuries of what he called an Anglican norm in such matters, Sykes said that the Tractarians broke with *Anglican* tradition when they tried to substitute an exclusive theory of episcopacy. It was the Tractarians, and not the (once again) much maligned Anglicans of the Enlightenment, who had innovated.

In so far as anyone could be said to have done such a thing, Sykes drove his opponents from their historical ground in this quiet, effective book. One may doubt whether the study of ecclesiastical history can ever do what he was trying to do here, shatter the standing of a particular doctrine: from the Anglo-Catholic point of view, no amount of Anglican historical error could constitute an Anglican norm, or to put it another way, what was doctrinally true could not be historically wrong. From the point of view of the secular historian, on the other hand, it might seem that Sykes was ignoring the historical nature and origins of Tractarianism, whose roots lay in an eighteenth-century sociological pattern different from the biblical, patristic and philosphical soil in which they were to flourish in the 1830s.[25] Sykes, however, was not seeking to penetrate the ambiguities of that background, any more than he was asking what it was in early nineteenth-century Evangelical families which made so many of the children welcome the Tractarian theory – hardly on rational or historical grounds – once the battle began. What Sykes did was to show in crushing detail that if the Anglican norm was to be defined by an appeal to Anglican history – and Anglo-Catholic theory insisted on appealing to history as well as to revelation – then all the historical events must be given their full weight, and that taken as a whole this evidence implied that the Tractarians (as Anglicans) were, what they had always claimed not to be, innovators.

Sykes did not shake Anglo-Catholic self-confidence: when Geoffrey Rowell wrote *The Vision Glorious* (1983) for the one hundred and fiftieth anniversary of the Assize Sermon which is usually regarded as having initiated the Anglo-Catholic movement, he ignored Sykes altogether, and with him the problem of Anglican (and Anglo-Catholic) history before 1800. As Rowell understood it, Anglo-Catholicism had been born in the 1830s as a response to threats to the Church of England, and was both a defensive reaction to protect the church from political interference, 'and an affirmation that the identity of the Church' – always the same problem of identity – 'was very much more than the religious aspect of English society'. Keble's Assize Sermon of 1833 also reflected (Rowell thought) an awareness that the Christian religion was ceasing to be regarded as the bond of English society. What mattered in response was a 'Catholic' vision of the ecclesia as a supernatural, episcopally-constituted community which derived from Christ and his apostles, and of which the Church of England was a true part. Sykes would not have agreed with Rowell's claim that 'it was the Catholic vision of a reunited, episcopally ordered, sacramentally centred Church, international in character, but to which local churches would contribute their particular genius and outlook, which was the inspiration of ecumenical endeavour';[26] this particular 'vision' hampered rather than helped ecumenical negotiations, which were inspired (if that is the right word) by more liberal hopes of compromise between 'Catholic' and 'Evangelical'.

Rowell's view may also be compared with that of W. R. Ward, in *Religion and Society in England 1790–1850* (1972), for whom the Anglo-Catholic 'vision' was a disastrous and authoritarian reaction against an open, 'ecumenical' revival of Christianity, including Roman Catholicism, at the end of the eighteenth century.

Rowell's reaction suggested that although Sykes had shown the difficulty of relating such a supernatural vision of the Ecclesia to actual historical events, he had not damaged the power of the sustaining myth itself – and if Professor Ward aspired to Sykes's mantle the same would be true of him. If anything diminished the strength of the Anglo-Catholic system in the long run, it was the steady decline in the authority and influence of the original intellectual sources of the movement, especially that of patristic writers in general (Augustine always excepted) and of English divines from Laud to the end of the eighteenth century: no doubt the reputation of Bishop Butler survived, but he gave no help to Anglo-Catholicism as such, whatever his contribution to John Henry Newman's 'grammar of assent', or theology of conscience. Anglo-Catholicism has never looked imposing intellectually since the older High Church mentality disintegrated under the pressure of late Victorian criticism, both biblical and theological. Keble (for whom see W. J. Beek's study, *John Keble's Literary and Religious Contribution to the Oxford Movement*, 1959) and the Tractarians in general (see *The Tractarian Understanding of the Eucharist*, by A. Hardelin, 1965) had no theological originality of their own, once Newman had abandoned them. This point has not been given quite the weight it deserves because the studies that have been done on Anglo-Catholic theology often seem to have been written in a critical vacuum as though patristic theology still had an unchallenged authority quite separate from that of the New Testament. It is one thing to respect 'pure scholarship' in fields like those of patristic studies and of the history of Anglican theology since the Reformation, but the texts involved cannot simply be analysed on the basis of the assumptions governing theological discourse at the time at which they were written. Even in the 1830s it was no longer enough to argue that Tractarianism was reviving positions which the Church of England should never have ceased to hold: the problem was whether these older positions could be revived simply by an appeal to the authority of the past.

Perhaps an awareness of these questions of method helps to explain why the one hundred and fiftieth anniversary of Anglo-Catholicism did not produce as much historical writing as had been the case in 1933. Apart from Geoffrey Rowell's work, *Pusey Rediscovered* (1983, edited by Perry Butler) was a collection of essays aimed at restoring Pusey's reputation, though this was hampered by Pusey's stubborn conservatism, which welcomed a sacral idea of monarchy and 'passive obedience', and involved him in opposing all useful change at Oxford University. Fresh detail apart, this was the Pusey with whom one was familiar: it was all very well for David Edwards to stick to tradition and say that 'he was revered as a holy man by those who knew him', but whether they (or David Edwards, for that matter) should have accepted this particular definition of holiness is another question.[27]

An American professor at Southern Colorado, J. R. Griffin, wrote a brief but ambitious revisionist essay, *The Oxford Movement 1833–1933* (1984), in which he challenged the normal view that the basic impulse of Tractarianism was a conservative defence of the Church of England as established. Between 1830 and 1836 Froude, Keble and Newman all advocated the abandonment of the Anglican alliance with the state, but Froude's early death, Keble's marriage and departure to a comfortable country parish, Newman's move to Rome, and what Griffin regarded as Pusey's incoherence dissipated this radicalism. The idea of a new look at Anglo-Catholic history was excellent and no doubt Keble and Pusey have been overpraised (an example might be A. M. Allchin's all too glowing account of Pusey's *Parochial Sermons* in the Perry Butler symposium), but the social historian has heard enough of these leaders, and would prefer a more detached examination of the Victorian movement at least, as a total group. At first sight more useful was *Clouded Witness: Initiation in the Church of England in the Mid-Victorian Period 1850–75* (1982) by Peter Jagger, which involved some examination of what was happening at the parish-level, where the conflict between Anglo-Catholic and Anglican Evangelical ideas and practices about baptism and confirmation made a coherent Anglican policy out of the question. Both parties wanted the rites taken more seriously by laity and clergy, and they agreed about godparents at baptism, and about the need to prepare people for confirmation, but they agreed about little else. Proposals for liturgical revision foundered regularly, and private baptism, which both groups abhorred, actually increased. All this was useful historical research, though Jagger took the clerical side of the argument very seriously, deploring the fall in the number of baptisms, which can be traced in part to the passing of the secular Registration Act of 1837 (because after this some parents felt that registration having been done, baptism was superfluous) and implying that the laity 'neglected' baptism and confirmation. Historically, this was to repeat one side of the argument only. On the other side, it should also be said that the Church of England had been deeply divided about the importance of confirmation since the early seventeenth century, while baptism has often been understood in terms of the church-state relationship. For all the talk about tradition and Catholicity, what some Anglican clergy were trying to do in the middle of the nineteenth century was to introduce a new set of attitudes, which many of the laity did not think were 'Church of England' at all, and which they therefore did not feel obliged to accept. In the long run – but that was after 1875 – the clergy had their way, and the laity went theirs. These are among the problems which have to be investigated before anything like a new look at Anglo-Catholic history becomes possible.

What we are not being given, of course, is a history of English religion, as distinct from the history of Christianity, in the eighteenth and nineteenth centuries. Norman Sykes, for example, thought of the Hanoverian Church largely in terms of its episcopate and priesthood, and made no attempt to discuss the history of eighteenth-century *religion* in England as a whole. Sykes sought to refute the Anglo-Catholic, and to a lesser extent, the Methodist picture of a degenerate eighteenth-century Church of England, not by showing that Protestantism was alive, creative and expanding, but by demonstrating that some Anglican bishops and priests took their roles earnestly and efficiently. The Evangelical Anglicans played little part in his argument, because to admit them to the foreground would have meant, as far as he was concerned, lowering the intellectual level of the apologia too far; and the Wesleyans hardly appeared at all, because their success in the eighteenth century seemed only to underline the Anglican failure which he wanted to call in question.

Not much has been written on the origins of the eighteenth-century revival of Protestantism, apart from John Walsh's essay, 'Origins of the Evangelical Revival', in *Essays in Modern Church History* (edited by G. Bennet and J. Walsh, 1966), which discussed the possible English sources of the various evangelical movements; and W. R. Ward's essay, 'Power and Piety, the origins of religious revival in the early eighteenth century', in *The Bulletin of the John Rylands Library* (1980), which set out to trace what happened in England back to European sources. Such studies extended our detailed knowledge of the revivals, but offered little new explanation. A wider kind of treatment is needed, less committed to the strictly 'ecclesiastical' sources. If one looks for this in Keith Thomas' *Religion and the Decline of Magic* (1971), however, one finds the confusing conclusion that by the early eighteenth century the rationalism inherent in the Protestant tradition had weakened both religion and magic in England. Thomas was justified in reasserting that the Reformation partly expressed a widespread rejection of the interventionist side of Catholic piety, but he left little ground in the early eighteenth century from which Evangelicalism could shoot. In the long run 'Enlightenment' Protestantism and 'Enlightenment' Catholicism have similar religious and social sources, though the pressure of Baroque religious absolutism in countries like France and the Austrian Empire hardened attitudes more than did the milder rule of the Hanoverians.[28] It would be difficult to interpret rank and file Wesleyanism in 'Enlightenment' terms, though John Wesley's own mind balanced uneasily between credulity and scepticism, with credulity dominant, but Methodism has not been deeply investigated by secular historians anxious, for example, to interpret it as a religious expression of the new, 'modernizing' seventeenth-century market economy; such historians might argue that the whole eighteenth-century Evangelical revival in England was not so much a resurgence of Pietistic elements in Protestantism (the approach favoured by the older school of Walsh and Ward), so much as further evidence of a new emphasis on the autonomous self which was the deeper characteristic of the period. Wesley and Anglican Evangelicals like the Venns would then have been contributing to the rich library of personal fictions of no significantly separate religious value, on which the new, Western, self-creating individual could draw. It was natural that this trend should have, among others, a religious form, because there is usually a religious expression of the dominant ideology of the period. And if one remembers that G. Josipovici, for example, in *The Lessons of Modernism* (1977), was saying that this 'self', which had seemed so 'real', so certain and so available to the novelist and the theologian, was only a mental construction with no permanent validity, one might foresee a future reinterpretation of Evangelicalism in general as no more than a part of this transitory invention of the individual as a necessary capitalist social fiction. Such ideas are important, because past study of English eighteenth-century religion has been dominated by ecclesiastical historians for whom the allegedly 'religious' content of Evangelicalism was to be taken for granted even if it was also sometimes criticized.[29] A general theory of the origins of Wesleyanism is badly needed from the social historian's point of view. The 'acculturation' thesis (see the discussion in Chapter 2 above) is implausible here, because Wesleyanism was a movement from below, always seen as such by the dominant classes. One might start from the hypothesis that eighteenth-century Wesleyanism should be thought of as a 'religious group' filling a given, and previously definable, space – one could have said, if one had known the society well as a whole, how far Wesleyanism was likely to spread, and even what its chief characteristics would have to be to do so. It was essentially the filler of a gap in the society left by the long-term consequences of (*a*) the final defeat of the Commonwealth in 1660; (*b*) the consequent marginalization of groups like the Quakers, many of whom willingly joined Wesleyanism; (*c*) the breaking-down of any serious hope of a Roman Catholic recovery after 1714 for many years, something which altered the total religious situation; and (*d*) the establishment, in the 'modern' sense, of a temporarily triumphant Anglicanism, which had to face two limitations: the need, for political reasons, to tolerate some degree of Dissent, however imperfectly, and the very gradual drying-up of the 'civic religion' which had seemed a preferable alternative to the High Anglican commitment of the Establishment to the interests of Stuart absolutism, a policy which had foundered on the Stuart preference for Catholicism. This restored Anglicanism was not seriously part of the 'Counter-Reformation', either in the old-fashioned sense – that was what collapsed in 1714 – or in Jean Delumeau's recent usage as a parallel Protestant-Catholic campaign for the christianization of Europe; but it claimed to represent the moral intentions of the Hanoverian state.

One has to be careful in generalizing about eighteenth-century Protestantism. There is a fascinating discussion of the possible varieties of Protestant behaviour in John Stroup's *The Struggle for Identity in the Clerical Estate* (1984), an analysis of north-west German Protestant opposition to absolutism in the eighteenth century; (and compare Mary Fulbrook's *Piety and Politics*, 1983). Stroup contrasted Christian Thomasius (1655–1728), of the Pietist centre at Halle, who said that the church ought to be completely subject to the territorial sovereign, and his great opponent, Johann Lorenz von Mosheim (1694–1755), who insisted that the church and its clergy had been instituted by Christ (which Thomasius denied) for the salvation of humanity, and ought to be independent; indeed, 'Mosheim contended that the clergy were of great importance in a monarchy because they could resist princely power'.[30] Stroup was talking partly about Hanover, which had the relaxing advantage of 'absentee-absolutism', while in England the Hanoverian kings were unable to set up either an enervating baroque court or an ascetic military machine which would increase royal power: the loss of the American colonies settled the issue. As a result, there was little sustained royal pressure on the Establishment, despite the Royal Supremacy, and no moves, in the Prussian style, to recruit Wesleyanism (as the equivalent of Pietism) to the support of a centralist state. Hanoverian Anglicanism drifted, withdrawing into a remote relationship with the mass of rural and urban people. Outside the Establishment a feeling of alienation affected the descendants of the defeated parties in the religious sub-culture, none of whom, round about 1730, really believed in their own possible restoration to social power. It was, after all, Anglicanism which had been restored – twice, in 1660 and 1688 – and which had escaped the dangers of a Stuart return in 1715. Anglican assertions of continuity concealed all this. It was not suprising that the impulse to form new religious institutions should have come from members of the dominant Anglican group.

It does not follow that there had been any important decline in the amount of religious or superstitious behaviour. Existing explanations of the origin of Wesleyanism always assume a 'decline in religion' between the 1690s and the 1740s, but this would need to be shown to have been the case on rather stronger grounds than the denunciatory language of preachers, and the sensible reluctance of the community as a whole to continue the wars of religion after 1714. Nor does it follow that there was a 'revival', led by the Wesleyan societies, if by 'revival' one means an extension of the religious sub-culture. Some of the new evangelical leaders, not least John Wesley, claimed great advances, but it is a reasonable hypothesis (in the manner of Richard Trexler's analysis of what happened at the Reformation[31]), that what occurred was a rearrangement of the religious sub-culture as a whole, a setting-up of new institutions with new bonds of association, including new forms of liturgical action, and the siting of these institutions in a previously undetected no man's land between Old Dissent and the Church Establishment, claiming the effective ecclesiastical independence of the first and some of the social position of the second. What slowly reconstituted itself (and shaped Wesleyanism in the process) was that part of the political, and therefore self-consciously religious, culture which remained alienated from the ways in which the society as a whole settled down after 1714. The contradictions of Wesleyanism, between the democracy of the societies, for example, and Wesley's personal authority, and between the pessimistic Lutheran concept of sin and the optimistic sectarian concept of perfection, reflected the contradictory nature of this environment. Wesleyanism offered a religious model of self-formation in line with the reluctance of some people to depend for their religio-personal identity on the Hanoverian civic religion and its attendant politics. I say 'some people' here because the obvious affinity of Wesleyanism for Anglicanism (an affinity which remained throughout the nineteenth century and repeatedly confused observers who could not account for it rationally) was really an affinity for social power in a period when non-Anglicans were powerless. Increasingly, the alienated wanted some degree of social authority to match their actual stability, emotional and financial, within the nation, but for generations they could find it only on Anglican terms. In the long run the emergence of Wesleyanism as the centre of a new, reinforced Dissent compelled the Establishment to redefine itself, dropping the Hanoverian assumption that the Church of England was still essentially the church of the English people, and instead falling back, between 1815 and 1850, on a version of the High Church position as it had been before 1660. Wesleyanism in its turn broke up in the 1850s, because industrialization and all its consequences were making a fresh rearrangement of the religious sub-culture inevitable.

Part of the responsibility for the comparative neglect of eighteenth-century ecclesiastical history in Britain lies with the historians of Wesleyanism and Anglicanism, who have concentrated on the study of the personalities of the Evangelical Revival, especially the Wesley brothers and George Whitefield. Nevertheless, attempts have been made to take a more general look at the period, and one of the most interesting of these was Bernard Semmel's *The Methodist Revolution* (1974), because Semmel put forward an alternative to the famous 'Halévy thesis', according to which Methodism became a vital conservative force in British society in the first half of the nineteenth century. In 1971 Semmel edited a translation of a long-forgotten essay by the famous French historian, Elie Halévy, called *The Birth of Methodism*: this had originally appeared as 'La Naissance du Méthodism en Angleterre' in the *Revue de Paris* in August, 1906. In this early paper Halévy had interpreted eighteenth- (not nineteenth-) century Methodism as developing as a response to popular disorder and potential revolutionary disturbance in the West of England manufacturing districts – in the woollen industry of Gloucestershire and Wiltshire, for example. In his *History of the English People*, which began to appear in French in 1913, the English translation following from 1924, Halévy extended his idea to the nineteenth century and interpreted Wesleyan Methodism as a fundamental stabilizing factor in British society which prevented an equivalent of the French Revolution from happening between the 1790s and 1850. The ease with which Halévy shifted his theory from the eighteenth to the nineteenth century suggests a certain airiness in the concept. At any rate, Wesleyan Methodism as Halévy presented it was a regressive, repressive agency, autocratic where the older Calvinist Dissent had been democratic, and intellectually inadequate compared with the systematic theology of the Reformed churches. (Halévy's thesis has become popular with sociologists of religion: see, for example, the discussion in *A Sociology of Religion*, by M. Hill, 1973.)

Semmel rejected Halévy's claim that a largely negative Wesleyan movement benefited English society by holding off the forces of revolution; instead, he interpreted Wesleyan theology as itself 'revolutionary', in terms suggested to him by R. R. Palmer's *The Age of the Democratic Revolution* (1959). Palmer argued that the period between 1760 and 1815 was the time when the traditional, hierarchical society which had characterized Europe for centuries was eroding, and when the Atlantic world rose to overturn the privileged governing classes, bringing the suppressed, inarticulate classes on to the stage of events. Semmel suggested that Wesleyan teaching constituted the liberal, progressive ideology which confirmed and helped to promote the shift from a traditional to a more modern form of society. Wesleyanism was therefore not the opposite, but the equivalent, of the democratic and revolutionary spirit which elsewhere produced both the American and the French revolutions. Semmel declared:

> Methodism may have helped to block a violent English counterpart to the French Revolution by preempting the critical appeal and objective of that revolution; indeed, it might be said that only because of what the Methodist Revolution was accomplishing

could the Methodist counter to revolutionary violence be effective.[32]

When Semmel tried to expound this theory in terms of John Wesley himself he failed, because Wesley's response to the revolt of the American colonies was to revert to a political ethic of obedience derived from seventeenth- and early eighteenth-century royalist and non-juring authors. In theory, Wesley always preferred central, autocratic control, but of course it is also true that when in practice he insisted on his own absolute authority over the Methodist societies he was offering the contradictory spectacle of the disobedient leader of a would be sect-within-the-Establishment. Semmel does not make enough of Wesley's example as himself the leader of a dissident movement from below; he exaggerated, on the other hand, the way in which Wesley's Arminianism, with its emphasis on certain kinds of religious freedom, provided his followers with an idea of spiritual egalitarianism which they could translate into political terms. Finally, Semmel said that Wesley's occasional pronouncements on economics suggested a bias towards laissez-faire. On this basis Semmel claimed that Wesley combined an economic and theological outlook which had 'revolutionary' implications with a political position which was counter-revolutionary in the extreme.

Like most writers on eighteenth-century Methodism, Semmel over-identified the movement with its master: there is little evidence that Wesley's political views had much influence on his followers even in his lifetime. After his death in 1791 Wesleyan Methodism seems to have become less a dynamic factor in British society (the view of Halévy and Semmel) than a religious organization which was inevitably subject to the external socio-political pressures of the society in which it was changing into a denomination. The emerging band of Wesleyan ministers, anxious to preserve their own authority in the newly-consolidated denomination, clung to the old leader's belief in the divine right of the priesthood and applied it to themselves; like him, they usually supported established power in secular politics. But the conservative ideology of the ministry did not stop many of the Wesleyan laity from taking a democratic, radical point of view, both in the affairs of the Wesleyan body itself, and in local and national politics. These choices were probably much more closely related to social background than they were to religious affiliation.

Neither Semmel nor Halévy really identified the Wesleyans with the working-classes as such; both thought of the Wesleyans as belonging for the most part to upwardly-mobile 'lower-middle-class groups'. Halévy sometimes spoke of Wesleyanism as depriving the proletariat of its potential leadership; Semmel even suggested that Jabez Bunting, the Wesleyan Metternich in Halévy's eyes, encouraged Wesleyan missionary work overseas in order to distract the laity from radical activity in Britain. Both these interpretations differed from the characteristic 'left-wing' analysis of Methodism: J. L. and Barbara Hammond (*The Age of the Chartists*, 1930, and *The Bleak Age*), for example, regarded Methodism, together with other forms of Evangelical Pietism, as weakening the power of the British working-class, and so actually making its conditions worse. Revolutionary change was avoided, but only because Methodism fostered submission. His was Halévy's result without Halévy's explanation, and with his moral judgment reversed.

These ideas were revived in E. P. Thompson's *The Making of the English Working-Class* (1963). Thompson's Marxism persuaded him that the absence of a working-class revolution between the 1790s and 1850 was a major historical problem which needed a drastic solution, though it must always be difficult (I think), if not actually illogical, to try to explain a non-event of such an abstract kind as a revolution which did not happen. Thompson accepted the reality of the willingness of a confident ruling class to suppress disorder, but he felt that revolution could have been prevented only if somehow the proletarian will to rebel had been shattered. Methodism offered a possible answer, though to make it plausible Thompson had to dress Methodism up in terms which it had rarely known before. He described Methodism as 'a ritualized form of psychic masturbation', a transforming power which disciplined the emerging working class. Methodist revivalism produced a psychic ordeal in which the character-structure of the rebellious pre-industrial labourer or artisan was violently recast into that of the submissive industrial worker. Methodism was 'a phenomenon almost diabolic in its penetration into the very source of the human personality, directed towards the repression of emotional and spiritual energies'. Methodism was 'the chiliasm of despair', the negative as opposed to the positive pole of the social process. Filled with a vision of a Methodism which no one else had ever seen, he even said that 'Methodism was permeated with teaching as to the sinfulness of sexuality, and as to the extreme sinfulness of the sexual organs': this was as wide of the mark as his statement that Methodism was chiliastic or millenarian, when one of the distinguishing features of the Wesleyan tradition, which marked it off (together with its belief in Christian perfectionism) from Anglican Evangelicalism, was the absence of that obsession with eschatology and adventism so typical of Pietism in general, and fringe Protestantism in particular.

There are wider objections to Thompson's revision of Halévy's thesis. Anyone acquainted with religious groups knows that conversion experiences rarely take place with the kind of seriousness which would be needed for Thompson's argument to have much force; in any case, the social consequences of even the most passionate conversion cannot be prophesied with the certainty that he implied. The Tory leadership of Wesleyan Methodism disliked revivalism, because they associated it with radicalism, not conservatism. Thompson's judgment did not develop from his study of the historical events but from the Marxist assumption that religion, shallow or intense, must be reactionary in its social results. Not many factory-workers were actually Methodist, however, and not all of those who were had been converted in this radical, regenerative sense, certainly not enough to have affected the psychology of the English working-class as a whole, so as to prompt its movement in a single direction, towards submission. It is true that the early working-class had to be disciplined in order to make it accept long hours of work under factory conditions with only brief week-end rests and little other holiday; but there is no need to invoke Methodism to show how this was done. The employers used beatings (more especially of children in textile mills), dismissal and threats of dismissal, blacklisting of awkward men in whole areas, heavy fines for absenteeism, the break-up of unions, and the building of factory villages in which the owners had large coercive powers; drinking and swearing were tackled by fines; incentive payments were sometimes offered as a positive alternative. If employers compelled their workforce to attend church or chapel, this was done more in the hope of persuading them to accept the idea of 'respectability' as a goal to be attained by hard work than in the hope of obtaining Methodist conversions.

Any assessment of the role of Methodism in the history of modern Britain is still overshadowed by the personality of John Wesley himself. The first volume of a new official *History of the Methodist Church in Great Britain* (vol.I, 1966; vol.II, from 1790 to 1850, in 1978; vol.III, from 1850 to 1970, in 1983), edited by Rupert Davies and Gordon Rupp, offered no important re-examination of the Wesleys, of eighteenth-century Wesleyanism, or of the traditional version of the relation between Wesleyanism and the Hanoverian Church of England. It was taken for granted that no revision was needed, and the same attitude affected a second new enterprise, *The Works of John Wesley*, edited overall by Frank Baker in thirty-four projected volumes, the earliest of which appeared in 1975. This edition will include seven volumes of letters (two have been published, in 1980 and 1982): in all there will be about 3000 letters by John Wesley, a third more than were printed in the old *Standard Edition*, edited by John Telford in 1931, and about 1300 letters written *to* Wesley. Two other volumes, *The Appeals to Men of Reason and Religion* (1975), edited by G. R. Cragg, and *A Collection of Hymns for the Use of the People called Methodists*, edited by O. Beckerlegge, J. Dale and F. Hildebrandt (1983), have also been produced. This hymnbook was originally published in 1780, and its most significant feature was the large number of hymns written by Charles Wesley; John Wesley edited the collection, and sometimes altered his brother's verse. A new edition of John Welsey's journals and diaries is in preparation, and there will be a two-volume bibliography of the writings of John and Charles Wesley.

Whatever their virtues in providing fresh information, these books all reinforced the Wesleyan myth, that the history of eighteenth-century Wesleyanism was essentially contained in the history of the Wesleys. Typical of the line taken by the new *History*, for example, was the assumption that Wesleyanism could be summed up in G. C. Cell's familiar formula, that Wesley's teaching was 'the necessary synthesis of the Protestant ethic of grace with the Catholic doctrine of holiness'.[33] Another contributor, in an essay on Methodist doctrine, said that the basic principle of Wesleyanism was anti-Calvinist Evangelicalism – an essentially Catholic synthesis, it was claimed – and the writer continued:

> John Wesley likewise is an admirable exemplar of the characteristic genius of English churchmanship: by inspired practical improvisation he was able to bring together the beneficial features of otherwise disparate forms of Church discipline.[34]

After this it is not surprising to find that although Rupert Davies recorded the obvious weaknesses of Wesley's teaching about Christian perfection – such as his emphasis on the possibility of freedom from outward sin, and his assertion that the divine gift of Christian perfection was given instantaneously – he did not find it necessary to re-examine the value of these constant claims to 'catholicity', or to enquire whether Wesleyanism's troubled history in the eighteenth and the first half of the nineteenth centuries might be more easily explained if one thought of Wesleyanism first as an unsuccessful internal attempt to reform the Church of England, and second as a kind of holiness sect (not least in the mind of John Wesley) which gradually shed the more sectarian features of its holiness teaching in order to achieve wider social acceptance. The suggestion (made here) that Wesleyanism was a vital ingredient in an eighteenth-century 'spiritual renewal of the nation'[35] obscured the issue: the Evangelical Revival was not 'national' in any simple sense but reflected the divisions in Hanoverian society, in which Wesleyanism itself was certainly not 'national' but seems, as I have already suggested, to have been primarily the product of certain alienated social groups.

Even at the less significant level of Wesley's personality, however, none of this historical writing seemed to have been deeply affected by a reading of V. H. H. Green's incisively critical portrait, *John Wesley* (1964), to which there had been a vivid fore-runner in the sharp chapter on Wesley which J. H. Plumb inserted in his eighteenth-century volume of the old Pelican *History of England* in 1950. Dr Green, who wrote as an Anglican, thought that Wesley's famous Evangelical conversion of 1738 was not an Evangelical conversion; he thought that Wesley's action in ordaining some of his preachers in the 1780s was unjustifiable. (It is interesting to find another senior Anglican ecclesiastical historian, J. R. H. Moorman, voicing similar disapproval of Wesley's ordinations in his *The Anglican Spiritual Tradition* in 1983: Moorman wrote as an Anglo-Catholic.) As for the Methodist movement itself, 'the private lives of the religious societies revealed so often an atmosphere of jealousy and intrigue that it is open to wonder whether the claim for conversion and rebirth really stood the test', an historical judgment central to one's view of the 'revival' and not obviously refuted in Wesleyan writing. Dr Green's image of Wesley differed completely from the canonical:

> Ultimately John Wesley, like so many of the Christian saints, was self-regarding. He was unwearied in his pursuit of the good, unwearied in charity, unwearied in well-doing, unwearied in the saving of souls, but John Wesley had under God's providence become the real centre of his interest. His life was built round his own experience, an experience glazed and insulated from the outside world by his confidence in God and in himself. Completely selfless and yet intensely egoistic, he had come to identify himself with his own creation. The carefully kept Journal was a record of self-giving, but for whom was it written? If it was penned for his own edification, then he was guilty of ministering to his pride. If it was written for posterity, then he was pandering to self-glorification. The diaries form one of the most consistently complacent documents ever written, and the more religious he became the more free from human frailty he appeared to be. Apart from the period of his early life his entries are almost entirely devoid of doubt and self-criticism. Self-satisfied and self-regarding, yet by his unstinted selflessness he made himself wondrously beloved. Nothing could justify the wild attacks of the neo-Calvinists and the writers in the *Gospel Magazine*, but their fury, like his wife's rages, may have been provoked by his untouchability, the hard core of his personality.[36]

Dr Green's paradoxical description of Wesley was the first convincing attempt to come to grips with all the evidence. No one has stated better the historical objection to the claim that what Wesley, Whitefield, Venn and others were doing amounted to a revival of 'primitive Christianity', unless, of course, one supposed that primitive Christianity resembled the eighteenth-century 'revival'. Any serious, as distinct from ecumenically sentimental, proposal for John Wesley's canonization would have to answer this critical analysis. Methodist biographers, however, have stuck to the image of Wesley as a combination of Paul and Francis of Assisi; Anglican and Roman Catholic historians have been less concerned with Wesley's personality than with showing that whatever was good in Wesley and Methodism really came from their traditions and that the later development of Methodism was degeneration. The Jesuit, Maximin Piette, in *John Wesley and the Evolution of Protestantism* (French ed. 1926, ET 1937) argued that the vital conversion in Wesley's life took place in 1725 and was the result of his study of Catholic authors like Thomas à Kempis: as long as Wesley was true to his original vision he moved away from the chaotic individualism of Protestantism in the direction of Roman Catholicism. V. H. H. Green regarded Wesley's career as the natural outcome of his Anglicanism, and said of the 1738 conversion that 'in the Moravian sense of an instantaneous change and renewal Wesley was not indeed converted . . . The ideas and habits of the next fifty years were already fixed'.

The more recent history of Methodism and of the Free Churches as a whole – from 1850 to the 1980s – has not yet been absorbed by church historians. Methodism shared in the slow but palpable decay of institutionalized Christianity which began in the mid-nineteenth century. The Victorian Free churches, like English Roman Catholicism before and after Emancipation, aspired to become self-sufficient sub-cultures; they came closest to success in the period between 1870 and 1914, when they broadly satisfied the not too exacting aesthetic, social and political aims of their adherents. Nevertheless, the mainstream culture, less narrowly tied to religious institutions (or religious obsessions, like teetotalism) pulled strongly against the cohesion of these smaller groups.[37] What sociologists in the 1960s and 70s often called the 'secularization' of organized Christianity may be interpreted as the failure of these religious sub-cultures, including not only

Roman Catholicism, but also Anglicanism in the forms of Anglican Evangelicalism and Anglo-Catholicism, to maintain their self-sufficiency. Unfortunately, the Free Churches, including Methodism, misunderstood the nature of their late nineteenth-century strength, which they attributed to the spiritual power of Evangelical Protestantism. A more significant source of their success was their base in upwardly-mobile elements in the population in the more prosperous industrial parts of Britain, like the north-west: as Britain declined economically and politically after 1920, this social base disintegrated, and the denominations which failed to adapt declined at the same time, with great rapidity after 1930, and with greater rapidity still after the Second World War.[38]

One recent attempt to give an account of what happened to the Free Churches was *The Nonconformist Conscience, Chapel and Politics 1870–1914* by D. W. Bebbington. The Nonconformist Conscience has often been invoked, briefly examined, employed for the sake of argument and then dismissed: no one had previously examined the label very closely, and not much had been written about Chapel and Politics in this period apart from Robert Moore's *Pitmen, Preachers and Politics* (1974), a discussion of Methodism in a Durham mining community, and Stephen Yeo's *Religion and Voluntary Organisations in Crisis* (1976), which concentrated on the town of Reading between 1890 and 1914. Both Moore and Yeo concerned themselves with local groups involved primarily in local politics; Moore, by extending his book into the 1920s, was able to show the disintegration of the Victorian Nonconformist pattern.

In contrast, Dr Bebbington looked at Chapel and Politics largely in national terms. His principal themes were: the Nonconformist quest for civil and religious equality; the Social Gospel movement, which is what people often mean when they talk about the 'Conscience'; the growth of the Free Church Council, which seemed very important about 1906 but then collapsed as a serious religious and political institution; Nonconformist attitudes to Ireland, then as now England's unsolved problem of conscience; international diplomacy; and education, the area in which Nonconformity sadly overestimated its strength. He would no doubt have echoed his most relevant predecessor at the national level, Stephen Koss, who, in his not very illuminating book *Nonconformity and*

Modern British Politics (1975), lamented that in case after case the private papers of leading Nonconformist political preachers no longer seemed to exist. Bebbington made use of printed sources, however, especially the *British Weekly* and the *Christian World*, though he paid too little attention to Methodism. He explained the rapid decline of a distinctively Nonconformist politics after 1914 partly in terms of the rise of the Labour Party and partly in terms of a Free Church recognition that political campaigning was secularizing the chapels without achieving major political results.

Bebbington defined the Conscience in terms of three convictions. First, that religion should have political implications; second, that politicians should be people of high moral tone; and third, that legislation could improve the character of a nation. These convictions usually meant the advocacy of teetotalism, and demands for legislation to limit as far as possible gambling, prostitution, and non-religious activities on Sunday. Bebbington found it puzzling that in the later nineteenth century Nonconformists should have turned to the state for a remedy against social evils, when in the earlier part of the century they had invested so much moral capital in voluntary effort, but the scale and goal of social programmes changed as the century progressed, so that wider state action became inevitable if what was wanted was to be accomplished. In effect, Bebbington exaggerated the extent to which Nonconformists were still free to choose voluntary action by 1900.

In recent years the Nonconformist Conscience has been interpreted either as a consequence of the broadening of the intellectual horizons of the chapels, or as a quest for increased political power to match rising social pretensions. Bebbington rejected these suggestions and said that 'it would be wrong to suggest that Nonconformity was lured into deserting its Evangelical tradition for the sake of new ideas or new social status in the years before the First World War. The politics of the chapels were primarily determined by the Evangelicalism that still gave them their reasons for existence, their message, their energy'. This conclusion left him in the slightly unsatisfactory position of wanting to attribute the 'Conscience' to residual Evangelicalism while saying that the chapels gave up political campaigning because this was secularizing the Free Church communities.

As one who takes a more sociological view of the formation and deformation of the Conscience, I would not say that Nonconformity deserted Evangelicalism for the sake of social status. Instead, I would argue that it was their steady acquisition of new social, political and economic status from about the middle of the nineteenth century which led to a temporary 'social aggression' by the Nonconformist middle-class groups, especially after the success of the long struggle to abolish the Contagious Diseases Acts, which had engaged the Free Churches at a deep, if confused, emotional level. Some Nonconformists promoted their own social choices to the level of moral judgments and then tried to impose the resulting way of life on both the aristocracy and the working classes, who were to be deprived as far as possible of the chance to devote their leisure to drink, gambling and sex. This willingness to impose a way of life partly explains the shift to state action which Bebbington found surprising: it was hardly probable that public-houses could be shut on Sundays with working-class consent – and Sunday-closing was at the heart of the Conscience. This social aggression deprived the Nonconformists of the working-class support which they might have found otherwise, and indirectly assisted the rise of the Labour Party, which had a different set of moral values traceable to the Enlightenment rather than to Christianity. At the same time, the success of the campaign to abolish the civil disabilities of Dissenters dissolved what was the true cement of Nonconformity, loyalty to a persecuted minority into which one had been born. In these circumstances it was not remarkable that by 1914 the Conscience, which itself ran wider than Dissent as such, and represented the moral code of some Anglicans and Roman Catholics, was running short of Nonconformist support.

A religious group's capacity to resist 'modernization' has always been bought at a very high price, even the price of extinction. From 1870 to 1930 two generations of church leaders and theologians thought that 'adaptation' meant some kind of 'liberal' adjustment in doctrine, and perhaps some degree of 'leftward' adjustment in politics. The high point of these tendencies was perhaps the Anglican report on 'Christianity and Industrial Problems' of 1923, which said that the fundamental error of modern industrialism was to encourage competition for private gain instead of co-operation for public service; and *Doctrine in the Church of England* (1938), the report of an Archbishops' Commission which was never officially accepted because it offered 'liberal' alternatives to orthodox, hard-line interpretation of such doctrines as that of the Virgin Birth, the divinity of Jesus, or the nature of the eucharistic action.

Neither of these reports had much influence, but they are the kind of evidence which would be used to support the characteristic view of the more traditionally-minded kind of church historian that the root cause of modern Christian decline in Britain was neither sociological nor intellectual, but an inner betrayal of the ecclesia by the priesthood. W. R. Ward, for example, in *Religion and Society 1790–1850* (1972) suggested strongly that in the first half of the nineteenth century Protestantism in England threw away a great opportunity for ecumenical expansion, and he blamed the self-interest of the priesthood, including the Wesleyan ministry under the leadership of Jabez Bunting, and the conservative doctrinal self-indulgence of the Anglo-Catholics. Left to the laity, he appeared to feel, Christianity would have survived more easily. E. R. Norman, whose *Church and Society 1770–1970* (1976) was perhaps the most vehement expression of the betrayal-thesis, said that by accommodating theology, worship and ethics to the secularizing trends of late nineteenth- and twentieth-century Western society the churches had merely 'secularized' themselves, repelling traditionalists without conciliating radicals. Norman wrote as the spokesman of a generation which had frightened itself with nightmares of a coming triumph of atheistic Russian Communism: by the 1980s the conservative wings of Protestantism and Roman Catholicism seemed to be establishing a religious front in a cold war of their own, an alliance, undeclared but militant, between Jerry Falwell, leader of American Fundamentalist Protestantism, and Pope John Paul II. Norman seemed to assume that Christian truth was both knowable and certain, so that those who had agonized over the intellectual difficulties and political conservatism of modern Christianity had no need to do so. His critique implied that the essentially supernatural ecclesia faced no major problem that could not be explained in terms of human sinfulness; the key to statistical recovery and therefore to socio-political power lay in ecclesiastical solidarity on an orthodox platform, and loyalty to the Establishment, whose mantle was sometimes extended to cover the South African state, and right-wing Roman Catholicism in South America.

Another example of this kind of committed and politically slanted church history was a study of the relationship between Dissent and English literature by Donald Davie, himself both an English academic and a minor poet: *A Gathered Church, the Literature of the English Dissenting Interest 1700–1930* (1978). Davie started from the popular view that Dissent had produced no important novelists or poets, the implication being that the ethos of Dissent was inimical to art of all kinds. This was not supposed to be true of either Anglicanism or Catholicism. Davie interpreted the cultural history of Dissent as a history of decline, and explained this in terms of the drift of the British Dissenting communities away from a Calvinist orthodoxy into Unitarianism and modern 'liberalism', a process which destroyed without replacement the solid and sustaining moderate Calvinist world-view which had lain behind the work of Dissenting writers down to the middle of the eighteenth century. Davie knew that William Blake, Robert Browning, Arnold Bennett and D. H. Lawrence would all have to be described as coming from 'Dissent' rather than from an Anglican or Catholic sub-culture, and he was therefore obliged to find grounds for depreciating Blake and Lawrence in the assumed weakness of Dissent. To add weight to his theory he also praised disproportionately 'Mark Rutherford', really William Hale White, whose novel, *The Autobiography of Mark Rutherford, Dissenting Minister* (1881), has been described as a compact and powerful account of the progress of nineteenth-century doubt (see *The Oxford Companion to English Literature*, edited by Margaret Drabble, 1985). Hale White was certainly a victim of early-nineteenth-century doubt, moving in the process through Congregationalism to Unitarianism and finally agnosticism, but that did not make him a reliable witness to the culture of Nonconformity. Politically, Davie's view seemed to be a variety of the explanation via clerical betrayal: the failure of sober, rational religious dissent had left its descendants (Davie's background was Baptist) exposed to 'revolutionary, irrational dissent' of the kind which had paralysed British universities in the year of abortive revolutions, 1968.

There were other explanations of decline than betrayal by the priesthood. William Strawson, for example, writing on Methodist theology from 1850 to 1950, said that Methodism had suffered from the pressure of a considerable anti-intellectual bias:

> it has been insisted that evangelism can only be on the basis of a simple gospel. But if evangelists never tackle the big questions they impoverish people who ought to be growing in Christian thought and action. Furthermore, the idea that Christians ought to be of one mind about everything has not been productive of creative theology . . . Methodists have also been afraid of extreme positions. In the 1930s they were afraid of Barthianism; in the 1940s and 1950s they were afraid of form criticism; in the 1960s they were afraid of the 'new theology'. They assume that the safe position is in the middle of the road.[39]

Strawson's criticisms would apply much more widely than to Methodism alone; the sources of such a failure must have lain in the noetic structure of the Christian sub-culture as a whole. There was constant unwillingness to come outside the protecting boundaries of familiar sets of concepts. The spectacle of Victorian Evangelicals, themselves obsessed with the sixteenth-century Reformation, denouncing the Anglo-Catholics as 'medieval', while the Anglo-Catholics themselves took for granted that the future of theology lay in the study of the Fathers, has been treated with too much respect by church historians, as though a scholarly grasp of either patristics or Reformation divinity guaranteed any theological relevance to either early nineteenth or late twentieth-century Britain. Similarly, it was largely British ignorance of the work of the mid-nineteenth-century German school of theologians on the doctrine of the Person of Christ which led to an over-valuation of late nineteenth-century English christology. In this case the record was corrected by the publication of *God and the Incarnation in Mid-Nineteenth Century German Theology* (1965) by an American scholar, Claude Welch, who also produced a useful account of nineteenth-century Protestant theology down to 1870 (*Protestant Thought in the Nineteenth Century*, 1972). As Welch said:

> For rigour and vigour in working out the implications of the (kenotic) conception, Thomasius (and the German kenoticists in general) make the later nineteenth-century British ventures into kenoticism (Gore, for example) look pallid indeed. It is all very well to praise the imprecision or vagueness of the British kenoticists as theological modesty and restraint before mystery, but the preoccupations on which the kenotic theory can really emerge are precisely those which demand pursuit to the limit of the metaphysical and even the psychological questions involved.[40]

The intellectual collapse of christology has been like the very slow disintegration of a desperately contested front in an old-fashioned infantry war: intelligence, tenacity and heroism were lavished on the crumbling defence, and in the imagination of some the struggle still goes on. But as Anthony Kenny said:

> No doubt it may reasonably be believed that Moses and Jesus did and said many of the things ascribed to them in the Scriptures; but can it reasonably be believed with a degree of certainty resembling that of knowledge? Unless the relevant stories can be as certain as the commitment which faith demands of the believer, the commitment, so far as it is faith, is irrational; and if the belief is a commitment which is rationally in proportion to the support given by the history, it is, so far forth as it is rational, something less than faith.[41]

Throughout the modern period the favourite theological method of coping with the difficulties of reconciling science, history and Christian doctrine has been to introduce metaphorical and symbolical meanings where, it has been argued, no such meanings stood before. This was the gulf which separated late Victorian agnostics like Leslie Stephen and Henry Sidgwick, who thought that a clergyman had no business to recite the Apostles' Creed unless he believed its statements in a highly traditional and therefore apparently literal sense, from liberal Anglicans like Hastings Rashdall, who thought that the Creeds could be used as poetic statements of truth. In Dr Kenny's terms, the agnostics emphasized the irrationality of faith and half rejected it; the liberals, on the other hand, argued for a description of faith which reduced both its irrationality and its certainty and half accepted it. Among church historians, Owen Chadwick devoted the first third of the second volume of his *Victorian Church* (1970) to the discussion of this range of subjects. He said that in the course of the nineteenth century people moved from saying that *the word of God is the Bible*, to saying that *the word of God is in the Bible*. 'But it made less difference to religion than might have been expected, for though earlier centuries professed that *the word of God is the Bible*, they had always acted and lived by the proposition *the word of God is in the Bible*.'[42] If Chadwick's answer were correct historically, then the history of Christianity (not of religion, strictly speaking), did not move into a new dimension of doubt in the late nineteenth/early twentieth century, but rather people began to see more clearly the limits of what they had always said and done, and this was a gain. This was a reconciling, 'liberal' conclusion, but I am not sure that Professor Chadwick wanted it to mean that 'something less than faith' to which Dr Kenny referred. As it is, he leaves us wondering just how successful the formula, *the word of God is in the Bible*, has proved in the twentieth century. A glance at Paul Welsby's *History of the Church of England 1945–80* (1984), with its account of theological bewilderment and ecumenical let-down, suggests that the formula needed revision.

All that was Left of Them

In fact, the treatment of Victorian church history as a whole needs a new perspective. The narrative needs to flow in fresh directions; theory needs to move further from theology and closer to the history of religion. This means giving less weight to what I have called the Anglican myth, and more prominence to events which have so far been left in the background. I have already suggested that as between Anglican and Roman Catholic the balance needs to be altered, because the most important events in ecclesiastical history occurred in the Roman, not the Anglican Church. The comparative liberation of Catholicism in 1829 was decisive: from it followed the impact of Newman's change of church; the restoration of the hierarchy; the absorption of Irish immigration in the second half of the century; and the condemnation of Anglican orders in 1896. But this is not the whole of the transformation which is required. Fresh importance might be given, for example, to (1) the restoration of the Roman Catholic episcopate in England in 1850; (2) the Divorce Act of 1857; and (3) the conflict over the Contagious Diseases Acts of 1864, 1866 and 1867, which were finally repealed in 1886.

1. Wiseman's arrival to head a new Catholic hierarchy was not really an 'aggression' which stimulated an uncouth, short-winded opposition from what survived of British anti-Popery: it was the symbol of a major change in British church-relations which was never reversed, and which in the long run affected the structure of British secular politics as well.[43]

2. The passing of the Divorce Act of 1857 began the reduction of divorce to a purely secular event and was a fundamental reverse for the conservatives of all religious parties. Clerical opinion held that the law of the land should reflect the church's law on marriage; in fact, the Act allowed the remarriage of divorced persons, whereas church law said that the 'guilty' party could not be remarried, and the position of the 'innocent' party was unclear. What was happening was that non-clerical opinion increasingly held that in sexual matters the law should reflect a consensus built on more than Christian assumptions derived from the Bible; this changing attitude lay behind the Act and meant that its provisions were bound to be extended as time passed. Just as Wiseman's arrival portended the end of the Anglican hegemony in the religious sub-culture as a whole, so the Divorce Act implied the approaching end of the religious sub-culture's wider social influence (one can hardly speak of hegemony by the mid-nineteenth century). It was hardly surprising that even so, the English Roman Catholic Church was still struggling in the late twentieth century to reverse the extent to which non-Christian views had become the basis of sexual morality as expressed in law.

3. The repeal of the Contagious Diseases Acts, which had made possible the compulsory medical examination of suspected prostitutes in a small group of seaports and garrison towns, figures in Anglican tradition largely as an example of a triumph of Christian campaigning, but Judith Walkowitz, in *Prostitution and*

Victorian Society (1980) showed that what happened was much more ambiguous. Both the Contagious Diseases Acts and the Divorce Act originated from concern about the position of men, not of women: in both cases men's interests were being protected. In the middle of the century Ruskin and others had created the powerful Victorian myth of woman as the guardian of a feminine principle of purity and of family-life: submissiveness became a major feminine virtue. The underlying intention was to protect masculine domination of society against the early wave of feminism which had lasted from the later eighteenth century into the 1840s.[44] Opposition to the Contagious Diseases Acts came to some extent from women deeply imbued with this ideology of Woman as a mysterious priestess of a nobler (and almost sexless but not quite childless) form of life; such women attacked the Acts (which were intended to protect young middle-class men and members of the armed services from venereal disease) because they legalized prostitution, and therefore endorsed a low view of the feminine. The Acts seemed to them to express a kind of social materialism. Other women, however, found that their experience of Josephine Butler's agitation against the Acts transformed their feelings about the relations between men and women. Judith Walkowitz even suggested that the violence of the suffragettes' movement in the following generation was retaliation for what had been felt as violence inflicted by men – police and doctors – when they enforced medical inspection on unwilling prostitutes. Compulsory examination came to be regarded as physical rape (see, for example, E. J. Bristow, *Vice and Vigilance, Purity Movements in Britain since 1700*, 1977). What began as a partly Christian protest against the tolerance of organized prostitution changed for some women into an attack on masculine behaviour and assumptions.

The best assessment of the relationship between Victorian Feminism and Victorian religion is by Olive Banks, who was professor of sociology at Leicester. In *The Faces of Feminism* (1981), she related Victorian Feminism to Victorian Evangelicalism, both in England and in the United States. It was actually in America that the emotions awakened by the evangelical revival led most obviously and directly to feminism. In England, there is little evidence that the early nineteenth-century evangelical passion for moral reform produced much change in the feminine consciousness before the 1870s.[45] Professor Banks emphasized the importance of Quakerism and of anti-slavery for feminism in the United States; the nearest English equivalent was teetotalism, but this movement remained very much in masculine hands.

> The London Anti-Slavery convention (of 1840) makes clear the difference between the American and British movements. In spite of the presence of women in the British movement there is no evidence that these activities extended much beyond the fund-raising that was their main (and strictly subordinate) function, and there is no sign of any demand for a greater degree of participation in the general movement. At no time does there seem to have been a British equivalent of the Grimke sisters, and even as late as 1853 the Bristol and Clifton Anti-Slavery Society appealed for a gentleman to organize public meetings, since this was still believed to be outside the scope of a ladies' society.[46]

Dr Bank's conclusion was that in Britain the Enlightenment tradition was more prominent than Evangelicalism in the formation of feminism, although Evangelicalism introduced some women to forms of political activity.[47]

This is relevant, because if one goes on to the twentieth century and asks oneself what the salient points have been in the religious history of the period so far, feminism in its third phase, that is, since 1945, obviously stands out. Feminism, which challenged the masculine-dominated structure of Western society, embarrassed the Christian churches, which had accepted that structure for centuries largely without criticism. Therefore, although modern Christianity produced its own varieties of feminism, it was not easy to claim that feminism had Christian roots.[48] Part of the problem was that the theology of the Virgin Mary, which glorified the obedience of the female to the apparently male deity, and which made Mary a symbol of Motherhood rather than of Woman, was irreconcilable with radical feminism. Moreover, the major Christian institutions, including the Roman, Orthodox and Anglican Churches, ruled that women could not become priests, while in the concluding years of the century Pope John Paul II was leading a kind of personal crusade against any weakening on this front, and even seeking to harden Catholic resistance to birth control and abortions. Feminism had become the most serious critical opposition Christianity had encountered in the modern world. Indeed, any history of modern Christianity has to face the fact that feminism has fatally weakened the impact of Christian symbolism. Any one who has grasped the nature of the feminist critique of a male-centred culture is bound to reject the figure and role of the Virgin Mary as a supernaturally-given revelation of the mind of God.

The damage done to modern theology, though not widely admitted, has been enormous. This was because feminism caught Christianity (as it also caught Marxism) unaware of the extent to which it was committed to an indefensible social order, just as both were ill-equipped to cope with the upsurge of nationalism, which proved stronger emotionally then either Marxism or Christianity. Both Marxism and Christianity had assumed that at least on the theoretical level they were socially beyond reproach. The leaders of Christian opinion thought that Christianity had solved the problem of its relationship to society by repudiating, in the course of the nineteenth century, the obvious structures of the *ancien régime*, but in practice the *ancien régime* was not so simply dismantled. British Anglicanism also suffered because the 'Catholic' revival reintroduced monasticism into the Church of England. First, because the Anglican hierarchy was less than whole-hearted in its acceptance of the new Anglican women's orders; and second, because the traditional theology of monasticism on which the Anglican nuns relied gave them little protection against the radical feminist critique as it developed in the twentieth century. After the Second Vatican Council similar problems spread rapidly through Roman Catholic convents and monasteries. This was extremely well-documented in Suzanne Campbell-Jones' *In Habit* (1979), an anthropological study of two orders of working nuns, which included an examination of their history since their nineteenth-century foundation.

5

Illustrative Interludes

Religion in Modern Germany

The history of Germany since 1800, and therefore the history of the Christian churches in Germany, is overshadowed by the Holocaust. No doctrine either of politics or of Providence has reduced the Nazi war against the Jews to an event which can be understood as part of an acceptable pattern, or be shelved theologically by a stock appeal to the problem of evil. There were large churches in nineteenth-century Germany, both Catholic and Protestant, and whatever their direct responsibility for the popularity of German anti-semitism (and they had some responsibility) what finally happened put a grim question-mark against their claims to be major sources of civilizing and moralizing influence. It is little consolation to remember that Marxism, locked into excessively self-limiting methods of explanation, could also make little sense of phenomena like racism, nationalism and anti-semitism.

Some historians have found the key to modern German history in the alleged failure of the nineteenth-century German bourgeoisie to develop 'normally', that is, to bring about changes in the socio-economic and political structure of modern Germany in line with an Anglo-Saxon model of advanced capitalism and parliamentary democracy. This failure was already apparent in the swift collapse of the German revolutions of 1848, a check from which 'democracy' did not recover before 1914. The German churches take their place in this account as supporters of the anti-democratic reaction after 1850: both Catholic and Protestant preaching was strongly anti-socialist, and played its part in drift of the working-classes away from the churches.

This kind of argument has been widely repeated, but some scholars, for example David Blackbourn and Geoff Eley[1] have disagreed, saying that despite what happened in 1848 the necessary conditions for the modernization of German society and industry were brought together by a 'bourgeois revolution' in the 1860s and 1870s. Imperial Germany between 1871 and 1914 was not just an archaic society, but one in which an effective Socialist Party formed before 1900, powerful enough to stimulate a hostile reaction from the middle and upper-middle class groups which feared any increase of working-class power. If the concept of linear development is dropped from a reading of German history (and with it irrelevant comparisons with Britain and the United States), it becomes unnecessary to suppose that twentieth-century Germany was compelled by a mysterious nineteenth-century 'bourgeois failure' to follow an inevitable path to Hitler and the Final Solution. What happened was decided by choices which were made in the 1920s, choices which were deeply affected by nationalism, anti-semitism and anti-socialism, as well as by the devastating shock of Germany's unexpected defeat in the First World War. The corrupting effect of these emotions on religious institutions has also been largely ignored. They mattered more than an alleged German preference for a mixture of obedience and irrationalism.

To some social historians of Germany, indeed, religion has hardly seemed worth mentioning at length, either because they feel that they can explain 'religious' intentions in terms of the underlying social 'reality', or alternatively, because they treated religious institutions as closed-off systems with an unimportant 'history' of their own.[2] (It is possible to sympathize with this attitude when the amount of time spent by students of 'new religious movements' on tiny sects which lack social or religious significance is considered.) Yet part of the conservative restoration after 1815 took the form of renewed Catholic and Protestant attempts to recover the social hegemony which had been endangered by the religious crisis which was at the heart of the French Revolution, and this 'religious restorationism' made headway in the European bourgeoisie as a whole as time went by.

Moreover, as R.J. Ross pointed out in *The Beleaguered Tower: The Dilemma of Political Catholicism in Wilhelmine Germany* (1976), Germany, unlike France and England, suffered from an unresolved conflict between Catholic and Protestant in the nation as a whole which went back to the sixteenth-century Reformation. The Reformation had been an 'incomplete revolution', and this meant that in attempting to cope with the problem of social and political modernization Germany had also to grapple with religious interests which refused to be reconciled. The defeat of Austria by Prussia in 1866, and the setting-up of an essentially Protestant German Empire in 1871 isolated the Catholic minority, which organized the Centre Party to safeguard its own distinct interests. If the Centre Party sometimes resisted social modernization it did so not so much in terms of class-interest, as in defence of the Catholic sub-culture as such.

A fascinating analysis of the situation can be found in Jonathan Sperber's *Popular Catholicism in Nineteenth-Century Germany* (1984). Sperber showed in detail how a German Catholic revival was mounted after 1848: a complete network of Brotherhoods, Catholic political clubs, peasant leagues and Christian Social Workers Associations was formed, as far as possible under priestly control, in order to make the Catholic sub-culture self-sufficient, and to mark it off from the Protestant society.[3] Evangelistic missions were carried out, and at the same time the 'undisciplined, individualised, traditional pilgrimage, with its combination of sacred and secular, was giving way to a highly organized, collective and clerically led public manifestation'.[4] The new-style pilgrimages were carried on at regional or national, rather than at local level, and concentrated on Marian shrines. The new Catholic working-class groups set up in the rapidly industrializing Rhineland and Westphalia were also usually dominated by the local priest and dedicated to Mary. These were not Catholic trade unions asking for change; they were established to safeguard the church's authority and solidarity, as well as to protect the existing kind of social stability; what they taught was the equivalent of the so-called Protestant work-ethic, that the worker owed his employer hard work and loyalty, but that energy, thrift and sobriety would find a reward from the caring capitalist. Less concerned about their social identity and future,

German Protestant institutions were at least a generation behind in this sort of social organization.

One aspect of this Catholic sub-culture which Sperber mentioned, but whose significance he did not emphasize, was the kind of political language which Catholic political and ecclesiastical commentators often used. It seemed quite normal, for example, to the *Sonntagsblatt fur Katholische Christen* to say in 1861 that

> it is unfortunately true that . . . at the elections many Catholics, as a consequence of their religious indifference, have left the field free for Jews and Freemasons . . . If the school is separated from the Church and turned into a state institution in which Christians, Jews and sectarians are taught and religious education is excluded . . . if all Christian institutions are robbed of their Christian character and a Jew can be judge and schoolmaster as easily as a Christian . . . then we will be on the edge of that abyss against which the watcher on the throne of Peter has warned us again and again.[5]

Similarly, the bishop of Paderborn could say that 'the secret and open leaders and followers of the worldwide subversive party think only of how they may destroy all authority in state and church . . .'.[6] This willingness to talk about world conspiracies was well-established by the middle of the nineteenth century, and had begun in Catholic counter-revolutionary circles at the time of the French Revolution. The conspiracy theory was first popularized by Comte Ferrand, later a minister in the government of the Restoration, in *Les Conspirateurs démasqués* (1790); the Jesuit abbé Barruel, in *Mémoires pour servir à l'histoire de Jacobinisme* (1798), added Freemasons to Ferrand's intellectuals (see J. Godechot, *La Contre-Révolution, doctrine et action 1789–1804*, 1961, ET 1972). Combined with the anti-semitic tendencies which had established themselves in German Protestantism it was to provide Hitler with a ready-made rhetoric of political hysteria which appealed to the religious sub-culture as a whole. In the long run the Catholic refusal to come to terms with the French Revolution was much more decisive for the modern history of Germany than its uneasy relationship with industrial capitalism.

Sperber carried this analysis down to the launching of the Kulturkampf, which was an outright assault on the Catholic sub-culture by the new Imperial government, which saw itself as the custodian of Protestant hegemony.[7] There are political explanations for this, but it is probable that Bismarck himself was reacting to the problems set for the new Imperial Germany by the presence within it of a sub-culture uncommitted to Prussian religious traditions. This frontal attack enabled the Catholics to dramatize their position as the defence of religion: 'the enemy of religion is Liberalism, whose faith is disbelief and whose mother is revolution';[8] the Masonic Lodges were 'all agreed in a twofold goal – everything Christian must go, all thrones must go';[9] Masonry was 'the epitome of Satanic subversion'; it was said to be the Masonic Lodges which fostered Social Democracy, and had been behind the Paris Commune in 1870.

Sperber's book, which ended in 1880 with the failure of the Kulturkampf, which Bismarck replaced with a campaign against the Social Democrats, a target much more to Catholic and Protestant taste, sought to establish that the Centre Party really was a *religious* party, not simply a cultural expression of economic interests; he argued that its history reflected an interplay between socio-economic factors and religious forces in which religion was often the dominant factor. He rightly objected to the secular assumption that religious groups need not be analysed politically in religious terms, because their politics would always be reducible to the sum of non-religious factors. There, however, Sperber stopped, as though it was enough to say, as he did in his conclusion, that the Catholic sub-culture's survival into and beyond the storms of the mid twentieth century was 'a testimony to the great success of the clergy and lay activists in constructing an edifice of religious beliefs and practices in response to a changing world'.[10] Survival, however, was hardly the point: what kind of survival mattered much more. At an earlier stage of his discussion, Sperber had said that the *political* implications of the mid nineteenth-century Catholic revival had decisively determined the shape of political Catholicism for the future. From the 1850s the clergy 'had, with few individual exceptions, perceived a connection between revolution and immorality. They saw radical ideas as sinful: democrats were to be placed in the same category as atheists, drunkards, or fornicators'.[11] This basic lack of enthusiasm for democracy was to remain, together with the temptation to invent world-wide conspiracies involving Freemasons, Jews and Socialists, and both attitudes had some responsibility for the failure of the Weimar republic. It was true, as Sperber himself noted, that even after the publication of the papal socio-economic encyclical, *Rerum Novarum*, in 1891, Catholicism still hankered after a pastoral vision of the *ancien régime* and was never completely committed to industrial capitalist society, but any tendency this might have had to draw Catholics closer to the Social Democrats was nullified in the 1920s by the priority given to protection of the institutions of the church, which the socialists were believed to threaten much more than the Nazi or Nationalist parties. Hitler's advance to absolute power depended on more than the Protestant votes which the Nazis obtained in the last Weimar free elections; it also depended on the reaction of Catholics as well as Protestants to the deep shock of Germany's total defeat in 1918 and the collapse of the monarchy which followed. Catholics were as responsible as Protestants for the hysteria which mounted in the 1920s, and the loyalty of the Centre Party's Catholic vote was not so much a sign of opposition to the Nazis as a continuation of the Catholic sub-culture's subjective policy of concentrating on what were believed, mistakenly by 1930, to be the best interests of Catholicism.

This becomes clearer if one considers Ellen Lovell Evans's *The German Centre Party* (1981), which brought the story down to 1933. She showed, for example, how in the 1920s the Centre Party remained monarchist in sentiment at the top, and criticized parliamentarism as 'divisive' and opposed to 'true democracy', by which was meant 'organic' communities. Efforts were made to revive Catholic corporativism, especially after the papal encyclical, *Quadragesimo Anno* (1931), had pointed in that direction. Corporativism never became part of the Centre Party programme, but was a convenient ground for criticism of the Weimar system. At the Munich Catholic Congress of 1922 the Archbishop of Munich, Faulhaber, called the German revolution of 1919 'perjury and high treason . . . eternally burdened and stigmatized with the brand of Cain'.[12] Between 1924 and 1926 the Centre Party effectively disengaged itself from Weimar republicanism; the decisive emotions seem to have been nationalism, fear of social change, and dread of 'Bolshevism'. The Centre entered the government of 1927, which was dominated by Nationalists and included no Socialists: the Centre was lured with hopes of concessions on Catholic education, and from about that time Cardinal Pacelli, the Papal Nuncio, was always in the background, seeking to negotiate a Concordat with the new German state.[13] This move to the Right alienated many Catholic workers hitherto loyal to Catholic institutions. The conviction that 'socialism' was more dangerous than 'nationalism' rotted the Centre's political position; its leaders did not identify Hitler as the shape of the future, but thought that a combination of priests, landowners, industrialists and generals could keep the extreme Right under control. Vatican diplomats like Pacelli put the achievement of a concordat before Catholicism's separate existence in German politics, as though the Centre Party had been formed only to protect the interests of the church. In an older, but still relevant book, *The Catholic Church and Nazi Germany* (1964), Guenther Levy said that although the *Fulda Letter* (June 1933, issued by the Catholic Bishops before the actual signing of the Concordat), was not alone in failing to perceive the totalitarian goals of the Nazi movement, it was significant that the bishops did not find much harm in Hitler's one-party state.

> Their pronouncement expressed little alarm over the supression of civil liberties except in so far as they touched the special freedom of the Church, its schools, newspapers and organisations; they spoke of moral renewal while the Brown terror tortured and murdered; the banning of the freethinkers' and nudists' magazines and the destruction of the godless Communist movement to Germany were welcomed even if achieved as part of the liquidation of all political opposition. It is hard to resist the conclusion that it was the attraction felt for certain elements in the Nazi ideology more than anything else that prevented the German episcopate from apprehending the true inhumanity of National Socialism in 1933 as well as in later years.[14]

A similar situation in the Protestant sub-culture was discussed by Daniel Borg in *The Old Prussian Church and the Weimar Republic, A Study in Political Adjustment 1917–1927* (1984). Borg made clear that Lutheranism was stranded by Germany's loss of the war of 1914–18. The Lutherans loathed the revolution, which had snapped their links with the Royal Family (for whose restoration they hoped for most of the 1920s) and had set up a 'religionless state' which worked through parliament, an institution which, in their eyes provoked disunity and fostered materialism. Although Luther's political legacy was much discussed it was irrelevant to what was happening: the Lutheran clergy had been politically quietist in modern Germany because authority had favoured them; they became activist after the revolution of 1919, Luther notwithstanding, because they feared a complete loss of cultural significance. Like the Catholics, Protestant leaders were hostile to Weimar, but their bitterness towards the Republic was greater because they saw the Centre Party combining with the Social Democrats in the government of the country – anti-Catholicism is said to have reached a new height of intensity in German Protestantism in the 1920s.

Borg quoted the Protestant leader, Otto Dibelius,[15] as saying that 'the religionless Republic, incapable of generating cultural values, might succumb to the anti-religious crusade of worldwide Communism'. It was a passionate belief of Protestant theologians that only the church, never the state, could promote a culture genuinely commited to love and justice. Dibelius declared that the church must have 'a unified will' – this opposition of 'will' to 'conspiracy' characterized right-wing rhetoric throughout the inter-war period. It was typical of the Old Prussian Church that in the 1920s it did not condemn as heretical the Deutschkirche, or German Church movement, which held that God had created a specifically German Christianity which could dispense with the Old Testament, and for which revelation took place through the People's intuitive recognition of Truth, and not through Jesus. Jesus was in any case Aryan, not Jewish; modern Jews were the source of a materialism which had corrupted Germany. All these ideas, together with the use in ritual of material drawn from the pre-Christian German past and from German folklore, were familiar by 1925.

For the most part the laity of the Prussian Church preferred a nationalism which was less religiously extreme, but theologians like Paul Althaus asserted that God gave the People (*das Volk*) an historical mission and judged them by their response: hence the popularity among Evangelicals of the stab-in-the-back explanation of Germany's defeat in 1918 – it was the Jews (who could not be German) and Socialists (who no longer knew how to be German) who were responsible, not the *Volk* properly defined. The Evangelical leaders campaigned vigorously against signing the Versailles Treaty, and against any acceptance of the so-called 'war-guilt' clause. The charge of war-guilt struck at their whole position, because it condemned the monarcho-Christian order which they vainly hoped to restore. If the *Volk* had any responsibility for Germany's disaster, it was to the extent that the People had rejected God's efforts to bring about religious renewal. Such teaching encouraged the Lutheran laity to reject the new democracy and cultural pluralism.

The Lutherans, moreover, had their own brand of what Borg called 'legitimate antisemitism', which demanded the removal of German citizenship from the Jews and their social isolation (a policy similar to that which the Catholic publicist, Hilaire Belloc, for example, was advocating in England in the 1920s). Orthodox Lutherans wanted to retain the Old Testament as a Christian book, however, and did so on the ground that it contained a supernatural revelation which was in no way 'Jewish'. 'Jewishness' meant materialism, and it was well-known that the Jewish 'folk-character' had degenerated since Old Testament times.[16] Modern secularized Jews had no right (it was said) to regard themselves as God's elect, but they still did so, and the belief lay behind their drive for world-dominion. Thus there was a widespread Lutheran anti-Jewishness available to supplement the racialism of the more extreme Nationalists. Everything worked against Protestantism in these decisive years for, as Borg notes, even a lively reformed (Calvinist) theologian like Karl Barth attacked any compromise between faith and socialism and every sort of 'hyphenated Christianity'. This resulted in 'theologically-based social anarchy' and religious indifference to the fate of the Weimar republic.[17]

The tragic aftermath, 1933 to 1945, has not yet been worked

over in this style, and we must be content with a list of books. There is E. Bethge's biography of *Dietrich Bonhoeffer* (ET 1970), the one persuasive figure in the German Protestant leadership, who died *sans peur et sans reproche;* J.S. Conway's *The Nazi Persecution of the Churches* (1968); and R. Gutteridge, *Open Thy Mouth for the Dumb: the German Evangelical Church and the Jews, 1870–1914* (1976). Ian Kershaw's *Popular Opinion and Political Dissent in the Third Reich* (1983), was not primarily about religious history, but in its discussion of Bavaria under the Nazis made clear how susceptible the Nazis were to any signs of public resistance to Nazi ideology. More directly relevant was a Swiss study by Bernard Reymond, *Une Eglise à croix gammée?* (1980), the first serious attempt to defend German Protestant Liberals against the claim that only Karl Barth and the Confessing Church genuinely resisted Hitler, and that liberal Protestant theology was the evil influence which explained the weakness of German Protestantism in face of the Nazi ideological enterprise.[18] Protestantism, Reymond claimed, resisted Hitler better than this view suggested, and this resistance was not simply due to the Confessing Church's rejection of alleged liberal Protestant 'heresies' – nor for that matter was it the result of concentrating on any other doctrinal position as such. It was the result of Protestant diversity, a pluralism of which the liberal tradition, when most true to itself, was the surest defender. French interest in recent German church history has grown since 1970: for example, Rita Thalmann's *Protestantisme et nationalisme en Allemagne 1900–45* (1976), was a discussion of G. Frenssen, W. Flex, J. Kleppen and D. Bonhoeffer which overemphasized the importance of Luther's political theology in determining the extent of Protestant opposition to Hitler, but was valuable for its study of the grip which nationalism had on *modern* Lutheranism between 1870 and 1939. For the earlier period, Uriel Tal's *Christians and Jews in Germany 1870–1914* (1975) should also be consulted.

Religion in Modern France

French religious history since 1789 has not been exhaustively studied, but there is an excellent French critical bibliography of what has been done: *L'Histoire religieuse de la France, 19e–20e siècle:*

problèmes et méthodes (1975), edited by Jean-Marie Mayeur. A basic French textbook on the period, by Adrien Dansette, *Histoire religieuse de la France contemporarine* (1948–52), was translated into two slightly abridged volumes, *The Religious History of Modern France* (1961), and covered the years 1789 to 1939. Dansette wrote under the influence of the post-war Catholic reform movement, whose ultimate check at the Second Vatican Council was already foreshadowed by the collapse of the worker-priest experiment in the 1950s.[19] This perspective still survives, and can be seen still at work in the writing of Jean Delumeau, the French Catholic historian, which is discussed in the Postlude.[20] There is no equally comprehensive treatment of French Protestantism since the Revolution, though Ernest Rochat's *Le développement de la Théologie protestante francaise au xix*^e^ *siècle* (1942) dealt with the central issue in the history of that small, withdrawn community – the struggle between liberal and evangelical orthodox theology which became acute after about 1850, as German radical theology penetrated deeply into French Protestantism.[21]

Any consideration of modern French church history has to begin with the revolution of 1789. As a religious event itself, the Revolution was not, as Catholic historians often suggest, an attack on religion in general and on Christianity in particular; it was the first serious evidence that the Western religious tradition was coming apart at the seams, and that the status of Christianity as 'the religion of the West' was breaking down. The radical republican reform of the French Catholic Church in the 1790s affected the more isolated parts of France like Brittany as an assault on what was understood as 'religion' – on the intensely local forms of rural Catholicism – but the attack was also in its own way 'religious'. World-views related to different understandings of 'religion' clashed in the civil war of the Vendée, where Republicans and Royalists, the latter supplied with British money and sometimes with British troops, fought in the 1790s. On both sides the war had elements of a renewed war of religion.[22] It is worth noting that the first serious internal violence in France after 1789 was the so-called 'bagarre de Nîmes', where the long-repressed Protestant minority of the south of France took the chance of political freedom and avenged the massacre of St Bartholomew in the blood of about three hundred Catholics.[23] Conflict between the two religious communities continued sporadically right down to 1815, when Catholic retribution took the form of the 'White Terror'. The revolution was in part the explosion of a religious tension which had been building up since the sixteenth century, when official Catholicism had beaten off the challenge of French Calvinism but, despite Catholic expansion in the seventeenth century, had failed, in the long run to set up a monochrome religious society.

In France, even more than in other countries in Europe in the nineteenth century, Catholicism never quite recovered from the shock of social and spiritual dispossession which it experienced in the 1790s. The sudden, official rejection of the Catholic Church in its classical, Tridentine form revealed how fragile Catholic social hegemony had become in France in the last stages of the *ancien régime* proper.[24] This fragility was recently illustrated in one of the best known works of French social historians. In *Piété Baroque et dé christianisation en Provence au xviiie siècle* (1973), Michel Vovelle used the form and content of about 16,000 wills as a measure of religious commitment in the eighteenth century among people wealthy enough to make wills, and concluded that after about 1750 there was a sharp decline in gifts to the church, requests for elaborate ecclesiastical funeral arrangements, and in the general use of religious language. In a later work, *Religion et Révolution: la déchristianisation de l'an II* (1976), Vovelle also challenged the view of the Catholic church historians that the dechristianization of the Year Two was a brief, chiefly urban phenomenon which soon gave way to the academic religious celebrations of the Directory.[25] He preferred to point out signs of a new religiosity and spoke of a 'massive feminisation on the level of the creations of the collective imagination; by putting the Father to death (God or the King), it crystallized the fixation of the new religiosity on maternal images'.[26] However, another recent historian of the period, Olwen Hufton, said that female sociability, which had revolved around mass attendance to a large extent in the eighteenth century, 'suffered an incredible blow during the Revolution and it was . . . the women of France who recreated their Church long before the Napoleonic Concordat, and that a church of no particular kind, one unconcerned with doctrine, instruction, confession, but immensely concerned with regular Sunday observance, the honouring of local saints, the parish bell, and a liturgy performed by an individual (not necessarily a priest) who was uncompromised by having taken the Oath'.[27] This feminization of Catholicism was not a temporary phenomenon: although the priesthood recovered its local authority after the Restoration, much of the power of the nineteenth-century Catholic revival came from the immense expansion of female orders in the first half of the century.

To the extent that there has been any revision of the standard Catholic understanding of French religious history – an understanding which put the destiny of Catholicism, as a supernaturally revealed religion, at the centre of the story – it has been the work of social historians who have taken up the study of French popular religion on a less committed basis. Maurice Agulhon, for example, in *The Republic in the Village: the People of the Var from the French Revolution to the Second Republic* (1982), analysed what he interpreted as a decline in popular religion between 1800 and 1850. Edward Berenson, in *Populist Religion and Left-Wing Politics in France 1830–1852* (1984), also studied the south, and linked religion more closely with the southern insurrection of 1851 against the coup d'état of Louis Napoleon. For the later part of the century we have a remarkable book by Eugen Weber: *Peasants into Frenchmen: The Modernization of Rural France 1870–1914* (1977), in which the making of peasants into full members of a French national society seemed to be largely dependent on their ceasing to be more than mildly Catholic. There was a point of no return after which peasant farmers stopped having masses said for the recovery of sick beasts and trusted in veterinary remedies instead.

Nevertheless, social historians seem to agree that between 1800 and 1850 French Catholicism revived, partly spontaneously, and partly because of the missions of the Restoration.[28] At the political level this revival was checked by the revolution of 1830, because the Orleanist tradition espoused a style of liberalism which conflicted with the Catholic Church's claims to various kinds of authority.[29] In France, as in Germany (see the previous section), the enthusiasm of the laity for processions to local saints and for a religion which protected agriculture, cured diseases and emasculated thunderstorms did not suit all the clergy, who disliked being used as supernatural power-brokers, and who also reacted against a democratic and anticlerical strain in popular religion. Edward Berenson said that

> on the eve of 1848 both peasants and urban workers represented a reservoir of religiosity which could be tapped for political purposes. During the Second Republic the democratic-socialist left would prove capable of harnessing the fervour of these anticlerical believers . . . Peasants and workers already believed in a populist Jesus: the Montagnards (Republicans) would simply suffuse that belief with republican imagery.[30]

Berenson criticized historians who regarded the popular religious element in the make-up of the 1848 Republicans as proof of no more than romanticism and naiveté: it was not, he said, naive of socialists to identify secular fraternity and co-operation with the fraternal message of the Gospels. François-André Isambert, in *Christianisme et classe ouvrière* (1961), analysed the contents of working-class periodicals published between 1830 and 1848 to show the existence of a marginal proletarian interest in Christianity as a social religion which ought to be committed to the side of the poor and oppressed, but which, in the case of the Catholic Church, was seen as supporting the destruction of revolutionary Poland, and the growth of the political power of the rich bourgeoisie in France.

Maurice Agulhon, on the other hand, stressed the decline in influence of the Catholic Church on the peasants and small-town workers of Provence, and the rise of alternative centres of sociability, notably the cabaret, itself the product of a vast increase in the European wine and beer market in the course of the eighteenth century. He also pointed out that in the 1840s Protestantism prospered temporarily as an alternative to Catholicism, but said that the political storms of 1848 diverted the current popular religion towards the democratic movement. Even so, he said, what the people who were critical of institutional Catholicism wanted was 'another religion', rather than pure rationality, and so the democratic movement assumed a 'crypto-religious' character. Isambert also thought that Protestantism had some influence on the liberalization of the religious ideology, but that this influence was limited, in Paris at any rate, by the obvious links between the

Protestant élite and financial and industrial circles: this utter respectability contrasted sharply, in the popular mind, with an image of the Christ of the Beatitudes as the greatest revolutionary preacher of all time.

A comparison between Berenson and Agulhon throws an interesting light on the ambiguities inherent in discussions of this kind. Emile Zola, for example, situated the first of his Rougon-Macquart series of novels, *La Fortune des Rougon* (1871), against the background of the Provençale insurrection of 1851. Berenson said that Zola's heroine, Miette, was intended to link explicitly populist Catholicism and republican politics. 'Miette grabs the insurgents' flag, and striking the symbolic pose of a republican goddess of liberty, declares: 'I feel as though I am the one who is carrying the banner of the Virgin at the procession of Corpus Christi'. Berenson added: 'Zola did succeed in depicting the transformation of religious processions into political demonstration, and of populist religious symbols (a peasant Virgin Mary) into republican imagery'.[31]

Zola, it may be said, did not paint quite so simple a picture. When Miette first raises the red flag, Zola says: 'A ce moment, elle fut la vierge Liberté'. This is early in the day, and during the march which follows Silvère, Miette's lover, is said to identify her 'avec son autre maitresse adorée, la République'. It is only at nightfall, as the insurgent column reaches the town of Plassans (based on Aix) that Miette says (to Silvère alone) that she feels as though she is carrying the Virgin's banner at the feast of Corpus Christi. Her remark was hardly meant to reflect the emotion of the column itself, or that of Silvère.

Agulhon examined the historical episode that lay behind Zola's fiction. He pointed out that the earliest anti-republican source, Hippolyte Macquan, who had been an eyewitness, described what he took to be 'a goddess of Reason', marching with the column: if this was really what had happened, Agulhon said, then the insurgents were deliberately recalling the anti-Christianity of 1793.[32] The first pro-republican historian of the insurrection of 1851, however, Tenot, dismissed the woman as more of a theatrical 'goddess of liberty', a role with no great religious overtone.[33] Agulhon concluded:

> The Var 'goddess' . . . did not stand for the archaic terrorism that Macquan so much feared, nor the timeless Provençale bent for the theatrical, as Tenot half suggested: she does epitomise the spirit and savour of '1848', somewhere in between archaic populism and the new socialism.[34]

If this were correct, then Zola's description of Silvère's association of Miette with the Republic would be the most pertinent interpretation of the symbolism. Eugen Weber, however, in his brilliant study of the French countryside in the later nineteenth century, was unimpressed by the argument that the peasants were politicized between 1848 and 1852. 'It is very doubtful', he said, 'that any countryman stirred to defend the republic or the constitution, to oppose Louis Napoleon's coup'.[35] He also referred to Zola's novel, but chose the incident of the peasant who, when brought to trial for taking part in the insurrection, could only stammer, 'I'm from Poujols' – 'for him, this was enough; and village solidarities . . . sufficed to account for most of what took place'.[36] Weber thought that the most desperate anxiety of the peasants was that Napoleon's seizure of power might mean a return to the servitude of the *ancien régime*, a sudden awareness that liberties which had only recently been won might also be taken away again.

If we are seeking to place the modern history of French religion in its wider Western context, Weber's concluding remarks are of great interest. Down to the seventeenth century, he said, the high and low cultures (we have already met this distinction earlier[37]) agreed on the fundamental interpretation of existence. In the seventeenth century this relative unity of Western society began to dissolve under the pressure of scientific advance and the development of critical rationalism. 'Coherent religious theories of life that had been accepted by most educated members of the community became survivals, superstitions . . . Deprived of the support of élite thought, popular belief broke into a thousand subsystems.'[38] The gap between these two cultures began to narrow again about 1800, 'largely because of the rural world's increasing intercourse with the towns . . . The more sophisticated people of the city . . . demonstrated to the satisfaction of more and more peasants that the world could be explained without evoking magic or supernatural interventions';[39] and by the end of the century the popular and élite cultures had come together again. Some errant customs might continue, or even be revived by middle-class sentimentalists, but they had ceased to be rites, to have the 'religious' overtone found in them by historians of Early Modern Europe. At Nice, for example, the old communal fertility rites were changed into flower festivals, and May Queens were revived as Rose Queens.

> Phosphates, chemical fertilizers and schooling had spelled the beginning of the end. In 1893, a drought year in the Bourbonnais, when many men were having masses said for their emaciated cattle (which died anyway), the priest reproached Henri Norre, a self-taught man who farmed not far from Cerilly, for not attending church. I haven't got the time', he answered. 'And really, I've not much confidence in your remedies for the beasts. My remedies are better. You can check.' Daniel Halévy quotes another story about Norre. This time the farmer was returning from the railway station with a cartful of fertilizers and met the priest. 'What are you carting there?' 'Chemicals.' 'But that is very bad – they burn the soil.' 'Monsieur le curé,' said Norre, 'I've tried everything. I've had masses and got no profit from them. I've bought chemicals and they worked. I'll stick to the better merchandise.' It was the requiem of nineteenth-century religion.[40]

Weber was right to the extent that he was thinking in terms of a high and low culture only, and of their eventual late nineteenth-century reunion in what amounted to the collapse of a whole system of traditional popular attitudes – though he probably exaggerated the importance of scientific innovations in provoking the change. He was not so correct if one thinks of late nineteenth-century religion not as something which was dying, but as a system of ideas and institutions and rites which was exchanging the role of social hegemony for that of a sub-culture, an alteration of status which was going on all over Europe at about that time. French Catholicism was modifying its relationship to society throughout the nineteenth century, partly because the counter-revolutionary forces of the political Right, which took Catholicism for granted as part of their ideology, and had done so ever since 1789, were never able to overthrow Republicanism permanently – a failure which, by the 1880s, was compelling the Catholic Church itself to contemplate an official reconciliation with the Republic. The social historian must treat the sociologists' concept of 'secularization' with caution, whether it is used descriptively or causatively. It seems to be certain that some kinds of observable behaviour, having masses said for sick animals, for instance, gradually ceased, but this does not mean that people therefore became less 'religious' than they were before, as distinct from following a particular style of Catholic piety.

Weber also underestimated, I think, the significance of the alleged appearances of the Virgin Mary at La Salette (1846), Lourdes (1858) and Lisieux (1883), on the basis of which new national centres of pilgrimage were created, serviced by the rapidly expanding railway system, which facilitated the clerical policy of depreciating the cult of local saints. These events have been more adequately documented (in French) than discussed, perhaps because those who accept their supernatural origin find no need to discuss them historically, and those who reject their supernatural foundation find no need to discuss them at all. Weber himself mentioned them, but passed on, because the dominant secularizing movement which he assumed could hardly accommodate a simultaneous outburst of popular religion. No one doubts, of course, that the Marian cults have to be studied in a political as well as a religious context: they are not simply religious events, and La Salette, for example, has been firmly annexed to Catholic right-wing extremism, and the same was true of the more recent Marian appearance at Fatima in 1917.

In France as in Germany after 1870 the Catholic sub-culture became alienated from the new regime, imperialist but Protestant in Germany, republican and anticlerical in France. This explained the renewed popularity in the 1880s of Catholic propaganda aimed at Jews and Freemasons, as in the popular books of the abbé E.A. Chabauty: e.g. *Les Juifs nos maitres* (1882). Chabauty built on the counter-revolutionary fantasies of the earlier nineteenth century and revealed that Satan was employing Freemasonry as part of a secret plan to destroy Christianity and establish world-wide Jewish domination. Between 1885 and 1897 the papacy itself fell victim to the snares of Leo Taxil and Diana Vaghan: see *Les Mystifications de Leo Taxil*, by Eugen Weber (1964), and Robert Byrnes, *Antisemitism in Modern France* (1950). Catholic groups were heavily involved in the campaign against Captain Dreyfus from 1894. These ideas were given wider circulation by the professional journalism of Maurice Barrès and Charles Maurras. Maurras's nationalist, royalist and cynically 'Catholic' organization, *Action Française*, embarrassed liberal Catholics from its foundation about 1899 until its papal condemnation in 1926, because Maurras asserted stridently that republicanism was incompatible with French nationalism, and that French Catholicism (in which he had no religious interest) was indissolubly bound up with French royalism. (See Eugen Weber, *Action Française*, 1962, and Zeev Sternhell, *Maurice Barrès et le nationalisme français*, 1972.) These writers reinforced the links between right-wing Catholicism and extreme anti-modernist nationalism, and helped to form the political ethos which briefly sustained Petainism and the Vichy restorationism of the early 1940s. Maurras was sentenced to life imprisonment in 1945 for bolstering up German power in conquered France. In France as in Germany, the inability of the leaders of ecclesiastical institutions in the first half of the twentieth century to understand the true nature of the modern political ideologies which confronted them condemned them to unfruitful political debate and unsatisfactory political action. Maurras's axiom was very wide of the mark: it was not true that republicanism was irreconcilable with French nationalism (in the past nationalism had often been the trump card of the Jacobins), but it was arguable that nationalism was incompatible with Catholicism – the attempt to mate the two produced terrible fruit both in France, Germany, Italy and Spain. This gulf was deeper than that between Catholicism and some brands of Marxist ideology.[41]

The strange patterns of European Catholic politics had some influence in England, where writers like Hilaire Belloc combined antisemitism and Catholicism, but had little influence on British Catholic voters, who probably felt less alienated from British mainstream culture between 1918 and 1939 than did some of their clerical and aristocratic leadership. Thomas Molony's *Westminster, Whitehall and the Vatican: The Role of Cardinal Hinsley 1935–43* (1985) gave a frank account of the strains produced for a local national Catholic Church by the foreign policy of the Vatican, especially towards Mussolini and Franco. Hinsley clashed with the Vatican over the Italian invasion of Abyssinia, but claimed to recognize in Franco the essence of the true Spain: he firmly supported the war against Hitler, however, and showed no sympathy for anti-semitism. Once Russia entered the war, his mood changed again, because he responded to the Catholic feeling that Communism was the real enemy, and at the time of his death he was demanding that Britain guarantee the restoration of a Poland independent of Russia after the war.

The influence of Maurras strayed beyond the borders of France and sometimes beyond the borders of Catholicism. The American poet, T.S. Eliot, for example, brought to England a variety of *anti*modernism which he had originally adopted at Harvard, where he heard the lectures of Irving Babbitt, and which was confirmed for him by the teaching of Maurras, whose writings he met in France before the First World War. Maurras's watchwords: Classicism, Nationalism, Royalism, Catholicism: appealed to Eliot, who echoed them in the late 1920s, but as an Anglo-Catholic he moved in Anglican circles where such a combination of ideas, with their overtones of violence, authoritarianism and antisemitism, had only muffled resonance.[42] England, moreover, lacked the tradition of political extremism which in France could be traced from the Ultras of 1815 through the Bonapartists to General Boulanger (Barrès's hero of the 1880s), and so by way of the nationalists (who courted Catholicism assiduously), to a climax more Bonapartist than royalist in Gaullism, where the Catholic content had become slight.

The United States

American and European writing on church history have gone separate ways. The best-known American church historians in the first half of the twentieth century, William Warren Sweet,[43] Sidney E. Mead[44] and Perry Miller,[45] for example, were not deeply influenced by contemporaneous European ecclesiology, that half-brother of ecumenism for which 'the church', as a supernatural institution, became the essence of the gospel. These Protestant historians thought much more in terms of a wide variety of self-justifying denominations, which they defined as voluntary associations of like-minded individuals, united on the basis of common beliefs (not too intellectually scrutinized) and vigorously committed to overseas missions[46] and domestic revivalism.[47] The ethos of these denominations was Puritan, Pietist, 'Methodist' – the last being the most difficult to grasp[48] – with a belief in the future which owed nothing to Hegelian metaphysics. European historians disapproved of this kind of theological description: in fact, Catholic and Anglican historians usually regarded 'denominationalism' as lying outside the significant line of Christian development, and for many years were apt to dismiss American church history as inevitably marginal – it was surely significant that America had no symbolic religious centre, no equivalent of Rome or Canterbury. The American religious style, on the other hand, at times seemed to assume that history, even Christian history, had begun in America in the seventeenth century, and that the Enlightenment, a regrettable European affair, offered the best available evidence for the fall of man. This quite non-European valuation of self-made, successful denominations, obviously analogous to a self-constituted and successful United States, enabled American historians to explain and justify the comparative indifference of American Protestants to elaborate doctrines of the church in particular and to any serious reworking of systematic theology in general. The role of this evangelical pietist rhetoric and of the institutions which it engendered in the growth of modern America has still to be adequately analysed, which is not to say that many writers have not tried to cope.[49]

As far as the writing of church history was concerned, what happened was that many American scholars, and especially those from the long-dominant Protestant stream of culture, preferred an almost supernatural concept of 'America' to the European notion of a supernatural 'church'. The triumphant history of American denominations was then united with this image of a Puritan and Pietist America, while bodies like the Roman Catholic Church were even sometimes assumed to be non-American. This was why Sydney Ahlstrom could say of William Warren Sweet, the Methodist historian who died in 1959, that in his work 'the older forms of nativism disappear, but Catholics, Eastern Orthodox, Jews, Negroes, immigrants and the city are on the periphery of his scholarly interest'.[50] American historians like Sweet often gave brilliant accounts of the development of particular denominations, but rarely saw any need to relate Protestant and non-Protestant to one another, and both to their European roots. Black history was a non-event except when it confirmed white evangelicalism's view of itself. This falsified the picture: American Lutheranism, for example, was always conscious of the shadow of Luther; Episcopalianism remained British enough to produce its own equivalent of Anglo-Catholicism; the history of American Roman Catholicism inevitably responded to European connections, quite apart from the decisive interventions of the Vatican, as when it froze American Catholic theology after the condemnation of the Modernists in 1907. The legend of American innocence, so strongly asserted by the sophisticated, fantasies about the frontier – whether physical, or, as more recently, psychological – the alleged uniqueness of the American idea of the denomination, as well as vague concepts like the 'Puritan-Pietist' ethos – these and similar ideas were combined to build many splendid edifices which, by the late 1980s, were beginning to look like empty chapels. Perhaps one needed some of the American social historians who have written so well on sixteenth-century European religion to apply their techniques to what has been happening in America between the Civil War and the Vietnam disaster.

One exception to this generalization would be the history of overseas missions. The loss of mainland China to Communism, and therefore, in a subtle sense, to 'Europe', and the subsequent expulsion of the foreign missionary enterprises, educational and medical as well as evangelistic, called in question what Protestant America thought that it had been doing, and what it had actually achieved, in the Far Eastern missionfields, and this revisionism broke through after the military, moral and political failure of the 'great game' in Vietnam. These reversals shattered any claim to some sort of American uniqueness, and suggested that in China the American missionary societies had made much the same mistakes as had missionaries from Europe, and had been similarly rejected as part of a political rather than religious choice.[51] Energy, competitiveness, fundamentalism, revivalism, anti-intellectualism, the hallmarks of the mainstream American religious tradition, had not proved enough to save the mission boards from disaster. What showed a difference between Europe and America, however, was the far-reaching political effects of the expulsion of the American missionaries from China. They fought a stubborn rearguard action against American recognition of 'Red China', and this became a potent source of the ceaseless Protestant fundamentalist campaign to make American foreign policy revolve around an eschatological interpretation of contemporary history in which Communism was translated into the Satanic enemy of the United States, the evil empire of a demiurge. This also harked back to nineteenth-century images of America's 'manifest destiny', but was now reinforced by the similar Catholic impulse to identify Russia and Marxism as the major threat to the survival of Catholic culture.

Attempts at historical reinterpretation have appeared. One example might be *Revivals, Awakenings and Reform: An Essay on Religion and Social Change in America 1607–1977* (1978), by William G. McLoughlin. McLoughlin interpreted American history as the story of five great religious awakenings: 1610–1640; 1730–1760; 1800–1830; 1890–1920; and 1960–1990(?). He related these religious revivals to corresponding movement for social reform, and presented American history as a whole as a millenarian movement which started in 1607 and had not finished yet. McLoughlin is a distinguished historian, but the traditional paradigm of American religious history had pushed him in the wrong direction. He was right in saying that historians needed a more coherent approach to the history of religion in America, but here he was sacrificing coherence to the prejudices of the tradition, and putting his faith in a romantic commitment to the concept of recurrent patterns. The history of American culture in the twentieth century, for example, did not support the claim that there had been two periods of great religious awakening since 1900; soberly, one would doubt that there had been one. And there was just as little ground for his confidence that by the 1990s a new American belief-value system would have established itself through the influence of the latest of the alleged religious revivals. Finally, although McLoughlin said that he wanted to relate religion and social change, he virtually ignored the Roman Catholic Church, as so many of his predecessors had done, despite the fact that by the middle of the nineteenth century this had already become the largest single American denomination.

McLoughlin had been much more conscious of the weaknesses of revivalism in 1959, when he wrote *Modern Revivalism, Charles Finney to Billy Graham* (1959): then he compared America's reputation as a church-going nation with its reputation as a highly materialistic society, while in his earlier book, *Billy Sunday Was His Real Name* (1955), about the baseball player turned revivalist, he has interpreted Sunday's popularity as social rather than religious – Sunday's revivalism, McLoughlin said, offered European immigrants a mode of entry into American culture, or at least, one might add, into the pietist subsection of the still dominant Protestant classes. The case was symptomatic of the decline of American politics through Nixon to Reagan: whatever American Protestantism had added to the struggle over slavery and the tragedy of the Civil War, it seemed to have nothing but a menacing premillennialism to add to the macho characteristics of late twentieth-century cowboy politics.

The pressure on most American church historians not to break with this Protestant consensus even at its most extreme still remains considerable. George Marsden, for example, in *Fundamentalism and American Culture: The Shaping of Twentieth-Century Evangelicalism, 1870–1925* (1980), was prepared to criticize twentieth-century fundamentalism as being more secular than its nineteenth-century predecessor:

> Theological and ecclesiastical issues seemed less important . . . Identification with secular nationalism and economic policies was often made with less qualification. One of the most persistent refrains, especially in the giant television ministries, was a gospel of personal success, reflecting the drift of evangelicalism generally away from Calvinist emphasis on depravity. As

> always, however, fundamentalists were highly ambivalent in their relations to the culture. Though the new fundamentalism was deeply involved in preserving or reforming aspects of the American way of life – salvation of souls, personal holiness as evidenced especially by avoidance of bar-room vices, witnessing as the primary obligation to one's neighbours, and the imminent end of the age – remained central to its message.[52]

Having made these criticisms, however, Marsden fell back on the basic position of the traditional church historian:

> In American church history many authors have pointed out the intertwining of Christianity with the various 'isms' of the times – nationalism, socialism, individualism, liberalism . . . Fundamentalism . . . incorporated some of these into its vision of Christianity. Yet God can certainly work through such combinations. Christians' trust in God may be mingled or confused with some culturally formed assumptions, ideals and values. Inevitably, it will. The danger is that our culturally defined loves, allegiances, and understanding will overwhelm and take precedence over our faithfulness to God. So the identification of cultural forces is essentially a constructive enterprise, with the positive purpose of finding gold among the dross.[53]

Looked at in this way, a more sociologically informed church history would protect extreme Protestantism against its worst extravagances, and encourage the fainthearted to believe that God was at work in unlikely places. Since 1945, however, events have destroyed the coherence of this Protestant-eye view of American religious history, a view which was always more relative than it supposed itself to be, and even Sydney Ahlstrom's cautious welcome for religious pluralism did no more than make new approaches possible.[54] By the early 1970s there were in the United States forty-eight million Roman Catholics, twenty-five million Baptists, thirteen million Methodists and about three million Anglicans; the situation was even more striking in Canada where in 1971 there were about ten million Roman Catholics, just over one million Anglicans and just under one million members of the

United Church (largely Methodists and Presbyterians). In North America church membership climbed virtually to irreligious heights in the 1950s but fell back swiftly in the 1960s. American religious history belongs with that of Western Christianity. There is no question of a single American tradition, conceived of as a coherent, unitary system, nor has technology united what demonology divided. But the problems of late twentieth-century Catholicism and Protestantism have become much the same: problems about the existence of God, the divinity of Jesus, and the resurrection of the dead. The historian of religion has to show how since 1800 America has slowly detached itself from the *ancien régime* and gone in search of a changed religious consciousness.

6

Newman and Catholic Modernism

Newman's sermon on 'The Second Spring', preached at Oscott in 1852, revealed nothing so much as his ignorance of eighteenth-century Catholicism in England: there had been, he said, no longer even a Catholic community, only 'a few adherents of the Old Religion, moving silently and sorrowfully about as memorials of what might have been'.[1] As J. C. H. Aveling said in *The Handle and the Axe* (1976), this judgment 'was right in seeing English Catholicism of 1570–1850 as a swirling mass of inconsistencies and changes. It was wrong as seeing such a state as uncharacteristic of Catholicism. The orderly English Catholicism of 1850–1950 was itself a period piece about which there was little intrinsic permanency'. He in his turn perhaps romanticized (because he admired) the pre-1850 English Catholics, who sat light to both the papacy and episcopate and lived very often on open terms with their Protestant neighbours.

> The Second Spring theorists also greatly exalted the priesthood as not merely the backbone and soul of Catholicism but as the Church itself. Cardinal Manning's extraordinary flight of fancy, *The Eternal Priesthood* (1883), imagines a church in which all alike are bound by the discipline of a strict religious order.

The Second Spring also reintroduced the idea of Catholicism as being an intensely sacramental, incarnational religion, an ethos which had been largely in abeyance during the eighteenth century. In the period between about 1770 and 1850 'English Catholic opinion was generally hostile to monasticism and the Orders in full decay. From the 1860s came a new and large rush' into monasticism. But this, Aveling said, and he wrote with the authority of a former Benedictine, 'was not a real wave of contemplation and radicalism of the kind which begot earlier monastic revivals', but a matter of dominant clericalism 'seeking to gather into useful institutions the pious laity needed as auxiliaries of the clergy to service the schools and parishes'. Finally, Aveling said that the Second Spring sharply altered the relationship between Catholics and Protestants:

> after 1850 it became unthinkable that Catholics had once been married and buried by Anglican rites, used inn rooms and public halls for Mass, allowed Dissenters to attend their chapels on occasion, let Catholic children go to Protestant schools and universities, let nuns go about in secular dress. After 1850 these informalities faded and a grim tension set in between Catholics and Protestants.[2]

Aveling's book, like John Bossy's *English Catholic Community 1570–1850* (1975), which covered a similar field, suggested that in the wake of the Second Vatican Council of the 1960s (which may be called the 'Roman spring' by way of contrast with the seemingly endless ultramontane winter which had preceded it), there was a growing awareness among English Catholics that they had lost as well as gained by the invasion of the English converts from the Church of England in the 1830s, that English Catholicism had, indeed, existed before Cardinal Manning and even before Cardinal Newman, and had had its own conventions and ethos quite apart from the dutifully repeated accounts of recusant casualties. (Earlier Roman Catholic historians specialized in recusant history, and in the history of English conventual houses founded on the Continent from the late sixteenth century.) Professor Bossy thought that Catholicism between Elizabeth I's reign and the 1830s should be regarded as a living part of English Dissent, because it formed part of a continuing alternative society which perhaps accepted the existence of Anglicanism more than its own existence was accepted by the Anglicans. The idea that eighteenth-century England was a deeply divided society before the advent of industrialism has not been popular among modern historians, who have preferred to emphasize the kind of social unity which they believe was destroyed in the first half of the nineteenth century. There is something of this mood in Bossy's work: why should one accept for ever the fortuitous combination of Irish Jansenism and Italianate Ultramontanism which had come to be the style of English Catholicism by 1900? Why not recover the freer spirit of a more English, even a more truly Catholic religious manner? The confident hopes for the conversion of England which had been expressed in the 1850s at the time of the restoration of the hierarchy had not been fulfilled. Was not at least part of the reason for this the unfortunate strategy of making Catholicism aggressively different from what it had been in the not so distant past?

In *More Roman than Rome* (1978), Derek Holmes, offered simpler explanations of the slow growth of English Catholicism in the last quarter of the nineteenth century. 'Englishmen did not welcome the definition of papal infallibility, the condemnation of Anglican orders and Modernism, nor did they sympathise with the Ultramontane attitudes to devotions and pilgrimages, relics and miracles.' However, even he admitted that Abbot Butler was too optimistic in 1925 when he said that Bishop Ullathorne, and not Wiseman or Manning, represented the progressive form of the older English Catholicism, and that this older form had survived and still dominated the English church after the First World War, (see his biography of *Ullathorne* 2 vols, 1925). Irish immigration, together with Ultramontanism, Holmes granted, had ultimately brought about fundamental changes in English Catholicism. And although Butler claimed in the 1920s that Newman would have been allowed at that time the academic freedom which he was so obviously denied in the nineteenth century, and that his intellectual powers would have been fully used in the service of the church, this was to ignore (Holmes added) that as a result of the Modernist crisis Butler himself had learned to avoid the critical questions. Nineteenth-century English Catholics had enjoyed a vigorous, if often ecclesiastically dangerous, intellectual life, whereas by the 1920s English Catholic intellectuals had largely taken refuge from authority in practical rather than critical religious activities. English Catholicism suffered no more in this respect than did Catholicism in the United States, where theology is said to have stood still in the fifty years after *Lamentabili* and *Pascendi*.[3]

It is arguable nevertheless, that the important events in nineteenth-century English church history were not Anglican, were not, that is, for example, Keble's Assize Sermon, F. D. Maurice's brief flirtation with Christian Socialism, the publication of *Essays and Reviews* in 1860 and of *Lux Mundi* (the Anglo-Catholic response to the Anglican Liberal manifesto) in 1889, but were events like Roman Catholic Emancipation in 1829, the restoration of the Catholic hierarchy in 1850, Irish immigration into England after the Irish famines – because this greatly increased the number of Catholics in England, and because the immigrants entered an English culture much more easily than seems to have been recognized – and the official Roman condemnation of Anglican orders in 1896 (after all, there has been no change in the situation nearly a century later), and the astonishing decline in British anti-Catholicism after the 1870s.[4] A change of emphasis of this kind follows from our position in the 1980s, a position from which the perspective of Victorian church history has altered, and no longer corresponds to the Anglican-weighted version which still satisfied E. R. Norman, for instance, in his study of the nineteenth-century Catholic Church in England.[5] It is clear that Anglo-Catholic and Anglican Evangelical efforts to revive Anglicanism were a comparative failure, that the collapsing English Free Churches have lost their critical edge with their belief in freedom and so have no influence on the outcome of the encounter between Anglican and Roman in the late twentieth century. Wiseman, Newman and von Hügel built better than they knew; in the long run the obscurantism of the elder Ward and Cardinal Manning counted for little. The self-conscious re-entry of institutional Catholicism into the mainstream of British culture and politics rests on Victorian foundations, and these should now have their proper position in an account of the Victorian churches, and not be treated as relatively unimportant adjuncts to what was going on in the Church of England. A new textbook, and not just an 'ecumenical' textbook, is overdue. Dr Norman's book was an Anglican confirmation of Manning and Vaughan's self-interested picture of the Catholic revival: both these approaches need to be replaced.

We have already discussed Catholic Modernism in terms of the general histories of the church.[6] We must now examine the subject as it is discussed in the numerous books which have been published since the Second Vatican Council relaxed the implicit ban on serious historical study of the field. The older view of Modernism was summed up in the introduction to the Catholic Truth Society's 1937 edition of *Pascendi* and *Lamentabili*, the official documents which contained the Vatican's condemnation of Modernism in 1907. The 1937 editor, Lewis Watt, said that the purpose of the Modernists

> have been described as the regeneration of the Church by its rejuvenation. But the methods which they adopted and the conclusions at which they arrived brought them into conflict with the fundamental truths of traditional Christianity. The danger to the Christian Church was particularly urgent because the modernists professed to be loyal Catholics. It was averted by the prompt action of Pius X in issuing the masterly encyclical which synopsised for the world the errors of Modernism and, by refuting and condemning them, made it clear that they were incompatible with the Catholic Faith. Outside the Catholic Church, however, they still exist and so long as they exist they are dangerous.[7]

Down to the 1960s nothing was likely to receive the *imprimatur* which did not take a similar view, and one finds the attitude still distantly echoed in the Anglican Edward Norman's account of Modernism in his *The English Catholic Church in the Nineteenth Century*. Norman said that the Modernists claimed for intellectual enquiry a measure of autonomy from ecclesiastical authority, and he interpreted *Pascendi* and *Lamentabili* as an attempt 'to protect the authority of the teaching office of the Church against academic individualism exercised without reference to it'.[8] Norman took Lord Acton, the historian, Friedrich von Hügel and George Tyrrell as typical of the movement in the English Catholic Church. He compared the ideas of conscience held by Acton and Newman to what he felt was Acton's disadvantage. Newman (he said) thought of conscience as exercised within a mystical community of faith, not as an individual criterion by which one could judge the magisterium of the church; Acton (Norman suggested) was claiming to have superior insight. One could also argue, however, that there was something unsatisfactory in Newman's willingness to identify his 'mystical community' with what was to be seen as Pius IX's Rome, and that Acton, as a historian, had good reason to believe that men could not trust the papacy in such an absolute fashion. (Tyrrell was to extend this argument by saying that the declaration of papal infallibility left all non-infallible statements from the Vatican in an uncertain area.) There is also more to be said about Acton's position than can be expressed in terms of 'individualism': by the close of the nineteenth century the liberal and historical-critical approach to the problems of theology and ecclesiastical politics had itself become an established tradition, to which individuals contributed, but which they did not invent individually for themselves. Acton might in some ways have been *sui generis*, but he was not alone.

Edward Norman swept von Hügel aside as a pompous German scholar of no fixed address. His fire was reserved for George Tyrrell, who 'had a degree of intellectual perversity'[9] which enabled him to feel that his congenital dislike of obedience was a principled objection to Catholic authority. That Tyrrell should have written a 'dismissive' reply to Vaughan's *Pastoral on Liberal Catholicism* (1900) was no more than an early sign of this perversity, this refusal to be told. Norman left the impression that Modernism was the result of the unnecessary self-assertion of undisciplined intellectuals, unwilling to accept the wisdom of a long-established institution: 'liberalism', in fact, was an illness of the human spirit which needed firm handling, a conclusion which would have satisfied Pius X himself. It has, of course, become a standard technique of orthodox apologetic to suggest that schism and heresy are the byproducts of psychological difficulties: orthodox theologians, no doubt because they are orthodox, have reliable, unflawed, personalities.[10] Occasionally, the technique is reversed, as in *How the Pope became Infallible* (1981) by Bernhard Hasler.[11]

Norman's support of the authoritarian position was in contrast with the stance of Derek Holmes in *More Roman than Rome* (1978). It was significant that he did not pass over the *Pastoral on Liberal Catholicism* with Norman's unquestioning approval, but underlined the significance of Vaughan's determination, encouraged by the powerful Roman official, Merry del Val, to make an end of Catholic

Liberalism as far as England was concerned. The condemnation of Anglican Orders in 1896, which had Vaughan's entire approval (see the French study by R. Ladous, *L'Abbé Portal et la campagne anglo-romaine* (1973), had emphasized the uniqueness of the Catholic Church in England, and now in 1900 the *Pastoral* described the authority of the church in extreme terms. As God had spoken through Christ, so he now spoke through the legitimate successors of Peter and the Apostles: theological authority belonged to the *ecclesia docens* (the teaching church), and must be accepted by the laity, as the *ecclesia discens* (the learning church). Moreover, the Catholic was to obey the non-infallible, ordinary authority of the church, which included episcopal pastoral letters as well as the decisions of the Roman Congregations. The *Pastoral* denounced any suggestion that 'the dogmas of the Catholic faith are not immutable but tentative efforts at the truth, to be formed under the inspiration of modern science; there was criticism of any appeal to the laity, however learned, in matters of theology. The church's continuity and indefectibility was that of a living organic being, animated by the Holy Spirit, and so the church's authority had in no way declined since the primitive period. It was not surprising that Tyrrell should have criticized the *Pastoral* on the ground that it envisaged the papacy as set above the ecclesia in the normal sense, dispensing an absolute power on which bishops like Vaughan could draw in dealing with the English laity. This style of clerical dominance had grown out of the policy of Pius IX, and there were obvious echoes of the *Syllabus of Errors* (1864) in the *Pastoral*. In England, it also grew, as Bossy showed[12] from the clerical drive to impose its authority on the laity after Emancipation in 1829. If we are to speak in Norman's fashion as though 'liberalism' was some kind of disease, what can be said of Vaughan's belief in the absoluteness of his own position? Holmes commented that 'a concern for a narrow uniformity out of a sense of pastoral responsibility or conceived as an apologetic weapon became almost typical of English Catholics as a result of the example of leaders like Vaughan'[13] – and, one may add, Cardinal Manning before him. Indeed, the tendency ran very deep: one also recalls von Hügel's letter to Wilfrid Ward in 1911[14] in which he said that Newman's 'apparently absolute determination never to allow – at least to others – *any* public protestation, any act or declaration contrary to current Roman central policy, cannot surely be pressed, or imposed as normative, upon us all'.

Much of the more detailed historical work that has been done in this area has been aimed at distinguishing 'Liberal Catholicism' from 'Catholic Modernism' – both of them changing notions, of course, rather than precisely defined concepts. The aim of these historians was to restrict the papal condemnation of Modernism to specific people like Alfred Loisy, who did withdraw from the Roman Church after 1907, and so leave room for an approved, or at any rate uncondemned, 'liberal Catholicism', which might also be linked with Vatican II. In making such a distinction 'Liberal Catholicism' would be taken to refer to a movement of Catholic dissent which grew between 1830 and 1870, was much concerned with the right of the laity to have a free part in the church's theological discussions, and which was brought up short by the First Vatican Council, with its stress on papal infallibility. 'Catholic Modernism' emerged rapidly in the 1890s, revived some of these older themes, but was especially anxious about the *intellectual* situation of Catholic *dogma* in a culture which, Marxists apart, was losing faith in the concept of dogma *per se*. It is sometimes said, without much evidence, that Newman, at least in part a Liberal Catholic, was vindicated by the Second Vatican Council; it is also claimed with equal uncertainty, that the Modernists laid the foundation of Vatican II.

Once again the importance of theological intentions in the writing of ecclesiastical history can be seen. William J. Schoenl, for example, in *The Intellectual Crisis in English Catholicism* (1982), argued that a moderate Liberal Catholicism which sought to reconcile 'modern thought' and Catholic tradition, had been compromised by the rise of a 'modernist' wing which asserted that such a reconciliation could be attained only by altering the meaning of dogma and reforming, that is, reducing, the authority of the church. In crushing Modernism, however, the Vatican also suppressed Liberal Catholicism which did not entirely deserve this fate. Part of the difficulty of an approach like Schoenl's lay in its simple identification of the papal position with orthodoxy; Pius X thus became the uncriticizable defender of the faith, who could be challenged only at the pragmatic level, in terms of the methods employed in the repression of the Modernists between 1907 and the death of Pius X in 1914. In an earlier, and not dissimilar, interpretation, Michele Ranchetti, in *The Catholic Modernists: A Study of the Religious Reform Movement 1864–1907* (translated by Isobel Quigley and published in England in 1969), said that although the theological condemnation of the Modernists could be justified in traditional terms, they had an ethical case against the Vatican because of the way in which these condemnations were handled.

This distinction had obvious convenience, because it implied that Pius X had judged the theological issues correctly; while the questionable treatment of individual Modernists could be blamed on others, though this became less tenable once Emile Poulat had shown, in *Intégrisme et Catholicisme intégral: Un réseau secret internationale antimoderniste: La Sapinière, 1909–1921* (1969), the direct links between Pius X and Mgr Benigni, who organized the pursuit of anyone remotely suspected of deviating from the conservative (integralist) line. Pius X, in fact, was consciously defending papal power as though it was seriously endangered. Yet Loisy, Tyrrell and von Hügel never really supposed that their challenge would compel the Vatican to summon a Council in order to reconsider the nature of dogma. All that they asked the authority to do was to tolerate the modernist publications. The Modernist intellectuals cared little for the older Liberal Catholicism which had always been more political than theological, and had reflected, in the English Catholic society of the 1860s as well as in Risorgimento Italy, the influence of the main body of bourgeois liberal ideas. As Ranchetti himself showed, after 1907 the shattered forces of Italian 'Modernism' regrouped, under Romolo Murri ('too scholastic ever to have been a *real* Modernist', Poulat said in *Alfred Loisy*, 1960), and Luigi Sturzo (for whom see the excellent and liberal-minded book by J. N. Molony, *The Emergence of Political Catholicism in Italy*, 1977). It was Sturzo who finally founded the Partito Popolare in 1919, from which the present Italian Christian Democratic Party emerged after the fall of Mussolini. The question of papal power was here as well, for the Vatican's dislike of the idea of a lay Catholic political party which rejected clerical control meant that Sturzo spent most of his later life in exile from Italy. This was not only a question of Modernism, however, but of the Papacy's reluctance to come to terms with a politically united Italy which did not think of ecclesiastical Rome as its true capital, but rapidly developed a secular Rome as the political centre of an increasingly secularized state. The papal Concordat with Mussolini in 1930 concealed what was happening, but John Paul II's revision of the Concordat (made official in 1985) made clear the decline of the papacy in strictly Italian terms. There was no English equivalent of this political 'Modernism' after 1907, and in France a Catholic political organization which was not identified with the extreme Right did not become effective until after the Liberation in 1945.

Many of the books which I have mentioned neglect the importance of wider elements in the Modernist crisis. One has only to look at Maurice Larkin's *Church and State after the Dreyfus Affair: The Separatist Issue in France* (1974), to realize that Pius X and Merry del Val saw themselves as fighting on a broad front against 'forces of evil' which they identified variously as the 'critical school', the 'advanced democratic school', international freemasonry and so forth. Merry del Val believed that what happened in France would decide what happened elsewhere. The Dreyfus Case had pitched some elements of the French Church against the State from the late 1890s: Alfred Loisy's *L'Evangile et l'Eglise* appeared in 1902, when the Republican government was already moving to separate the State from the Church. The papal reply to the French policy was contained in *Vehementer nos* and *Gravissimo officii*. Published in 1906, before the official condemnation of Modernism in 1907, they urged French Catholics to a total resistance from which many of them, including some of the bishops, drew back. In such an atmosphere, the Modernist intellectuals were bound to be disciplined as part of the effort to purge French Catholicism.

Modernism, in fact, has to be considered in its own right as more than just a heresy which good Catholic historians can deplore and pass over quickly: its roots lay in the intellectual difficulties of Christianity as they had grown in the nineteenth century, which does not mean that Modernism was only a Catholic version of Liberal Protestanism. Ranchetti[15] became an unintentional witness to this when he argued that there was no continuity between the earlier crisis and Vatican II. Modernism, Ranchetti said, was theoretically inspired by the wish to free Catholic dogmatics from the limitations imposed by an out-of-date scholastic philosophy, bad history, and antiquated science. Modernism set out to restore doctrinal relevance, and therefore authority, to the Catholic Church by creating a sounder relationship between Catholicism and modern culture as a whole. Unfortunately, the theological outcome was heretical, and had to be rejected by the papacy. On the other hand, Vatican II was regarded by Ranchetti as being not deeply concerned with doctrinal questions: there was therefore no kind of 'modernist' revival at the Council, no sense in which the *salon des réfusés* of 1907 became the Académie Catholique of 1964. There was even a naive belief, characteristic of the earlier liberal Protestant, but not of the Modernist tradition, that the Christian intellectual crisis was not profound, that 'progress' in biblical studies pointed to solutions, not problems. Each generation of intellectuals is tempted to announce that it has overcome the difficulties which proved too much for its predecessors. In some branches of science this is actually the case; in most humanist studies, including theology, it is rarely if ever the case. But the Vatican sanctioned freer biblical studies in the 1950s on the assumption that liberated Catholic scholars would bring this field of inquiry into line with official dogma. This is the real explanation of the conflict which has gradually broken out between Catholic biblical scholars and the new 'Holy Office': see, for example, *The Schillebeeckx Case* (ed. T. Schoof, 1984), an official exchange of documents during the official investigation of the Dutch scholar. In fact, when told that dogmatic conclusions belong to the church, not to the scholar, Schillebeeckx seems to me to give way and assent. Modernism, that is, had failed completely to change the position.

It is not surprising that for Ranchetti the Modernist theological propostions remained condemned, and even, Ranchetti suggested, partly answered by the Second Vatican Council's emphasis on faith, which he contrasted with *gnosis*, that is, with an alleged Modernist search for a perfected state of Christian doctrine. The Second Vatican Council, he said, was concerned with liturgy rather than with doctrine, a conclusion which might have pleased von Hügel in his post-Modernist vein, when he had moved aside from the crisis in his study of Catholic mysticism, *The Mystical*

Element in Religion, but would not have impressed Loisy, who seemed to become more interested in the relationship between religion and politics after 1907. As for George Tyrrell, presumably he would have sympathized with the later Catholic rebel, Hans Küng, the critic of John Paul II and an exponent of Vatican II: Küng not only shared Tyrrell's detestation of papal power as such, but, in *On Being a Christian* (1982), for example, was grappling with the same intellectual problems of christology which had fascinated some of the Modernists.

Schoenl tried to legitimate similar conclusions to Ranchetti's by concentrating on the English Catholic lay theologian, Wilfrid Ward,[16] who claimed to stand in a liberal Catholic tradition which drew its inspiration from Newman. In order to sustain this position, which was not immediately obvious, Ward had to argue that Newman was both 'ultramontane and liberal', an interpretation rejected by Lady Blennerhassett, on the ground that 'no complexity or sublety of mind can reconcile Yes and No in one and the same argument'.[17] As a matter of ecclesiastical, not intellectual, politics Ward had to protect Newman from *Pascendi* in order to protect English Liberal Catholics from 'Modernist' contamination; the alarm in England over the Encyclical was such that the superior of the Brompton Oratory had to write to the *Times* that he had been assured on the highest authority that Newman had not been an intended target, and Wilfrid Ward believed, or chose to believe, that Merry del Val himself, was the authority in question. Nevertheless, the *Times* also published a letter from Robert Dell, a more Liberal Catholic than Ward, asserting that *Pascendi* condemned 'development' and therefore, inevitably, Newman himself. When Ward finally pronounced on Modernism in the *Dublin Review* (January 1908), he avoided the boggy ground of Newman's undeniable support for an official consultation of the laity in Catholic theological debate; he instead, defined Modernism as subjectivism in religion: 'the identification of religion with sentiment or emotion rather than belief in objective truth, issuing in the concept of a deity immanent in man and not transcendent, and of dogmatic formulae as no longer the expression of facts'.[18] (The best *theological* study of Modernism, Gabriel Daly's *Transcendence and Immanence* (1980) showed how the barren intellectualism of late nineteenth-century neo-Thomism generated a counter-emphasis on immanence among dissatisfied Catholic philosophers – this shift was characteristic of the period, in which non-Christian philosophers like Henri Bergson and William James reacted in a similar but more secular fashion to a sterile invocation of 'science'.[19]) For if the 'Modernism' rejected in *Pascendi* could be identified with 'subjectivism' then Newman (a few paragraphs of the *Grammar of Assent* apart) was in the clear. Schoenl's approach may be added to those which aim at the creation of a 'Liberal Catholic' tradition running through thinkers like Newman, von Hügel and Wilfrid Ward up to the Second Vatican Council, which seemed for a time to have set limits on the theological freedom of action of the papacy, and even to have blessed the idea of consulting the laity in matters of doctrine.

The most vigorous attempt to release Liberal Catholicism from the embrace of Modernism was made by T. M. Loome in *Liberal Catholicism, Reform Catholicism, Modernism* (1979). Loome claimed to be setting out a fresh orientation for modernist research: he wanted to put the Modernist crisis in the context of a conflict, recurrent since the seventeenth century, between two mutually antagonistic intellectual traditions in Roman Catholicism. The antagonists were scholastic and ahistorical on one side, historical and scientific on the other. This would be true enough, though hardly as original as Loome suggested. In any case, his work turned on a distinction between the years 1895–1903 and 1903–1914. In the earlier period, he said, men like von Hügel and Lucien Laberthonnière (1860–1932) were led mistakenly to identify themselves with Loisy; after 1903–5 they and others, having realized the true, negative nature of Loisy's religious position, abandoned Modernism (here very much identified with Loisy's point of view), and the movement passed into the hands of 'third-rate Catholic scholars, no-Popery Protestants and "Old Catholics" '.[20] Loome attacked von Hügel at some length for his weakness in supporting Loisy, and praised his subsequent recovery of an orthodox equilibrium.

The obvious criticism of Loome's book is that the substantial intellectual case made by Loisy betwen 1895 and 1905 about the problematical relationship between history and dogma, was largely ignored: once again the controversy was transformed into an analysis of personalities. At this level the behaviour of the Vatican and of its supporters could safely be deplored, with supporting quotations, in Loome's instance, from the papers of Edmund Bishop, the lay Catholic liturgical scholar, whose capacity to believe that he had suffered the lash of the Ultramontanes far exceeded any risks that he had ever taken in the liberal cause.[21] The impression given by this and other versions of Modernist crisis was that no serious theological problems existed in the Catholic Church in the first half of the twentieth century: what happened could be explained in terms of Loisy's alleged private loss of faith and public duplicity, an explanation similar to that of the sixteenth-century Reformation in terms of Martin Luther's alleged inability to live as a good monk, and of the excesses of right-wing Catholics, which (it had to be admitted) slipped out of control by the Vatican after the death of the worldy-wise Leo XIII.

On Loisy's personal position wiser judgments were made by Alec Vidler and Emile Poulat. In *Histoire, dogme et critique dans la crise moderniste* (1962), Poulat said that to discuss Modernism simply in terms of Loisy's honesty was to suppose an uncomplicated man and an uncomplicated book (*L'Evangile et l'Eglise*): in fact, not only were both complicated, but the universe of faith in which Loisy worked had its own manifold layers of belonging and expression. Just to say that Loisy was 'dishonest' when he wrote *The Gospel and the Church* because he knew that he no longer 'believed' in traditional Catholic Christianity, was to simplify unduly. By 1900, belief was no longer first and foremost a matter of deciding on one's personal attitude to some brief standard statement of doctrine. It was no longer even a question of a right of private judgment. Instead, Loisy was acting as a member of a religious community made up of people whose states of religious consciousness were by no means identical, but who shared, however indirectly, in the consequences of the advance of a general pattern of research. Loisy was not only an individual scholar, but also consciously part of a changing movement of thought.

This seems to me to be fairer to Loisy than Loome's assertion that Loisy deliberately deceived people like von Hügel about the state of his faith. Poulat appreciated, as Loome did not, the problems of intellectual honesty in modern religious thought, the difficulty of describing what is believed, and of defining the degree of certitude involved in believing it. Only for those for whom these problems did not exist, and who could not really imagine them as genuinely existing, for whom 'honesty' was a matter of confessing total acceptance of a standard creed, was there the option of insisting that Loisy ought, at any moment which suited his critics, to have taken and made known an irrevocable decision, and said that he was no longer a Roman Catholic. It was a criticism of the rigidities of Catholic institutionalism, rather than of Loisy himself, that he hesitated as long as he did. It is as well to remember that he was excommunicated for what he had printed, not for what he might have concealed. Vidler's words in *A Variety of Catholic Modernists* (1970), are as apposite as Poulat's:

> At a time when traditional theological concepts could no longer be treated as absolute or final by anyone who had become aware of their inevitable relativity, and when they needed to be reconsidered and re-interpreted, Loisy's reticence or suspension of judgement was not only creditable in itself but consistent with his intellectual integrity and continued allegiance to the Church. He still believed that the Church had a unique mission for the moral and spiritual education and guidance of humanity, whatever might be the future of its more speculative and metaphysical doctrines. This attitude may be described as pragmatic, but it was one that was perfectly respectable in a scholar who confessed his metaphysical incompetence and speculative agnosticism.[22]

A failure of historical judgment has confused most accounts of modern Catholic history, and therefore judgments about the role of Modernism in it. This failure may be described as the view, widely held in the Edwardian period, and often still assumed in progressive and Marxist interpretations of history, that the stream of events has a goal which can be recognized, and that, for example, the advance of science and the growth of an educated (and perhaps socialist) community is bound to culminate in a paradisal society in which (in the religious form of the argument) Christianity will take a comfortable, comforting place – though in the Marxist form it will have withered away. This view affected Bernard Reardon's judgment on Roman Catholic Modernism in *Nineteenth-Century Religious Thought in the West* (3 vols, ed. N. Smart et al., 1985), when he said that although the Second Vatican Council had been called 'Newman's Council', it would probably be nearer the mark to characterize it as the Council which the Modernists, other than the most extreme, would gladly have welcomed if they had lived to see it.[23] Reardon said that Modernism and its old opponent Integrism (this is the English form of 'intégrisme', the French word which refers to the hard core of the Right-Wing of Roman Catholicism) were 'phases in a process of abiding change, in which progress and reaction, liberty and restraint, are abiding features'.[24]

Twentieth-century history, however, has not proved a benign medium of either divine or Marxist revelation, except for those ruthless souls who read the will of God into every fresh human experience of catastrophe. Newman had been more cautious in his use of the idea of development; he used it only to explain the luxuriance of Catholic theology, traditionally a ground of suspicion in Protestant eyes. He had dismissed the history of Western secular society, especially since the sixteenth century, as a story of degeneration (see especially, *The Idea of a University*). The Catholic reformers, however, saw themselves as part of a cultural revolution, combining Christianity and human self-discovery, which would transcend the past of the Roman and Anglican Churches.

This sort of optimism has been the constant temptation of secular as well as religious reformers in modern times. Throughout this century they have persuaded themselves that change was bound to occur according to a pattern which they had discovered; they have been sure that they knew how to read a kind of revelation in history. Long after Victorian ideas of 'progress' had disappeared, they assumed that the political and reforming Left was inherently stronger than the forces which resisted change: they believed that freedom and enlightenment were permeating Western culture. That misunderstanding has had long-term consequences in political miscalculation, and the Modernists were far from being the only people to suffer. In reality, indeed, it can be argued that from the beginning of the nineteenth century the Right, conventionally defined, has been stronger than the reforming Left, that change (which has certainly happened) has been socially and politically neutral, and that freedom and enlightenment have gradually been declining, not increasing, in the social democratic as well as the Marxist West.

Above all, what dominated the Roman Catholic sub-culture between 1860 and 1914 was not a modernizing movement which had to be resisted at all costs, as Pius IX and Pius X believed, but a vigorous anti-modernizing movement which took and held the initiative. It was not potential liberal change or socialist revolution which made the running; instead, the church was being governed by a counter-revolution which nevertheless always presented itself as the underdog and the victim. The actual historical role of the Modernists was not to lead a liberalizing group which would introduce into Roman Catholicism a series of institutional and theological changes which had already happened in some of the Protestant churches; their role was to protest unsuccessfully at the steady consolidation of religious forces which were politically centralist and theologically anti-critical. The clergy were mistaken in hoping that 'history' would release them from the often intolerable intellectual tension which they experienced in these years: events stepped up the tension, but did not resolve it dialectically.

This historical judgment, which has *not* been the guiding-line of the study of modern Catholic history, affects one's assessment of the relationship between Newman's generation and that of the Modernists, and that of the Modernists and the Second Vatican Council. In the past historians seem to have assumed that since the 1860s it was the Liberals who were forcing the pace in the religious sub-culture, so that Pius IX was striving to hold down forces which were bound to break through sooner or later. These historians somehow interpreted the sustained conservative pressure which stretched from Pius IX to Pius XII as a long parenthesis, after which John XXIII released the by now irresistable liberalizing forces which found expression in Vatican II. Even ecclesiastical conservatives, of course, sometimes thought of themselves as delaying the inevitable, like Metternich. If we look at the series of events in this way we are bound to ask, how far did Newman agree with the Modernists, and judge him accordingly. A more accurate interpretation of the historical events however, may be to say that there was in the religious sub-culture as a whole, and in the Roman Church not least, a slow growth of anti-modernizing, centralizing, populist attitudes, which consolidated themselves at the popular level in terms of Marian devotion and speculative theology, while at a more sophisticated level critical methods which had been borrowed from Protestantism were used to promote a return to the authority of the papal office in an ecumenical ecclesia. When events are interpreted in this way, and Vatican II is understood as more like a stage in the containment of reforming tendencies than a victory for them, the question about the part which Newman or the Modernists played as fore-runners of Vatican II changes. What useful and effective continuity, one is driven to ask, was there in the critical, reforming tradition?

The answer to that question suggests that Vatican I mattered more than Vatican II, because Vatican I forced the issue of religious certainty by proclaiming the dogma of papal infallibility, an act which Vatican II was unable to reverse. Newman restricted his criticism of papal infallibility to a persistent plea (from the 1860s) that consultation of the laity should be added to the existing processes for deciding official dogmatic pronouncements. The Modernists, however, were reacting against Vatican I (which has to be seen as a cause of the movement), but they had no programme for reforming institutional authority; they tried instead to show at the intellectual level that dogmatic certainty had become impossible. Theirs was a grammar of dissent which put down no roots in Catholic popular belief, and this meant that the Modernists saw themselves as in discontinuity with Newman. Newman's had been a grammar of restraint, a clinging to the hope that the future would bring better weather. The most committed Modernists, however, Loisy and Tyrrell, faced not only the full force of the uncertainty of Christian belief in the modern world but also the full weight of the anti-modernism of the Vatican under Pius X, and we should not minimize the tragic element in their situation, and not only theirs, for Modernism had many casualties, like Hebert, etc. Bernard Reardon said that the Modernists were convinced that only Catholicism, once it had been 'modernized', could preserve the values and even the institution of historic Christianity. Protestantism could not respond, as Catholicism could, to the diverse needs of the human spirit. 'The humanism of the Catholic tradition, which Protestants were so ready to deplore, was in fact, as Tyrrell always held, its actual strength.'[25] The strength of such an argument, however, depends upon what is thought to be surviving, a Catholicism of the spirit, at once Erasmian and ecumenical, or a Catholicism of the Vatican, at once political and Marian.

7

Failure of a Mission: Christianity Outside Europe

Historians have often been tempted to see Christian missions as the spiritual arm of Western imperialism, and some missionaries, though far from all, would have liked to have been thought of in that role.[1] China offers an excellent example, for mid-nineteenth-century Protestant missionary societies forced their way into the Treaty Ports and then into the Chinese interior by exploiting the Opium Wars. Yet the evidence for a close connection between missionary and imperialist is of the vague kind much employed in such cases by Marxist historians, and there is countervailing evidence that Western politicians for the most part did not regard Christianity as more than an incidental part of a Western package. Western governments could not exclude missionaries from colonial territories without having to face persistent and embarrassing lobbying.

In fact, however, the most important function of Christian missions from the point of view of those who sent them was ecclesiastical, not political. Nineteenth-century European and American churches had recovered to some extent from the losses inflicted by the Enlightenment and the French Revolution, but they nevertheless recognized the limits of their recovery and that they were not able to re-establish Christendom; but would have to accept the role of powerful pressure-groups and sub-cultures. In this situation Christian missionary expansion provided what turned out to be a shortlived compensation for the diminution of social, political and religious influence at home. The missions also helped to stabilize the churches from which they came, because the mission-fields presented an opportunity of escape from some of the moral, theological and social problems faced by individuals and by the religious sub-culture as a whole in Western 'modernizing' society. An alternative ecclesia, even a substitute imperium, seemed to be possible even as late as 1900, a dream which helps to explain the slogan, 'the evangelization of the world in this generation', which was popular in youth movements at the time, and which had premillennialist, adventist overtones.[2] John Mott, the most famous student leader of that period, claimed in 1902 that it was the destiny of the United States and Britain to set working in the depressed, neglected races of the world 'those influences which alone can ameliorate the conditions of mankind, build up a lasting civilization and make possible the evangelization of the world'.[3]

This point of view reached a climax at the Edinburgh World Missionary Council in 1910, when the mission-field 'younger churches' helped to set up the original institutions from which came the World Council of Churches in 1948. The ecumenical movement was a logical consequence of seeing missionary expansion as a means of recovering Christianity's influence on Western society itself. A kind of 'Christian imperialism', in fact, affected the development of missionary work much more than did the political aggressiveness of Western states. And on the whole, where the missionaires achieved some degree of penetration, they owed this less to Western prestige and political power than to their own encounter with social groups already, quite apart from Western pressures, deeply alienated from the ancient societies in which they lived.

The war of 1939–45 brought a sudden end to this whole historical pattern. The complete communist triumph in China, the rapid emergence of a self-governing black Africa, the British withdrawal from India and Ceylon, the bitter collapse of Dutch and French colonial power in the Far East, the American stalemate in Korea and eventual defeat in Vietnam, changed the situation irrevocably. The removal of the protecting European powers closed an era of Christian missionary activity which had started in the 1790s, and the historian was left to ask the inevitable questions: why had this astonishing episode of cultural aggression happened, how had it been carried out, and what effects had it had, both on the sending bodies and the societies which received them? These were not the only questions which were asked. Missionary theorists were anxious to analyse the past in order to modify missionary policy in the newly independent states. Sociologists thought that the mission-fields, objectively studied, offered an opportunity to examine the relation between religion and society, and to analyse the role of society in religious behaviour, for Christianity entered non-European cultures as a fresh, competitive religious movement, whose communicability, influence and basic meaning could be studied against a background which was not soaked in centuries of Christian assumptions. American historians were interested in the growth of Russian power in the Far East, in the conflict between American and other imperialisms, in the nature of communist and nationalist movements and their successful challenge to Christianity; over everything else brooded the shadow of the Vietnam debacle. And so a new branch of church history developed, which transformed the study of missions from what it had still been as recently as 1939, an excuse for not very critical biographies and for complacent accounts of the work of the missionary societies.

The history of Christianity in modern China, for example, has been the subject of a number of excellent studies. Apart from the initial period, from the sixteenth to the end of the eighteenth century, when Roman Catholic missionaries had China almost to themselves, there have been four broad historical phases. First the years in which the Western powers forced an entry into China, taking the Protestant missionaries with them, say from 1830 to about 1860; the Taiping rebellion started in 1851. Second, the period from the sacking of the Summer Palace at Peking in 1860 by European troops to the Boxer troubles of 1900, a period in which the Chinese *ancien régime* fought to survive in Confucian terms; it put down the Taipings by 1864, who combined Confucian Christian and 'modernizing' elements; in these years China became a principal target of an American evangelical youth movement committed to an eschatological understanding of missions. Third, from 1900 to the Second World War, a time when a republic replaced the empire and a wider range of Western influences, including Liberalism and Marxism, penetrated China;

as the Nationalist movement (the Kuomintang) emerged from the chaos, the missionary movement found itself steadily pushed to the margin. Four, from the Communist takeover in 1949 to the present: the Communists expelled all foreign Christian institutions from mainland China.

The implications of this historical work gave small comfort to church historians who found the clue to the analysis of history in the alleged supernatural nature of the church. A typical summary of what might be called the secular case was provided by John Fairbank, a distinguished Harvard professor of history who specialized in Far Eastern studies.[4] In his introduction to *The Missionary Enterprise in China and America*(1974), he said that by 1949 it had become evident in any case that few of the Chinese people were likely to become Christians and that the missionaries' long-continued effort, if measured in numbers of converts, had failed. They had entered China not only as spiritual reformers, however, but also as part of a Western invasion. This invasion combined the technology of an early iron warship like 'the incredible *Nemesis*',[5] with the power of unfamiliar systems of ideas, not only Christianity, but Liberalism and Marxism as well. It was true that once they were in China, the Protestant missionaries began to realize the need for material improvement; they fostered it by means of medical, agricultural and educational institutions: and in doing so they helped to foment the Chinese revolution. As foreigners, however, they could take no part in that revolution, much less bring it to a finish: instead, it finished them. Always outsiders in old imperial China, they had their heyday *after* the Boxer rising in 1900, in the nationalist period proper, when many of the intellectuals whom they had trained in their schools and colleges held some degree of power. But this heyday was illusory: the floundering, corrupted Nationalists, themselves fighting both the Japanese and the Communists, became increasingly conservative, but Chinese opinion grew impatient with the concept of reform and shifted to the Left. Forced to choose, the majority of the missionaries clung to an anti-Communist position: even when their attitude combined the pursuit of individual salvation with schemes for social change, it offered no theological basis for mass mobilization in the cause of violent revolution. The missionaries could not move towards the revolutionary position, and so they were finally condemned by the new government as an aspect of the Kuomintang. Missionary thinkers underestimated the speed with which China could change; they also found their own idealism less attractive to the Chinese than that of the revolutionaries.

The Chinese Republicans, including Sun Yat-sen, regarded the Taipings as their revolutionary predecessors, and popularized their story in order to stir up anti-Manchu feelings.[6] The inter-war Nationalist leader, Chiang Kai-shek, on the other hand, identified in his later years with the conservatives who defeated the Taipings and saw himself as a defender of 'chinese' values against the Communists. When the Communists took control of China in 1949 the Taipings became heroes again, for Chinese Marxist scholars interpreted the Taiping rebellion as an example of the chief historical force in Chinese feudal society, peasant class-struggle against the landlord class. All these views obscured the older, and to some extent mid-nineteenth-century missionary reaction, that the Taiping ideology was a kind of Christian heterodoxy which drifted into undesirable political extremism and corruption. In fact, the founder of the Taiping movement, Hsiu-ch'an (1813–64) had been taught about Christianity by an American Baptist in Canton, and the leading Taiping 'Westernizer', Hung Jen-kan (1822–64) had been an evangelist with the London Missionary Society (which was Congregationalist) in the early 1850s. Both missionary groups stood in a slightly ambiguous relation to Western society. Taiping acquaintance with the Christian scriptures helps to explain certain elements in their programme, including the radical demand for the abolition of private ownership of land. This 'Christian' influence has been re-emphasized in modern Western treatments, but with the rider that the Taiping rebellion was essentially another, perhaps the very largest, of the long succession of peasant revolts which had relieved the almost intolerable pressures of the imperial regime (see, for example, C. A. Curwen). Historians like Paul Cohen see the missionaries as having done no more than teach the Chinese something of the religious and political language of a Western civilization from which they wanted to borrow: 'what the missionaries did not manage to convey was a new spiritual outlook, one that would produce Christian solutions to Chinese problems'.[7]

This comment seems slightly unrealistic, for the missionaries could not draw on a body of agreed Christian solutions to the new problems of the West's industrial-urban society which they could apply to the collapsing Chinese imperial regime as it foundered in the gap between a feudal, agrarian past and a modernized, industrial future. When the early nineteenth-century missionaries entered China they initially took the social system for granted but regarded themselves as divinely called and entitled to preach a religion of salvation to 'heathen' who, if they rejected this 'gospel', would be punished eternally for their 'sins'. The missionaries' belief in the absolute authority of their message explains their willingness to use political and military methods to gain entry into China. Their political ideas amounted to support for the existing forms of order and justice, as long as these operated in Christianity's favour, and this was why they rallied to the Empire against the Taipings, and to the Nationalists in the 1920s. As the nineteenth century continued, some missionaries took more interest in agricultural, educational and medical institutions, and here the tradition of the 'enlightenment' and 'Christian values' briefly combined to produce what has been called a programme of 'Christian reform'. This was the stage at which the Protestant missionaries failed to convince the Chinese intellectuals that Christianity was an essential ingredient in the West's apparent superiority, and one reason for this was that the missionaries themselves rarely possessed a spiritual outlook which would have enabled them to transcend the dominant Western attitude – which shaded from paternalism to contempt – for all non-white races. Chinese xenophobia, so often dismissed in the literature as a bizarre phenomenon, was only the other side of the coin of Western cultural intolerance. It was not so much that the missionaries failed to offer the Chinese a Christian solution to their problems, as that they did not foresee that the Chinese would be able to work out their own solution, using only what Western material they thought was valuable. At the same time, it should be remembered, that the older and larger Catholic mission in China, which had 1.4 million members in 1912, and was protected by French imperialism, then enjoying its Third Republican heyday, was equally unable to conciliate the Chinese governing classes, and suffered heavily in the Boxer troubles.[8]

Paul Cohen, moreover, showed that a Chinese tradition of anti-Christianity went back to the seventeenth century (some of whose anti-Christian writings were actually widely used again in the nineteenth century), so that hostility to the nineteenth-century missionaries could not simply be explained as a by-product of Chinese resentment at the Western powers, including the United States, which were exploiting China. In fact, the Roman Catholic missions had been severely persecuted as recently as 1784–5, and the Jesuit 'edifying and curious letters' from China, which covered most of the eighteenth century, told a similar story of slowly growing hostility and persecution. The statement made in 1900 by the Protestant missionary societies that there 'is no evidence that the persecution of the Christians and the attacks on Christians have any religious basis such as was so prominent a feature of the Indian Mutiny', cannot be accepted. It belonged to the unchanging and mistaken missionary belief that the ordinary Chinese, as least in the rural areas, were friendly towards Christianity, and that opposition came from the Confucian gentry, anxious to safeguard their social privileges. Purcell, with whom Cohen and Wehrle agreed, quoted the famous sinologist, Joseph Needham, to the effect that

> four times in history was China offered the possibility of adopting organized Christianity . . . but the missions always failed, and the fact must be faced by Westerners that the Christian religion in its organized forms has been decisively rejected by the Chinese culture . . . this necessarily follows from the highly organic structure of the Chinese humanistic morality which could not but view with distaste a religion placing so tragic an emphasis on transcendence, and which was therefore so dogmatic and ecclesiastical . . .

Needham's argument belonged to the history of ideas, but was in agreement with the line taken by historians like Cohen and Irwin Scheiner (see the latter's *Christian Converts and Social Protest in Meiji Japan*, 1970), that an important difference betwen China and Japan in the late nineteenth century was that whereas in Japan Protestant missions made many converts among the samurai élite who had recently been deprived of their social privileges in Japanese society, in China the effect of the Taiping rebellion and Westernizing influences was to increase the solidarity of the Confucian gentry in their resistance to Christianity. They were in no way impressed by the confidence with which the Protestant missionary societies, even after the Boxer rising, talked about China's need for Christian civilization and dismissed Chinese society as a 'huge anachronism'.[9]

That China needed the Christian missionaries whether the Chinese wanted them or not, was the case that the missionary apologists (nowadays usually called missiologists) had to make in order to justify the whole extraordinary episode.[10] One has only to look away from China to the West itself to find oneself asking the inevitable question: why should Christianity be able to do for China what it had so palpably not done in the West? By the 1920s the argument begins to sound ominously familiar: China must be saved, not just from sin, but from Communism. Right down to 1945 the missionaries regarded the economic and social problems of China as not their business (see Varg, Fairbank), but they were still able to regard support for the Nationalists as on the divine side of history. They clung to the unequal treaties to the end. Some of the politicians knew better. Varg quoted Walter Adams, then consul-general at Hankow, in 1932, as saying that the Nationalist government was trying to eradicate communism by means of military drives, but that the use of military force would not suffice. The Soviet movement in the area was deeply rooted in economic distress, he said, and its eradication would be possible only through a change in the conditions which had produced it. He concluded: 'So far as I have been able to ascertain the Chinese (Nationalist) government is not now effectively executing any programme which will result in such appropriate change'.

The missionary pretension, in fact, was greater than it seems at first sight. It meant a claim to have a divinely-given right to keep China out of modern history. They wanted, without much reference to the realities of the 1920s and 1930s, to fix the country in the Chinese equivalent of a Christian medieval world picture. Purcell underlined the extraordinary nature of Timothy Richards's choice of *The Nineteenth Century, A History* (1880) by a Scottish journalist from Dundee, Robert Mackenzie, as the book best calculated (in 1893) to convey to Chinese readers in translation the essence of Western achievement. Perhaps a million copies of this all too mediocre work were circulated in the last years of the century, and it was a principal source of Chinese information about Europe at that time. What it, very temporarily, concealed was the existence of powerful non-Christian traditions within Western culture itself.

Here, as in other mission-fields, missionary leadership was not equal to its pretensions, and one is bound to ask whether the claim to divine direction was sufficient ground for the enterprise? Stuart Miller, for example, thought that the furious missionary reaction to the Boxers illustrated the serious dangers of assuming a position of moral absolutism, and he listed this among other occasions when the American sense of mission had degenerated into an aggressive missionary impulse: the Philippines, Vietnam. On the other hand, Irwin Hyatt transformed Charlotte Moon from a Baptist cardboard missionary heroine whose memory is much employed for money-raising campaigns, into a much stranger figure, a woman who in her later years almost abandoned mission-as-evangelism for a self-negating identification with the miserable existence of Chinese peasant women in a time of war and drought: at the end of her life she stopped eating out of sympathy with Chinese Christians whom she believed to be starving. Charlotte Moon was not a great creative leader, but she was much more than a reflection of the aggressive aspects of American society in the nineteenth century, as was the case with so many of her fellow missionaries.[11]

Chinese missionary history suggests how much remains for historians to do to break down the over-simplified concept of a 'Christian missionary' who preaches the 'gospel', and to replace it with a pattern which expresses the interaction between missionaries who often preached many things besides the 'gospel', and alien, self-sufficient societies which, however, usually contained alienated social groups which were willing to use new ideological positions as a means of changing their social role advantageously. In a discussion of the relationship between the cargo-cults of the

South Pacific and missionary Christianity, Mircea Eliade, the famous social anthropologist, gave a brilliant analysis of how this confrontation might on occasion have taken place:

> If so many cargo cults have assimilated Christian ideas, it is because the natives have rediscovered in Christianity their old traditional eschatological myth. If the natives came to feel disappointed in the missionary, if the majority of the cargo cults ultimately turned anti-Christian, it was not on account of anything in Christianity itself, but because the missionaries and their converts did not appear to conduct themselves as true Christians. The disillusionments that the natives suffered in their encounter with official Christianity were many and tragic. For what attracted the natives to Christianity the most powerfully was the preaching of the renewal of the world, the imminent arrival of Christ and the resurrection of the dead; it was the prophetic and eschatological aspects of religion that awakened in them the most profound echo. But it was precisely these aspects of Christianity that the missionaries in practice seemed to ignore or not take seriously. The millenarist movement became savagely anti-Christian when their leaders realised that the missionaries, who had indirectly inspired them, did not really believe in the arrival of the ships of the dead bearing gifts, that in effect they did not believe in the imminence of the Kingdom, the resurrection of the dead, or the establishment of Paradise.[12]

This was certainly not what the older school of missionary historians meant by missionary history. They were chiefly concerned with the history of the mission institutions, and were too close to their material to understand how bizarre an episode was the invasion of the South Pacific by evangelizing Victorians.

We, however, at a greater distance in time, can see that the inner content of the religious behaviour stimulated by the intervention of the missionaries in the existing native cultures mattered far more than what happened to the missionary societies themselves. The missionaries, that is, estimated their success in terms of the rate at which they set up and expanded a new, separate church; modern critics are much more concerned about the fate of the new society, Christian and non-Christian, which the missionaries helped the administrators and businessmen to form, with or without the consent of the indigenous inhabitants. We are also in a position to see how many different strands were woven into this religious behaviour, and how easily the Victorian missionaries deceived themselves about the kind of Christianity adopted by their converts and contacts.

The history of the Wesleyan Methodist mission to New Zealand will illustrate the argument further. Wesleyanism was never a great success in New Zealand. The first missionary phase ended in 1827 with the Maori sack of Whangaroa and the flight of the missionaries. A second phase foundered in the tragic Maori Wars, which went on intermittently from 1845 to 1869, and which represented a second conquest of the islands: subsequently, white New Zealanders knew that they occupied the land by force. In the second half of the nineteenth century the Wesleyan missionaries turned chiefly to the European invaders and built up a small denomination. The Maoris were said to be dying out, but in fact they survived and still make up about ten per cent of the population.

In his valuable study of the religious aspects of the encounter between Maoris and Europeans, John Owens stressed that this was not a simple struggle for dominance between two groups, but a mutual grappling in which each deeply affected the other.[13] The Maoris had to rework their world-view in order to incorporate immense stores of fresh information and experience; the missionaries had to come to terms with the overall failure of their evangelism. In itself, the failure was not surprising. The Maoris had a highly developed sense of kinship, which meant that they could not accept the 'revealed' truth that after death people were separated into heaven and hell – the idea of individual salvation made little sense to them. They did not mind keeping the tabu of the Sabbath, but were upset to find that even when they had kept this tabu the angry Jehovah, or Christ, still allowed newly-planted potatoes to die in the ground. There seems to have been little in the Maori religious vocabulary which could have served as a basis of the communication of a Christian atonement theology, which was the heart of the missionaries' piety. When the first Wesleyan leader, Samuel Leigh, proved a failure, the inexperienced society in London sent out two inexperienced batchelors – Hobbs and White – who suffered sexual torments which finally compelled White to return to London without permission.

Owens played down the element of cultural conflict between Maori and Wesleyan societies, arguing that the conflict took place between individuals and not between 'cultures' as such. In reality, however, the basic situation in New Zealand was one of racial conquest, not of cultural persuasion, and this conquest, which involved setting up an elaborate, swiftly changing Western type of society, was as drastic in its effects as the military occupation, though that had cruel enough results in the Maori Wars. This external conflict of weapons and ideas decided the Maori view of Christianity, and as in Africa, the genuinely indigenous conversions were probably to fringe, separatist churches, in which a local Maori group made its own use of 'Christian' concepts and rituals. The relevant question about the missionaries, however, is not whether they 'converted' anyone even in their own sense of the term, but whether they helped to soften relations between the two races: as far as the mission to the Maoris went, it can hardly be said that they did. A similar conclusion can be drawn from Judith Binney's fine biography of Thomas Kendall (1778–1832), *The Legacy of Guilt* (1968). Kendall was the first ordained agent of the Anglican Evangelical Church Missionary Society to go to New Zealand (in 1814); his contact with the Maori destroyed him, and helped to damage them. And the same picture is found in *The History of the Tahitian Mission* by John Davies, an original source reprinted by the Hakluyt Society in 1961. In his account of the Protestant missionary invasion of the islands between 1799 and 1833 Davies never showed himself aware of the degree to which his presence had altered the Tahitian situation and contributed to the decline of a culture.

In the cases of India and Ceylon, historical research has concentrated on two fields: first, on the role of Christianity in the development and collapse of British rule in the East; second, on the investigation of religious behaviour, and more especially with the same problem of conversion to Christianity. This work has necessitated a revision of the older account according to which Christian missionary societies had gradually made triumphant headway against a combination of the darkness and idolatry of Hinduism and the cynicism and obstruction of the British administration – a version which still appeared in Stephen Neill (1964), who dismissed the Indian Mutiny as an unimportant interruption in the steady advance of the gospel in India. In fact, as Ainslie Embree showed in *Charles Grant and British Rule in India* (1962), this picture of India as a land of moral darkness and idolatry owed much to the efforts of Charles Grant and his friend William Wilberforce, who perhaps succeeded better in moulding the average Englishman's opinion of India and the Indian peoples than they did in converting the Indians themselves to Anglican Evangelical religion. Charles Grant's 'Observations on the State of India among the Asiatic Subjects of Great Britain' had an influence beyond its author's wildest dreams. He wrote the original essay in 1792, when he was trying to ensure that the new Charter of the East India Company should include what was called the Pious Clause, which would have both enabled and obliged the Company to take active steps to christianize India; Wilberforce popularized Grant's arguments in England; the essay was reprinted in 1813 and by 1820 had become the Evangelical source-book and final authority on India and Indian policy. Grant denounced Indian society as corrupt and traced all its evils to the Hindu religion: the evangelization of India was a necessary preliminary to its good government. He said that there was no foreseeable future 'in which we may not govern our Asiatic subjects better than they can be governed by themselves' but that the Indians could not be expected to suffer British rule indefinitely unless they were christianized.

All this material was given great publicity in 1813 when the East India Company's Charter came up for renewal. Grant and Wilberforce, who wanted the legalization of the entry of missionaries into India and the appointment of an Anglican bishop, mobilized British public opinion in a campaign of a type which was to be repeated again and again through the nineteenth century. Those who opposed the work of the missionaries were said to be ready to trample on the cross of Christ. An unprecendented number of petitions was gathered, and the government gave way to Wilberforce, but much more important than this local victory was the fact that the propaganda used in this struggle was to colour the British attitude to India for generations. And one found combined together the assertions, that the missionary was divinely entitled to preach the gospel to the Indian, and that the British seizure of India was somehow providentially directed to make the missionaries' task more successful.

These views were inevitably challenged at the time of the Indian Mutiny. Thomas Metcalfe, for example, in *The Aftermath of Revolt in India 1857–1870* (1964), showed that once the revolt had been put down there was general agreement in non-missionary circles that Dalhousie's well-meant reforms had been mistaken, and that the spread of Christianity, which had had the apparent support of the British administration, had thoroughly alarmed both Hindus and Muslims for the future of their own religions. These conclusions, which meant that official circles held the missionaries partly responsible for the Indian rising, were denied by the missionary societies at the time. They still repeated Grant's argument that British rule in India required the christianization of the country – without admitting that this implied a British withdrawal, since the christianization of India was improbable in any likely future. They insisted that Indian Christians had remained loyal to Britain during the rising, which they attributed to the failure of the administration to support Christianity more openly. They actually demanded a more pro-Christian policy, just as Grant had done after the Vellore sepoy mutiny in 1807, and said that the Government should ignore all caste distinctions, sever all connections with the rites and customs of Hinduism, introduce the Bible into Indian schools as a class-book, and take whatever other steps were needed to propagate the faith of the occupying power. This policy was advocated by famous missionary leaders, like Alexander Duff. In fact, however, the administration drew quite the opposite conclusion from the revolt: official opinion would have agreed with S. B. Chauduri's diagnosis that there was considerable civil as well as military discontent in 1857 (see his *Civil Rebellion in the Indian Mutinies*). In practice, the Indian Mutiny marked the end of the real power and influence of Christian opinion in India, a power which had depended on Anglican Evangelical laymen (in the Punjab, for example), at least as much as it depended on the missionaries themselves. From the 1860s official circles, when liberal at all, agreed with Matthew Arnold's brother, Henry, that Britain held India in trust for the Indians themselves, and had no special divine mission to replace the existing religions of the country with Christianity.

The extent of missionary influence after 1857 was also discussed in *Social Protest in India: British Protestant Missionaries and Social Reforms 1850–1900* (1979), by G. A. Oddie. Oddie discussed the permanent hostility of the missionaries towards the caste system, and their part in the anti-nautch movement and in the campaign against child marriage. The missionaries also intervened in agrarian problems, including that of the oppression of indigo producers, in the mid-nineteenth century; in the late nineteenth century some, but by no means all, of the missionaries took part in temperance crusades and in a campaign against opium. Oddie concluded that missionary involvement in social protest was influenced by three major considerations: first, they were often moved by humanitarian feeling; second, they reacted sharply against social institutions, such as the caste system, which made evangelism itself more difficult; third, as Indian Christianity grew, they sought to change social conditions which might predispose converts to return to Hinduism. Their protest campaigns had little effect, however, except when their aims coincided with those of Hindu reformers acting for their own non-Christian reasons. On the specific topic of caste, Oddie should be compared with D. B. Forrester: *Caste and Christianity, Attitudes and Policies on Caste of Anglo-Saxon Protestant Missions in India* (1980). Forrester brought the story down to the present and showed how often all mission churches in India were still frustrated in their efforts to weld together congregations of different caste origin. Caste, however, is surely no longer a problem to which a 'Christian' solution counts for very much: in the new, independent India caste is an 'Indian' problem for which only a 'Hindu' solution remains relevant.

All this may sound a little ungenerous, as though the revisionist historian undervalued the missionary's self-sacrifice, his patient attention to an unfamiliar culture and language, his willingness to endure alien climates and the danger of persecution, his persistent attempt to translate one world into the language of another. There is truth in this criticism, nor should one be blinded by the masculine image of the missions into ignoring the extent to which women as missionaries helped to stimulate the movement for women's emancipation in the East. Nevertheless, the historian would not entirely accept this counter-claim: the missionary, he would reply, was doing what he wanted to do, his sufferings were usually no greater than those of many isolated, dedicated (and even humanist) administrators, and he sometimes seemed to expect a high return in the form of praise for his self-sacrifice and recognition of his superior moral insight. With hindsight, the historian was bound to suspect that this constant urge to deny the autonomy of a foreign society, an impulse which seems to have been as marked a feature of the missionary movement as it was of imperialism, this conviction that one was divinely entitled to intervene outside one's own culture with the aim of controlling other people's behaviour, was part of a wider social intolerance which developed rapidly into twentieth-century totalitarianism.

This impression is reinforced by K. M. de Silva's study of *Social Policy and Missionary Organization in Ceylon 1840–55* (1965). De Silva showed in great detail how after 1805 Anglican Evangelical pressure, directed more especially by James Stephen from his central position in the Colonial Office in London, achieved, against the better judgment of the British administration on the spot, a complete severance of the links, dating from the Kandyan Convention of 1815, between the ancient Buddhism of Ceylon and the newly arrived British government. 'Stephen's attitude on this subject', de Silva said, 'is a study of the darker side of Evangelicalism – its confident assumption of moral superiority, its intolerance and its bigotry.' Central to the Evangelical position was the assertion, first made in the case of India, that a Christian government ought not to associate itself in any way with an idolatrous religious system, such as Buddhism was held to be. In the background lay the belief of the missionaries that the withdrawal of what they regarded as official recognition of Buddhism would accentuate what they took to be its inevitable decline in Ceylon. De Silva contrasted this campaign, sustained over a long period and absorbing much energy, with the comparative lack of interest which the same missionary societies showed in

Ceylon's social problems: caste, slavery and immigrant Indian labour. 'It was unhappily characteristic of the missionary movement in Ceylon at this time,' he concluded, 'that they seldom interested themselves in a social problem if it was not likely to bring a dividend of converts.'

De Silva's conclusion brings us back to the historical question of conversion to Christianity. In India it is commonly agreed that the higher castes were largely unaffected by the Christian missions, and K. M. Pannikar, in his famous book, *Asia and Western Dominance* (1959), insisted that the missions failed. His views were echoed more recently by K. P. S. Gupta, who said that 'the matter of Indian converts was very insignificant as compared to the vast population. The majority of them were from the lowest strata of Indian Society, outcastes, half-castes and even beggars. Their behaviour after conversion scarcely reflected any change in their character or way of life. Thus the missionaries failed to achieve their object'.[14] A milder, pro-Christian verdict was given by Sundararaj Manickam in *The Social Setting of Christian Conversion in South India* (1977). This was a study of the impact of Wesleyan Methodist missionaries in the Trichy-Tanjore diocese between 1820 and 1947, with special reference to the Harijan communities of the mass movement area. Trichy-Tanjore had given the Wesleyans hardly any significant return from 1820 until 1913, when a mass movement into Christianity happened among Adi-Dravida pariahs; a second movement took place at about the same time among pariahs working in the tea and coffee plantations in the Anamalai Hills; in 1923 a third movement occurred in another outcaste community, the Madharis, who were village workers. Manickam asserted that the missionary work among these outcastes produced permanent and fundamental changes:

> The most important good that Christianity has done to the Adi-Dravidas and the Madharis is the conviction it gave them that the God who was revealed in Jesus Christ cares for them as individuals. By saying realization of the value and worth of the individual, I do not mean merely understanding it, but making it real and actual, so that it is not just a matter of belief but of experience . . . (This) has resulted in a feeling of self-respect

and self-reliance which they never had before. There is no doubt that there was and still is a growing awareness of injustice in the minds of the Depressed Classes themselves.[15]

For a more sociological analysis one may turn to J. Boel's *Christian Mission to India* (1975). Boel pointed out that although it was natural for Hindu writers to think of Christianity as invading the territory of another religious culture and seeking to impose an alien religion, yet religions have to be accepted as well as offered. That Hinduism was vulnerable because of the moral and social injustices of the caste system was indisputable, if only because outcaste groups had left Hinduism, not only for Christianity, but for Buddhism and Islam as well. Hinduism did not altogether lack the impulse to treat all human beings equally but had given it no institutional expression; in practice the institutions reinforced inequality and injustice. In the past, groups which had managed to acquire wealth or power have succeeded in moving upwards in the system, a process which M. N. Srinivas has called 'sanskritization', but this path was never open to the lower groups in Hindu society, and this explained why in the late nineteenth and early twentieth century they sometimes adopted Christianity in order to try to better their position in Hindu society. Christianity was therefore *one* of the factors (for the influence of the Western humanitarian and socialist traditions should never be left out of the picture) which contributed to changes in Hindu values and beliefs and helped to stimulate Hindu reform movements. The coming of Independence changed the situation again, because the Christian bodies lost their subtle relationship to the occupying power and even tended to turn into a kind of accepted caste; moreover, the new Indian government denied the christianized outcastes their former Harijan status, which meant that they could not easily benefit from policies designed to alleviate to some extent the lot of the outcastes. Boel concluded that although the adoption of Christianity had resulted in a relatively high number of Christians improving their social position, the Christian community as a whole, and especially in Delhi, the Punjab, and Medak, was still among the poorest groups and lived on the margin of Indian society. This made Indian Christians very uncertain about how they should behave in the future, now that it was clear that theirs would always be a minority church.

Africa is a different case, because Protestant and Roman Catholic missions played a considerable part in the Western occupation of Africa south of the Sahara, and not only set up their own denominations there but also stimulated the Africans to establish an immense number of churches of their own. It is indicative of Western, rather than African, attitudes that in the literature these are often called 'separatist' or 'independent' churches, as though they must by definition be deviant; or they have been called 'Sects', not a kind description even in the prose of a sociologist. In 1950 there were perhaps twenty-five million African Christians of all descriptions south of the Sahara; by 1975 upwards of one hundred million: over the same period virtually all the Christian institutions involved passed into African control, a shift which altered the balance of power in the largely Protestant World Council of Churches, and also affected the Roman Catholic Church, as could be seen at the Second Vatican Council.

A comprehensive attempt to survey the recent ecclesiastical history of Africa is to be found in Adrian Hastings's *A History of African Christianity 1950–75* (1979), which should perhaps be read in conjunction with *Christianity in Independent Africa* (1978), edited by E. Fasholé-Luke, R. Gray, A. Hastings and G. Tasie. On modern Roman Catholic history in Africa the Jedin *Handbuch* was disappointing:[16] the missionary section did little more than list constitutional changes and assert, rather blandly, that Catholic missions had in the long run supported African independence.

Many good studies in African church history have appeared in recent years, and what follows is inevitably only a selection from the more important works.

J. F. A. Ajayi, *Christian Missions in Nigeria 1841–91* (1965), and E. A. Ayandele, *The Missionary impact on modern Nigeria 1842–1914* (1966): written from an African point of view, they show how the early mission succumbed to imperialist influences in the generation after the Indian Mutiny (see T. E. Yates, below).

F. L. Bartels, *The Roots of Ghana Methodism* (1965): the Methodist

Church in Ghana had become autonomous in 1961, and this was a semi-celebratory, semi-critical history.

J. H. Boer, *Missionary Messengers of Liberation in a Colonial Context* (1979), a case-study of the Sudan United Mission which covered the history of Northern Nigeria from the 1870s.

Willy de Craemer, *The Jamaa and the Church* (1977): the Jamaa was a Bantu 'Catholic' movement whose early history involved a group of Flemish Franciscan missionaries.

M. L. Daeel, *Old and New in Southern Shona Independent Churches* (2 vols, 1971, 1974): was concerned with African religious movements in what used to be Rhodesia.

D. Lagergren, *Mission and State in the Congo:* a study of relations between Protestant missions and the Congo Independent State authorities, with special references to the Equator district between 1885 and 1903 (1970).

I. Linden, *Church and Revolution in Rwanda* (1977): an account of the French Catholic White Fathers mission to the former German colony which had passed into Belgian hands in 1919, and which was to become the scene of perhaps the most bitter of all recent Africans civil wars, that between the Tutu and the Hutu.

J. McCracken, *Politics and Christianity in Malawi 1875–1940* (1977): the impact of the Scottish Livingstonia Mission in the northern province of what was then Nyasaland. This should be compared with K. N. Mufuka, *Missions and Politics in Malawi* (1977), which discussed much the same material from an African point of view and brought the story down to the collapse of the Federation of Nyasaland and the Rhodesias in 1963.

M. Markowitz, *Cross and Sword* (1973): the political role of Christian missions in the Belgian Congo between 1908 and 1960, a study which completed Langergren (see above).

J. D. Y. Peel, *Aladura, A Religious Movement among the Yoruba* (1968): another basic study of an African religious movement which adapted Christian material to its own purposes.

R. Rotberg, *Christian Missionaries and the Creation of Northern Rhodesia 1880–1924* (1965); and *The Rising of Nationalism in Central Africa*: the making of Malawi and Zambia 1873–1964 (1967).

G. Shepperson and T. Price, *Independent African: John Chilembwe and the origins, setting and significance of the Nyasaland native rising of*

1915 (1958): a classic account of the tiny rebellion which was a portent of the future of much of Africa, and which actually antedated the Dublin Easter Rising of 1916 as well as the Russian revolution of the following year.

J. V. Taylor, *The Making of the Church in the Buganda* (1958): one of the earliest serious analyses of what the missionaries had actually achieved in the way of conversion to Christianity.

M. Wright, *German Missions in Tanganyika 1891–1941* (1971): an analysis of the Lutheran and Moravian missions in the southern part of the country.

T. E. Yates, *Venn and Victorian Bishops Abroad* (1978) was a sympathetic discussion of the missionary policies of Henry Venn of the Anglican Evangelical Church Missionary Society, and their repercussions on the Anglican episcopate in the British colonies between 1841 and 1872. Yates's book confirmed the earlier work of Ajayi and Ayandele (see above). Venn made an African, Samuel Crowther, bishop of the Niger Mission in 1864, an experiment not tried elsewhere, and so Crowther became a symbol of the African capacity to evangelize and govern. After Venn's death the CMS missionaries on the West Coast turned against his policy, which had really been to create a self-governing indigenous church as quickly as possible; Crowther was conveniently disgraced in 1891, no African was appointed to succeed him, and his alleged shortcomings were used for years afterwards as proof that Venn's policy was wrong in principle. Indeed, S. Neill was still taking this line in *Colonialism and Christian Missions* in 1966, but Max Warren, the most distinguished CMS Secretary in this century, said that Venn's critics were 'missionaries of lesser vision'[17] The change in missionary attitude which was implied here was in line with the general hardening of the British attitude to their subject races in the generation after the Indian rising of 1857. It was also true that as the Western missionaries established themselves they became less eager to surrender their authority over their converts.

Many of these books stand very close to the events which they describe and try to analyse; this is contemporary history, and a longer perspective will modify the judgments which have been made. It will become easier in the long run to distinguish between the future of religion in Africa and the future of Christianity in Africa. Nevertheless, an overall historical picture of the Christian missions does appear. In the early stages of the nineteenth-century Western occupation of Africa the missionaries justified their intrusion partly by an appeal to a divine commission, partly by their success in forming African congregations (which was alleged to be a confirmation of the commission), and partly by the assertion that the extension to Africa of Western civilization – which included both commerce and Christianity – was for the benefit of Africa as well as an extension of the kingdom of God. Along this last line of argument they were easy victims of men like Livingstone, Lugard and Leopold of the Belgian Congo, (see, e.g., Boer, Lagergren, Markowitz). Even the hyper-Calvinist, Abraham Kuyper (1837–1920), than whom no man could have been more orthodox in his own opinion, could talk about the Dutch colonies in terms of 'trusteeship', that is, of a three-fold divine mandate of the occupying power to teach morals, to look after the economic estate, and to prepare the natives for ultimate self-rule.

In other words, in Africa, as elsewhere, the missionaries chose to see Western expansionism as a means of entry, and yet at the same time they resented the developing African view of them as one aspect of a foreign conquest. They were conscious that they brought to Africa some education, some medicine, some effort to improve agriculture, and they knew that in East as well as in West Africa they had helped to form African élites which in their turn supplied many leaders to the nationalist movements. They did not always realize that the extent to which this work seemed to be superseding African culture also made the Africans think of them as part of an invasion which was tearing traditional African society apart. Above all, there was no irrefutable case for conquest, no completely satisfactory answer to the question, 'Why are you here at all?' Once the missionaries had accepted, to however slight a degree, a role inside as well as outside the colonial system, they could not avoid moral criticism, no matter how many resolutions were passed on biblical grounds in ecclesiastical meetings to proclaim their innocence. Most missionaries undoubtedly believed in their divine commission and clung to varieties of the trusteeship theory, and this meant that even in the closing decades of direct

Western rule, between 1930 and 1960, they acted on the assumption that it would and should still be a long time before the Africans became fully self-governing.

After independence, in what may be called a post-missionary situation, the institutions which the missionaries had established declined in political importance; they played a socially conservative role which sometimes attracted the favour of new African régimes which desperately needed to stabilize society. There is some evidence[18] that the African Independent Churches also declined once political freedom had been obtained, which was not what some historians, who emphasized an image of these groups as the 'true' African expression of Christianity, had expected. In fact, however, once the religious groups neither acted as the agents of an occupying power nor as stimulators of nationalist emotion, their social significance was bound to suffer. In some of the new African states, moreover, independence turned out to be more political than economic; the consequent attacks on 'neo-colonialism' inevitably affected institutions which had surviving Western connections. Projects for church union in Ghana, Nigeria and Zambia faded out, at least in part because Africans regarded them as expatriate affairs. At the same time, Islam appeared as a strengthened religious rival with a political programme: in states like Nigeria the status of Islamic law became a subject of public controversy. Islam and Catholicism resemble one another in their conviction that the state ought to enforce their sectarian views of law; that there is no area of private morality in which the individual may properly refuse to be told either by the state or by a religious institution what are the permissible limits of his behaviour. Both would reject the proposition that the state should protect the individual against the tyranny of extreme sectarian opinion.

The decline in the political influences of the African churches coincided in the period between 1960 and 1980 with a growing enthusiasm for political Christianity among Western church leaders, and theologians, especially those who wanted to combine a Christian spirituality with a Marxist analysis of the socio-political future. There was much talk of *praxis*, a holy kind of thinking after the event. This attitude led to much criticism of the missionary movement and its past policies. Boer, for example, said that missionaries involved themselves in colonialism out of 'pietistic dualism and class blindness':[19] that is, they acquiesced in a tacit division between a religious sphere governed by a private ethic, and a public sphere of economics and politics outside religious control, and dominated by economic acquisitiveness. Boer thought that the missionaries ought to have been able to maintain a critical distance from the colonial situation. Like most of the historians we are discussing, however, he was assuming that another kind of colonialism, ethically defensible, would have been possible, that is, he held a variant of the trusteeship theory himself. Yet the conquest of another people is indefensible, and the classic ground for the Western advance into the interior of Africa had been the need to liberate the inhabitants from Islamic slavers. Here the irony ran deep, for although the Western rulers usually abolished slavery, they introduced their own forms of forced labour as time went by. The Congo was a case in point, for Lagergren and Markowitz agreed that the Protestant and Catholic missionaries in the Belgian Congo were more anxious to obtain concessions for their missions from the administration than they were to criticize the brutal exploitation of the country.

The assertion that historically the missionaries accepted the colonial system, were attracted by imperialist theories of trusteeship in the later nineteenth century, failed to develop African-controlled institutions quickly enough, did little to equip Africans for political life, and switched to support for independence only when change became politically irresistible, was largely accurate. It is not easy to see, however, how affairs could have taken a different course. To suppose that the missionaries could have changed colonial economic policies which involved questions of race, labour relations and education, seems to depend on the fallacy of ecclesiastical power. Marxist and other Western historians have often exaggerated the social reality of churches and missions, and have therefore exaggerated their political influence. The missionaries probably understood their practical weakness better than some of their critics have done. Nor were the African Independent Churches necessarily stronger: on the eve of Zambian independence in 1964, for example, the government used force to break up Alice Lenshina's Lumpa Church, which had seemed to be the soul of the nationalist movement, because Lenshina's stockaded villages now wanted to contract out of the political society altogether. It has been one of the illusions of the South American 'liberation theologians' that one can remedy this political weakness by committing the ecclesia to the side of the peasant and working classes: the African equivalent was perhaps to be found in D. McGavran's *How Churches Grow* (1960), which argued that an aggressive orthodoxy would produce the massive increase in the number of African Christians which would be needed to transform the social situation in religious terms.

Given, however, that the missionaries' potential political influence was always slight, and given that independence broke up the brief alliance between the nationalists and some of the churches, the calculations of the missiologists seemed irrelevant. There was no ideal missionary policy, either before or after 1860, which would have transformed the African situation. What was open to question was the quality of the missionary critique of what happened in Africa from the later nineteenth century down to the 1960s.

Several factors operated here. First, most of the missionaries lacked the training and interests which would have given them a firmer grip on the realities of African religious and political life. Secondly, the missionary societies relied too much for policy on central officers ('missionary statesmen') whose influence on the ground was apt to be limited. Writing in the 1970s, Elliot Kendall, who had worked in East Africa, said that missionary policy often appeared to be discussed far away from the situation of the 'younger churches'.[20] Western missionary societies still sought to perpetuate themselves and to protect their existence with a theological rationale. Thirdly, after 1917 both Protestant and Catholic missionary societies, like other Western institutions, were deeply affected by anti-communism, and this frequently distorted the judgment of those making policy (for example, in the Camerouns, but also in other places such as China).

Finally, few missionaries came entirely to terms with what had happened in Africa. In the article quoted above, Kendall distinguished between European colonialism, which had damaged (he said) the African soul, and the grafting of the Christian church on to Africa, which he believed had had a very creative influence on the development of society in the whole continent. However convenient such a distinction may be to the missionary, and to Christian apologetic in general, it should not be accepted. Christian institutions entered Africa as part of Western expansionism; they were an integral part of 'colonialism', and they would have had to behave very differently to be entitled to separate the good from the bad in the African experience of the West and attribute the good to themselves.

What produced such judgments was precisely the notion that we have already encountered in discussing the nature of 'church history', the notion that the history of the Christian church is a special case which is obedient to laws of its own. Boer, for example, asserted that the unity of history was a biblical doctrine. This unity was constituted by God's own work of redeeming human beings through the ordinary events of history which were themselves moving towards the eschaton, the climax of the process. It followed that the missionary, like the church historian, had to judge the course of events, as it might be African modern history, from the standpoint of this unity. Boer, wiser in this than some other church historians, admitted that this formula had its own problems. 'Though surely guided by God's providence, history is an ambiguous affair.' Neither history nor the Bible, he added, supported the idea of steady historical progress in one direction. The fact of providence remained unarguable: 'it is the interpretation of it in a specific historical context that is difficult, for we have no norms for such'.[21] The absence of norms, however, must limit the freedom of even the historian who believes in the divine unity of history to treat the history of the ecclesia as a special case. This means that the historian of Christian missions should be cautious about criticizing the missionaries because they did not guess what the historian has guessed about the divine guidance of affairs. And when Boer delivered his own general judgment on the missionaries, that they did not demand structural change in society but preferred a 'relief approach', one suspects that he was not keeping the critical distance which he himself required, but repeating the accepted wisdom of his own generation. It seems to be the structure of African mission Christianity itself which has begun to disintegrate into what Adrian Hastings has called 'village Christianity'.

8

Ecumenism, the Light that Failed

The Ecumenical Movement has been the great ecclesiastical failure of our time. The churches throughout the world remain broadly as divided in the 1980s as they were in 1910 when the search for institutional unity was first systematically organized. To the extent that the movement was originally Protestant it reached its climax in 1947 in the formation of the Church of South India. Here there united on the basis of episcopacy the South Indian province of the Methodist Church; the South India United Church, which had started in 1906 as a union of Congregationalist, Presbyterian and Dutch Reformed missions, and had been joined in 1919 by the Malabar District of the Basel Mission, which employed both Lutheran and Reformed missionaries; and the larger part of four dioceses of the Anglican Church of India, Burma and Ceylon. For the moment it looked as though a way might have been found of uniting bodies which claimed to possess the 'historic episcopate' with bodies which lacked this distinctive ingredient. However, a sizeable group of Anglicans in the Anglo-Catholic missionary tradition refused to join the Church of South India, and the Church of England itself never extended full intercommunion to the new church. Although the World Council of Churches was constituted at Amsterdam in 1948 out of the older separate sections known as Faith and Order, and Life and Work, it was clear by the time that a World Faith and Order Conference met in Lund in 1952 that the original movement had run out of energy. Indeed, in retrospect, the creation of the Church of South India seems to have been a disaster. No further unions of the same kind followed, and subsequent events, as for example the long and unsuccessful negotiations between the Methodist Church and the Church of England in Britain, which finally collapsed in 1982, confirmed that Anglicanism was too deeply divided within itself to be able to unite with a Protestant non-episcopal body. One was left with the impression that the enthusiasm of the churches for unity was about equal to the enthusiasm shown by the Great Powers for the avoidance of a Third World War with atomic weapons.

The movement, however, which had begun in circles which were not only Protestant but largely Anglo-Saxon, was more than an expression of Anglo-American expansionism. As the Protestant movement slowed down, ecumenism became fashionable in the Roman Catholic Church. The Second Vatican Council (1962–65) released a powerful Catholic impulse for closer relations with other churches, and a series of semi-official theological discussions took place in the 1970s between Catholic theologians and their opposite numbers in several other bodies, including the Lutherans, Methodists and Anglicans. However, if it is looked at it in terms of the whole Christian ecclesia, the Catholic ecumenical movement was no more successful than its Protestant predecessor. What followed, in a third, really post-ecumenical, phase was a renewed series of diplomatic negotiations between separate churches, in which each was to bargain as firmly as possible for the protection of its own fundamental identity. The rhetoric of ecumenism continued, but the reality of ecclesiastical politics was much less concealed. By the 1980s, when it was certain that there was no longer any serious possibility of union between the Church of England and any of the English Free Churches, the only negotiations that mattered were those between Canterbury and Rome. The wheel had come full circle from the 1890s to the 1980s: throughout the intervening years the underlying, permanent influence on Anglican behaviour had been the fact of the encyclical, *Apostolicae Curae*, issued by Pope Leo XIII in 1896, in which he condemned Anglican priestly orders as invalid through defect of both form and intention. Much has been said about how simple it would be to make this encyclical nugatory, but to the present day it remains unmodified.

Attempts at historical description and analysis have been few. On the Protestant side Ruth Rouse and S. Neill edited a symposium with the title *A History of the Ecumenical Movement 1517–1948* in 1954, which had a useful essay by Miss Rouse herself on the nineteenth-century movement. A second volume, edited by H. Fey and called by the unpromising title, *The Ecumenical Advance 1948–68*, appeared in 1970. Lukas Fischer edited a *Documentary History of the Faith and Order Movement 1927–63* (1963). The chain of events in India was recorded by Bengt Sundkler in *The Church of South India: the movement towards union 1900–47* (1954). G. K. A. Bell, one of the most distinguished figures in the ecumenical world, patiently collected and published, without commentary, the mass of public, official statements which the negotiations about unity inevitably produced: *Documents of Christian Unity* (1924, 1930, 1948, 1957) charted the most hopeful period of the enterprise, when it seemed as though the ecumenists had generated the momentum needed to carry them close to their goal. Visser't Hooft, for years at the centre of the ecumenical system, wrote his own brief account of the early stages of the struggle to give the movement institutional expression: his book, *The Genesis and Formation of the World Council of Churches* (1982) virtually ends in 1950.

Biographies have filled in the background of some of the principal actors. Among the more important of these are: *George Bell, Bishop of Chichester*, by R. C. D. Jasper (1967); *Dietrich Bonhoeffer* by E. Bethge (1967, ET 1970); *Randall Davidson*, by G. K. A. Bell (1952[3]); *Arthur Cayley Headlam*, by R. C. D. Jasper (1960); *Hendrik Kraemer: Pionier der Oekumene*, by A. Th. van Leeuven (1962); *Red Tape and the Gospel*, by Eleanor Jackson (1980), a study of the significance of the ecumenical missionary career of William Paton. Eleanor Jackson also created the nucleus of an ecumenical archive centre at Selly Oak, which was formally opened in 1979. Other biographies were *Nathan Söderblom, His Life and Work*, by Bengt Sundkler (1968); *William Temple*, by F. A. Iremonger (1949); and *Memoirs*, by Visser't Hooft (1972).

There are two sorts of interpretation of this historical material, the first ecclesiastical, and the second that of the social historian.

The first approach is that of George Bell, for example, who was already a famous Anglican ecumenist when he delivered his Olaus Petri Lectures at Uppsala in 1946: these were published as *Christian Unity, The Anglican Position*, in 1948. Bell said that the ecumenical movement was one of the most urgent issues of the age,

> for in a world divided and tormented as we see it today, the witness of the Church, the help and inspiration of the Churches, given not through one communion alone, but through all the communions working for God's Kingdom together, could by God's blessing, do more for the recovery of mankind than any other single factor or force.[1]

Despite this exordium, however, Bell understood very well the ambiguity of the Anglican attitude to ecumenism: on the one hand, the evangelistic expansiveness of its foreign missions and on the other, the tendency to insist on what was distinctive and exclusive in Anglo-Catholicism. This insight remains just as true a generation later. Bell repeated the widely-held view that the first impulse of the ecumenical movement came from the mission-fields; the next stimulus to Christian co-operation, however, had been the cause of peace (even before 1914). He underlined Anglican hesitation about the growth of Life and Work as a separate ecumenical institution, because this meant co-operation with mainly Protestant European churches and so fostered dreams of 'Pan-Protestantism'. Some Anglican support for the other ecumenical institution, Faith and Order, was given because there it was easier to insist on the distinctiveness of different churches.

Bell, however, thought that the World Conferences which were held in the 1930s had impressed on the leaders, including the Anglicans, the possibility of a Christian unity transcending barriers of race and nationality and bringing to the rescue of the kingdoms of the world the saving energies of the Kingdom of God. This conception of the church as one body in ideal, if not yet in actual fact, seemed to Bell to have been what led to the formation of the World Council of Churches as a concrete expression, however premature, of what had to come: there must be a body, however weak, which demonstrated the ultimate cohesion of the church. Pressure in this direction mounted during the Second World War, which many Christian leaders interpreted as a war in defence of Christianity. In the light of later sociological analysis of the World Council, it is fascinating to find Bell saying that although the Council's utterances would not have *ecclesiastical* authority, they would be bound to carry great weight because they would reflect the mind of leading members of the churches, and also because the Holy Spirit might *to an unlimited extent* speak and exercise influence through them.[2] This was a perfect illustration of the assumption that the ecclesia was a special case within the general historical system. Part of the later history of the World Council and part of the explanation of its relative failure, was the drive to assert its ecclesiastical status as a kind of 'super-church': as late as the Montreal Faith and Order Conference in 1963 there were some who wanted to determine how the Council manifested the *notae ecclesiae* of the classical creeds. Once the momentum of institutional growth slackened the Council lost some of its sense of ecumenical purpose and became more of an instrument for the political theology which had developed in Life and Work.

If Bell's presentation of the ecumenical movement reflected a European attitude to unity, Sundkler treated the problem from the Indian end. The idea of at least Protestant unity in South India could be traced back as far as 1900, when a conference in Madras had brought together one hundred and fifty missionaries from forty-five different organizations whose total membership came to three hundred and fifty thousand. Sundkler wrote as though conditions in India made the denominational divisions of the West seem irrelevant; the point has often been repeated and was no doubt true about a particular group of missions and European missionaries. Nevertheless, nearly a hundred and fifty thousand of the Christians in South India belonged either to the Church Missionary Society (Anglican Evangelical in tradition) or to the Society for the Propagation of the Gospel (which was Anglo-Catholic), and in the long run the majority of the Anglo-Catholics did not enter the united church. Sundkler regarded the presence in the same area of substantial numbers of Roman Catholic and of Syrian Christians as making no difference to the form of the argument, but these bodies, though they experienced the same Indian environment, showed little interest in the search for some kind of Christian unity.

Among the purely Indian factors which favoured unity, Sundkler pointed out that economic pressure, and especially the severe famines of 1876–78, had stimulated mobility in the Indian population and had spread members of the same Indian communities through different Protestant missions. In the 1885 Indian nationalism had coalesced in the National Congress, and the growing desire for freedom and national political unity inevitably affected Indian Christians. Well before 1914 Indians were complaining about the European monopoly of real power in the Protestant mission churches, and were referring with approval to Henry Venn's policy of transferring power to the local community as soon as possible. The missionaries responded to the growth of nationalism and said hopefully at the inauguration of the South India United Church in 1908, for example, that a united body would have a greater appeal to the people. The disestablishment of the Anglican Church in India, finally achieved in 1927, was partly an admission that the Free Church missions in India would never unite with an established form of Indian Anglicanism and partly a recognition that the political scene in India had reached a point when Anglicanism had to become as 'Indian' as possible. Even so, the Church of South India began with eight British diocesan bishops and six Indian. And the failure of the scheme to break the ecumenical logjam was determined by an obdurate Anglo-Catholic opposition which drew its strength from England and which, however often it was reminded of its minority status, wore its badge of 'catholicity' as proof that it represented the real majority.

The value of Sundkler's account was that it stuck to the details of the long drawn-out negotiations, in which the missionaries played the dominating role. This should not be allowed to conceal the fact that the Indians themselves were only partly affected by the factors which influenced the missionaries and their ecclesiastical leaders in the West, for whom the South India schemes often appeared to be a useful test of strength between non-Indian opinions. In this sense the negotiations were not so much about ecumenism as about the terms on which the occupying churches would consent to leave Indian Christianity to the Indians. To *Indian* ecumenism nationalism was central, but Sundkler undervalued these elements and ignored the possibility that it was the imminence of Indian independence which led to the over-riding of Anglo-Catholic hostility, an over-riding which was not to be repeated in later Anglican ecumenical negotiations, in England for example. The Western missionaries still had sufficient authority in the 1940s to push through the kind of settlement which they wanted, and which they believed would serve the purposes of ecumenism elsewhere. By the 1970s, in an independent Nigeria, they found their ecumenical assumptions completely rejected by the African church leadership.

An attempt to suggest a broader basis for the Ecumenical Movement can be found in Visser't Hooft's *The Genesis and Formation of the World Council of Churches* (1982). He had been General Secretary of the World Council from its inception until 1966. Anxious to show that the movement had always been more than pan-Protestant, he began, not with the Edinburgh Conference of 1910, but with an encyclical which the Orthodox Church of Constantinople, the so-called Ecumenical Patriarchate, sent in 1920 'to all the Churches of Christ everywhere', calling for the formation of a 'league of churches' on the analogy of the League of Nations. There was irony in the Orthodox gesture which Visser't Hooft did not register, for one of the stronger motives which prompted the encyclical was a desire to stop Western churches and missionary societies proselytizing among the Orthodox, who resented being treated as pagans in need of a sound conversion. This was another instance of the cultural aggression to which reference has been made before.

Once again the political implications of ecumenism mattered greatly. The collapse of the ancient Ottoman and Russian empires had made the Orthodox anxious and uncertain about their future; they hoped that contact with the West would help them to preserve the freedom which was theirs for the moment in 1920. Ecumenism was part of the foreign policy of the Orthodox Churches. There was also, in these few years when the League of Nations stood for a slender chance that the problems of nationalism and sovereignty might be solved, a feeling that the divided church was being left behind by an idealism in which it had only a small part. Visser't Hooft hardly mentions Roman Catholicism, but however noble Benedict XV's attempts at bringing about peace during the World War of 1914–1918 may now look on paper, the belligerents, whether Catholic, Orthodox or Protestant, had taken no notice of them whatsoever. In practice most ecclesiastical leaders had thrown themselves enthusiastically into war propaganda. It is not entirely surprising, therefore, that in the same year, 1920, the Anglican Lambeth Conference should be found appealing for church unity in England, and the Swedish Archbishop, Nathan Söderblom, urging on Protestant ecclesiastics in the West the need for a permanent organ of the churches which could be the voice of the Christian conscience, though without having any kind of jurisdictional authority.

Any chance of such a development taking place quickly had vanished by 1925 and the Stockholm Conference of Life and Work: the immediate explanation was institutional inertia, the long-term explanation that a majority of the institutions involved feared that any such Council would seek to add jurisdictional powers to its initial constitution. By the 1950s there was no more enthusiasm for the new Council of Churches than there was for the United Nations organization which had replaced the old League of Nations. And although ecumenical momentum certainly recovered in the 1930s this must be attributed in large measure to the drastic changes in the political scene. To see this it is only necessary to read, for example, Adolph Keller's excited remarks, written in 1936 in preparation for the Oxford Conference on Church, Community and State which was to gather in the following year:

> A judgement was passed (in the 1917 Russian revolution) on the old society and Church in Russia. But that judgement was at the same time a *mene tekel* on the wall of the same civilization in all lands . . . The flaming churches in Spain and Mexico, the indifference and hostility to the Church in many countries, the sudden and open growth in paganism, all go to prove that these events are not solely a Russian phenomenon, or generally, a revolutionary phenomenon, but a deeply significant apocalyptic sign of the times, an announcement – *Maran atha* – to the whole of Christendom. The plan of an anti-Christian world revolution is no longer a vague idea, but a concrete programme in execution, which is combatting the Christian ecumenism by a spreading ecumenism of class-war and hatred and replacing a transcendent heavenly message by a this-worldly materialistic gospel.

The published accounts of the Oxford Conference were full of the same pessimism, which was always directed more against Communism than against the varieties of Fascism. Historians will have to consider how much the emergence of the ecumenical movement between 1910 and 1950 owed to the growing middle and upper-class fear of social revolution, and of a threat to what many Catholic and Protestant ecclesiastics still thought of as the church's right to tell modern nation states what their moral code ought to contain. Visser't Hooft belonged to the school of church historians for whom the *ecclesia* remained a special case: he regarded the formation of the World Council as part of a divine historical pattern in which political forces had to take a subordinate part.

There is a fuller discussion of these problems in the literature of the sociology of religion. Bryan Wilson, in his *Religion in Secular Society* (1966), approached ecumenism in terms of theory. He said that 'the pristine values of religious movements are attenuated over time' – a statement which seemed to ignore the complicated history of theological and liturgical revival in Anglicanism since 1800 – and that 'amalgamation and alliance occur when institutions are weak rather than when they are strong'. When Wilson wrote of 'weakness' he was thinking particularly of the British Free Churches, which he saw as having weakened themselves in a vain struggle to match in 'religious' terms the increasingly secular nature of British society; this self-secularization was also an example of what he meant by the attenuation of original religious values. If the Free Churches wanted to remain 'religious' they had no option by the mid-twentieth century but to revert to a more hieratic and sacramental version of Christianity, and this meant a move in the direction of the Church of England, either liturgically or intentionally, or both.

Wilson had read Sundkler[3] and assumed that the formation of the Church of South India showed that ecumenism was gathering strength. His discussion of the British negotiations between the Church of England and (*a*) the Presbyterian Church of Scotland and (*b*) the Methodists was based on the further assumption that what he called the religious professionals (priests, ministers) were committed to unity and would persuade the laity, more conscious perhaps of surviving differences between denominations, to accept amalgamation.

Wilson's assumptions were unfortunate, because the Scottish negotiations broke down completely in the late 1960s, when Scottish nationalism showed itself stronger than ecumenism, and when Glasgow revolted against Edinburgh, and the Anglican-Methodist schemes for unity finally collapsed in the 1980s. In so far as there was anything to explain sociologically it was the failure of ecumenism, which in seventy years (from 1910) had not significantly altered the religious map of Western Christianity.

There are two omissions in Wilson's analysis which seem to be important. First, although he repeated Sundkler's reasons why many Indian Christians supported the ecumenical movement, he did not examine as thoroughly why other Indians, especially those in the Anglo-Catholic mission areas, did not. He did not ask whether there might not have been valid Indian reasons for division, as well as valid reasons for unity. Nor did he consider seriously the possibility that if the European occupation of India actually favoured ecclesiastical unity in the long run, the departure of the Westerners left a new set of historical conditions in which the appeal of unity might decline. In Britain, the urgency with which unity was pursued waned after 1945, because the leaders of the Christian institutions no longer felt the direct external threat to the survival of religion which they had felt in the 1930s. Wilson's neglect of the broader political scene is the first of his significant omissions.

The second omission is that of Roman Catholicism. In India, as has already been said, the Church of South India was a 'Protestant' body from which the Indian Anglo-Catholics dissented and in which Indian Roman Catholics took little interest. The Second Vatican Council was meeting at about the time that Wilson was writing his book, and he must be forgiven for not recognizing that the Council marked the Vatican's change of policy towards the reunion of the churches. But any attempt to account for the failure of the ecumenical movement in England after 1945 has to put at the centre of the pattern the ambiguous relations between Rome and Canterbury, which rose to a vivid climax in the Pope's visit to England and to Canterbury itself in 1982. From the 1960s the Vatican sought to make ecumenism revolve around Catholicism, and as far as possible around the papacy. A vital new element in this campaign was the availability of international television. The 'Protestant' ecumenical 'moment' had passed, and an accurate description of the relationship between the major Christian bodies in Britain in the 1980s would have to eschew the ecumenical language which was still reflected in Wilson's analysis, and to talk instead about a direct struggle for the control of the British religious sub-culture as a whole between Anglican and Roman.

Nevertheless, in the 1960s and 1970s the sociology of religion was dominated by the view that religion in the West was in terminal decline and that the churches were reacting to their own weakness and to the impact of a secular society by seeking to resolve their differences in a search for corporate unity. A British example may be found in Robert Currie's analysis of the forces which led to the merger of three Methodist denominations in 1932, in *Methodism Divided* (1968). A more formal example was Peter Berger's *The Social Reality of Religion*, the English title of a book first published in America as *The Sacred Canopy* (1967). Berger suggested that the bureaucratization of modern institutions, including religious ones, had meant the emergence of a similar social-psychological type of leadership in most of the major churches. He gave a flattering description of this bureaucratic personality – activist, pragmatic, skilled in personal relations, 'dynamic' and conservative at the same time – an 'ideal type' if ever there was one. Berger might have added that the internal conflicts of the World Council of Churches after 1950 took place between the bureaucrats who wanted to organize a world-church in the name of ecumenism, and the less committed who only wanted a central committee which would act as an international Christian conscience. This bureaucratization of religious institutions, Berger said, had laid the psychological foundations of ecumenicity, while the need to rationalize competition in the existing state of the religious market provided the social stimulus to collaboration. Ecumenists reduced the number of competing units through mergers, and the survivors organized the market through mutual agreement.

Berger's appeal to the market economy model was only relevant, however, if it were true that religious motives were rapidly being replaced by practical 'capitalist' motives. The market analogy added no force to his argument, but only emphasized his conviction that the prevailing historical conditions, as he interpreted them, made the success of ecumenism inevitable. In reality, the areas in which something like 'competition' took place – between fundamentalist organizations and the traditional denominations, for example – were not areas in which mergers were ever remotely likely. Then again, the economic concept of rationalization proved less attractive when it had to compete with strong emotions like nationalism. Above all, the substitution of the economic model for the religious was unconvincing: as Robert Towler said, in *Homo Religiosus* (1974), Berger talked as though an explanation of what made ecumenism possible must also serve as an explanation of why reunions took place (if, indeed, they did). Towler argued that an ideology as apparently powerful as ecumenism deserved careful study in its own right, whereas the sociological account of the movement was usually presented with a disregard of the explanations given by the ecumenists themselves worthy of a nineteenth-century anthropologist. An actor's account of his own behaviour ought not to be treated as mere delusion, even if as a sociologist one believed that a more cogent account of what was going on could be given. Even so, Towler himself was tempted to locate the principal ground of ecumenism in the social effects of scientific and technical innovation. The consequent waves of 'modernization' had broken down established social groups and had blurred the boundaries between the socio-religious bodies which comprised the total religious sub-culture. There had resulted a decline in the credibility of discrete traditions of religious symbolism, and so a decline in specific religious beliefs and symbols had facilitated the progress of ecumenical ideas.

All this seems remote from the actual history of the churches. It is instructive to return to the case of Africa, as seen by the African historian, Ogbu Kalu, in an essay on 'Church Unity and Religious Change in Africa', which he contributed to *Christianity in Independent Africa*. Kalu took it for granted that church union movements in Africa had been an aspect of missionary strategy. They started as a survival tactic among Protestants: 'Protestant missions huddled with Protestant missions and defined themselves in contradistinction against Roman Catholicism.'[4] In Africa the ecumenical movement came as an external force just like the denominations it was trying to destroy. As in the case of the Church of South India negotiations for unity in Nigeria had been going on since the beginning of the twentieth century. The scheme was stopped in 1965 at the point when the inaugural ceremonies had already been arranged. The whites had brought denominations and the whites wanted to take them away, but the blacks demurred. Some blacks at least did not identify the end of denominationalism with the triumph of some kind of Africanism. Kalu himself traced the failure to the ecclesiastical leadership's inability to convert the local communities, whether Anglican, Methodist or Presbyterian, to the final scheme. Unity had become a bureaucratic end in itself, and as such it had little to offer to those who lived at the local level, the level of Adrian Hasting's 'village Christianity'. The ideal of Christian unity, Kalu wrote, had to be presented as only the first stage of a quest for religious change in Africa. In other words, whereas the sociologists of religion ascribed the alleged popularity of ecumenism to religious decline and 'secularization', Kalu, more realistically perhaps, traced the failure of ecumenism (and schemes have failed, of course, in other parts of Africa as well as in Nigeria) to the absence of Christian renewal. And sociologists who want to account for the *failure* of ecumenism will have to pay attention to the growth of Anglo-Catholicism and of Anglican Evangelicalism over the very period in which the credibility of sharply-defined traditions of religious symbolism was supposed to be in decline; the Protestant movement for unity might just have succeeded if the Church of England had not been effectively divided between Evangelical and Anglo-Catholic throughout the period of negotiation. Ecumenism has suffered from excessive self-consciousness: its leaders were always telling each other and the world in general what the historical significance of the movement was, and attempting to create a school of historical interpretation by sheer assertion.

9

Postlude, or After the Barbarians

Let us, in conclusion, look at two different judgments on the historical face of modern Christianity. One comes from the Catholic French historian, Jean Delumeau, in a book called *Le Christianisme va-t-il mourir?* (1977); the other from Hugh McLeod, a social historian, in *Religion and the People of Western Europe* (1981).

Writing in a liberal Catholic tradition, and starting from the assumption that Christianity was true, Delumeau interpreted the history of modern Catholicism as primarily the outcome of clerical misgovernment: Counter-Reformation Catholicism adopted the wrong, authoritarian institutions in order to instil the wrong religious emotion, fear. The historical development of the Roman Catholic Church had enveloped the power of the supernatural in secular bondage. Roman Catholicism had remained too hierarchical, too dogmatic, too willing to ignore the opinion of the laity in religious matters. If the dogmatic burden of the laity were reduced to belief in the divinity and the resurrection of Jesus (one may wonder, however, to what extent this could still be thought of as a reduction), if the papacy were reduced to the role of representative leadership, and if the government of the church was reformed so as to free the laity from the control of the priesthood in questions of private sexual behaviour, all might yet be well. As long, however, as the Catholic Church refused to relax its insistence on a wide area of dogmatic assent and moral obedience, and sought the support of the state to enforce this clerical definition of righteousness, it would continue to dwindle into a hard core, solid perhaps, but small and without much influence, a reminder of Tridentine Catholicism, and of its mirror image, Baroque

Protestantism, the Protestantism of 1517–1789. Liberal Protestantism, one is bound to add, does not really appear in Delumeau's historical survey: like Catholic Modernism, it vanished in 1914, and nothing has been heard of these *folies libérales* since then. Equally, however, Catholicism has not been changed by the Second Vatican Council: writing nearly twenty years after John XXIII's *démarche*, Delumeau was sceptical of sudden transformations from above. There could not be a 'Vatican Three' solution; instead, gradual reforms would have to culminate in a Council. He summed up his attitude in a remarkable paragraph:

> Because Christianization, in countries described as being part of Christendom, had never been completed, and could not be;
> because christianization always met resistance;
> because official Christianity betrayed the Gospel in becoming part of the power-system;
> because the good news of Liberation had become menace and constraint;
> our present dechristianization – certainly something serious and grave – must not become a motive of discouragement among Christians. Dechristianization really represents a return to what is sane and normal from the point of view of the Gospel. And it will be good if, thanks to dechristianization, the Word of Salvation is presented in humility, in poverty and in charity to people who are free to refuse what they are offered.

Hugh McLeod, on the other hand, in a book which discussed the relationship between Christianity and the people of Western Europe since 1789, did not offer a guide to ecclesiastical recovery. He preferred to limit himself to comments on why Christian institutions had declined: his stress fell on what had happened outside, rather than inside, the ecclesia – once more, social history is to reveal the secret of religious history. Since 1789, he said, the Western forms of Christianity had shown two kinds of dependency. First, they had persevered, in the style of the *ancien régime*, in trying to use the power of the state to maintain their influence. In Britain, for example, where the Church of England was still more established than disestablished, Christian teaching was nominally compulsory in state schools. That is, the churches had refused to accept the changing direction of Western social history between the Reformation and the French Revolution, a period in which the dominant social groups had gradually reduced the role of religion in society; the churches had clung to the idea of the political ecclesia, backed, and if possible, financed by the state. This applied just as much to the self-styled Free Churches as it did to the directly 'established' churches. Public feeling did move in the churches' favour after 1800, however, and as a result reliance, and even dependence, on the assumed 'official' nature of Christianity ('after all, this is a Christian country') had weakened the religious institutions.

Second, after 1815 institutional Christianity did adjust, however awkwardly, to the urban-industrial development of the West. All denominations built large numbers of churches in the Victorian period; they increased the numbers of the clerical profession; they experimented with fresh methods of evangelism, and even, helped by the growth in population, seemed to expand. This process, McLeod argued, embedded the churches in impermanent social situations on which they became dependent, so that when the socio-economic context altered, the religious institutions showed little capacity to alter as well. In England, for example, whole communities – railwaymen, fishermen, miners, rural labourers – rapidly decreased after about 1920 both in numbers and in social solidarity. There were thus two kinds of dependency in McLeod's analysis: first, a theoretical (and clerical) dependency on the past (symbolized by the present state), and second, a less voluntary dependency on socio-economic conditions. Once again, the critique suggested that there was not much to be done except to wait and see if the inevitably fresh social groupings would create an equally new Durkheimian religious community, which might or might not relate itself to the Western religious tradition.

The historical evidence was therefore interpreted in two rather different ways. Delumeau took 'secularization' for granted as a fact in itself, made more pervasive by the errors of an ecclesiastical hierarchy which had been corrupted by the opportunities of social/secular power. The implication of McLeod's argument was that the policy of the churches had not made a vital difference, because the transformaton of the urban-industrial scene would have produced decline in any case. The more conservative church historian instinctively formulated a moral critique of the institution, alleging ethical failure to co-operate with 'providence'; the social historian contented himself with a social critique, which suggested that religious institutions could not impose themselves indefinitely without political power, which they had now (whatever might have been true in the remote past) to buy on secular political terms. And this was true, whether the terms were fixed on the right or on the left of the political spectrum. There was not as much difference as has often been claimed between the clerical groups which hoped to benefit from the Revolution, and those for whom the only possible future was counter-revolutionary. Delumeau regarded any serious recovery as dependent on the release of the supernatural energy which he believed to be somehow bottled up in the Roman ecclesiastical system; McLeod implied that the churches would have to let Western society go its own way, in the hope that a freer relationship would restore relevance to religious institutions which might, in the meantime, be able to get the *ancien régime* out of their system once and for all. This is analogous to the American position, where the traditional idea of a relationship between church and state has been effectively replaced by a pluralist conception of civic and religious communities which may overlap but don't easily combine into an identifiable 'national' identity. Unreformed, or conservative Catholics cannot really accept this conclusion: American Catholic bishops still lecture American Catholic politicians on their duty to fit American law to Catholic moral teaching. This is an example of the Catholic Church behaving in what Delumeau saw as an authoritarian, unacceptable manner. The bishops, not being church historians of any school, believe in the autonomy of 'the church', that is, that it cannot be reduced to any other form of historical reality, that it acts in and on 'history', but that 'history' does not act on it. They are apt to think of themselves as representing, if not actually releasing, supernatural energy. Delumeau knows that the historical churches are shaped by economic and cultural forces, but in his heart be believes that for a certain kind of church, one which had purified itself, perhaps purified itself of 'history', the bishops would be in the right. McLeod does not believe in this ideal of the 'church', and he therefore finds the historical churches of the nineteenth/twentieth centuries less unacceptable.

Perhaps both Delumeau and McLeod have missed the point. The historian who neglects the present may misunderstand the future. The Western religious creativity no longer works happily with orthodox Christian symbols. Even the cult of Mary, Our Lady of Popular Religion, finds feminism at its most sophisticated impossible to assimilate. Religion is far from withering away, however. A second death of religious images, not unlike that which took place in the eighteenth century but more complete, is occurring in Western culture, leaving the religiously-minded to grapple with ideas of *im*personal theism, of religion in a valid Buddhist style, which takes little account of older Western ideas about God. The barbarians have arrived, twilight has descended, and this time when it lifts the Western churches will probably have ceased to function . . .

Notes

Introduction: To Serve, rather than Seduce, Mankind . . .

1. Emile Poulat, in *Histoire, dogme et critique dans la crise moderniste*, Paris 1969; he was actually referring to Catholic Modernism (Ch. 6, below) circa 1900, but intended to raise the wider question as to whether Christianity and the other world religions can come to terms with the 'modernist' criticism of any kind of absolute.

2. See R. F. Atkinson, *Knowledge and Explanation in History*, 1978, pp. 90–92.

3. F. Nietzsche, *The Twilight of the Idols*, 1889, trs. R. J. Hollingdale, 1968, p. 54. 'We invented the concept "purpose"; in reality purpose is lacking.'

4. M. Creighton, *Historical Lectures and Addresses*, 1903, p. 22. Creighton established modern church history as a discipline in Cambridge, but when he left the university in 1901 to become Bishop of Peterborough he showed how ambiguous his attitude was to historical studies.

5. See R. Niebuhr, *The Nature and Destiny of Man*, New York, 1941; but he, in a respectable theological tradition, fell back on the assertion that however much people suffered, God suffered more in Christ. After Auschwitz and Hiroshima this lacks moral persuasiveness.

6. R. Niebuhr, *Faith and History: A Comparison of Christian and Modern Views of History*, 1949, p. 161.

7. H. Butterfield, *Christianity and History*, 1949, p. 146.

8. Ibid., p. 98.

9. Ibid., p. 136.

10. See, for example, the agonizing on this subject by E. P. Thompson in *The Poverty of Theory*, 1970, and Perry Anderson's reply, *Arguments within English Marxism*, 1980, which sought to reassure humanists that Marxism was on their side. In both cases, religious and secular, the question becomes: what is to be done?

11. A. Harnack, *What is Christianity?*, Berlin 1900, ET 1901, pp. 276–7.

12. *Catholicity: A Study in the Conflict of Christian Traditions in the West*, 1947, p. 13, a report presented to the Archbishop of Canterbury by the Anglo-Catholic party in the Church of England as part of the process of ecumenical

negotiation in England which finally broke down with the failure of the Anglican-Methodist scheme for union in 1982.

13. Ibid., p. 11.

14. D. Sutherland, *The Chouans*, 1982, p. 311. The Chouans were peasant guerrillas in Western France in the 1790s.

15. J. Morrill, 'The Attack on the Church in the Long Parliament', in *History, Society and the Churches*, ed. D. Beale and G. Best, 1985, p. 105. This was a commemorative volume for Sir Owen Chadwick.

16. T. C. W. Blanning, 'The Role of Religion in European Counter-Revolution 1789–1815', in Beale and Best, op. cit., p. 196.

17. J. Obelkevich, *Religion and Rural Society: South Lindsey 1825–75*, 1976, p. 311.

18. See, for example, J. F. C. Harrison, *The Second Coming, Popular Millenialism 1780–1850*, 1979, especially for Southcott; W. H. Olver, *Prophets and Millenialists, The Uses of Biblical Prophecy in England from the 1790s to the 1840s*, Auckland 1978; and E. R. Sandeen, *The Roots of Fundamentalism, British and American Millenarianism 1800–1930*, Chicago 1970, especially for the Brethren.

19. Obelkevich, op.cit., p. ix.

1. Acceptable Faces of the Church: General Histories

1. S. E. Ahlstrom, *A Religious History of the American People*, 1972, p. 763.

2. K. S. Latourette, *A History of the Expansion of Christianity*, 7 volumes, 1938–45; and *Christianity in a Revolutionary Age*, 5 volumes, 1959–63. The role of Christian missions, Catholic and Protestant, in misleading the churches about their historical situation has not been properly examined. Latourette's career started with a *History of Christian Missions in China*, 1929. China was often the graveyard of Christian commonsense.

3. E. J. Hobsbawm, *The Age of Revolution 1789–1848*, 1962, p. 220.

4. See, for example, O. Chadwick, *The Secularization of the European Mind in the Nineteenth Century*, 1976, pp. 264–66.

5. See below, pp. 218–20.

6. R. Aubert, *Le Pontificat de Pie IX* (vol. xxl of *Histoire de l'Eglise*, ed. A. Fliche and V. Martin, second edition, Paris 1963, with bibliographical supplement; the Italian translation, second edition, Turin 1969, had fresh material on Italy).

7. *The Christian Centuries* was to cover the whole history of the Catholic Church in five volumes. For the modern period, only *The Church in a Secularized Society*, 1978, edited by R. Aubert, has appeared.

8. R. Aubert, *Le Pontificat de Pie IX*, Paris 1963, pp. 466–68, my translation. The curé d'Ars and Don Bosco were canonized in the twentieth century.

9. *The Christian Centuries*, vol. 5, Paris 1978.

10. Aubert had originally expected to write the section on Pius IX and Leo XIII, but the deaths of David Knowles and Louis Rogier meant that he played a large part in editing the complete work.

11. *The Church in a Secularised Society*, p. ix. The darkest moments, he said,

were the First Vatican Council and the encyclical *Mortalium animos*, (1928) issued by Pius XI.

12. For more detailed discussion of the problems of modern Roman Catholic history, see below, pp. 158–76.

13. Or of Emile Léonard's *Histoire générale du Protestantisme*, 3 vols, Paris 1961–64, which had to be corrected and supplemented bibliographically when an English translation was begun in 1968. Léonard thought that if Protestantism travelled light both ecclesiastically and theologically it could still offer itself successfully as a layman's religion for laymen.

14. *The Oxford History of the Christian Church* commenced publication in 1976 with R. T. Handy's *A History of the Churches in the United States and Canada;* and continued with O. Chadwick's *The Popes and European Revolution* in 1981. About twenty volumes were projected. Handy was professor of church history at Union Theological Seminary, New York; Chadwick was professor of modern history at Cambridge.

15. Chadwick, *The Popes and European Revolution*, p. 610.

16. *Die Kirche im Zeitalter des Absolutismus und der Aufklärung*, Freiburg-im-Breisgau 1970, appeared in English translation by Gunther Holst in 1981. Nine authors contributed, among whom Lous Cognet wrote on France, Burkhardt Schneider on the Papacy, and Oskar Köhler on the Enlightenment.

17. Jansenism was not always treated so sympathetically; but in its early form Jansenism relied on Augustine as a guarantee of its orthodoxy, and recent Catholic historians and theologians have come to feel more and more that to accept the traditional condemnatory line on Jansenism brings the church close to a rejection of Augustine himself. In the late nineteenth century, however, Augustine, Francis of Assisi, and Pascal all came under a cloud when official, thomistic, theology emphasized the primacy of the intellect.

18. P. Pourrat, *La Spiritualité chrétienne*, 4 vols, Paris 1920–28; there is an American version, Westminster, Maryland, 1953–5. Owen Chadwick compared Pourrat unfavourably with Henri Bremond as an historian of spirituality, in *Christian Spirituality*, ed. P. Brooks, 1975, pp. 203–231. The *Handbuch* makes little of the Bossuet-Fénelon-Guyon controversy, beyond supporting Fénelon, and is less satisfactory still with the case of the Spanish quietist, Miguel Molinos, who was warmly defended by Chadwick in *Christian Spirituality*.

19. See G. E. Cell, *John Wesley's Theology*, Cokesbury 1950. What made the synthesis fragile was Wesley's assertion that sanctification, like justification, could be obtained through faith in an instantaneous experience. Nothing could have been further from the views of the Catholic mystical theologians he studied.

20. Piette's book was not included in the bibiliography of the *Handbuch*, which needed revision for the ET. For discussion of John Wesley's sources see the essays by J. Orcibal and E. G. Rupp in *A History of the Methodist Church in Great Britain*, vol. 1, 1965. It is easier, however, to show that Wesley read books by Catholic writers than to show in what ways he was influenced by them; what impressed him in the lives of seventeenth-century Catholics like Fénelon and Madame Guyon was the intensity of their devotion rather than

its methods and theories. See also *John Wesley. An Anthology of His Writings*, ed. A. C. Outler, 1964.

21. V. H. H. Green, *John Wesley*, 1964; the best biography of John Wesley, though not the most detailed.

22. *Die Kirche in die Gegenwart: Die Kirche zwischen Anpassung und Widerstand*, Freiburg-im-Breisgau 1973, translated as *The Church in the Industrial Age* by Margit Resch, 1981: nine writers took part, but much of the volume came from Roger Aubert and Oskar Köhler; a useful essay on Catholic Missions (1878–1939) was by Jakob Baumgartner.

23. *The Church in the Industrial Age*, pp. 216–19. Although Köhler recorded the part which Catholic antisemitism played in the Dreyfus Case, he left the wider issues unexplored. The Dreyfus Case, the classical modern example of European antisemitism before the time of Hitler, took place in France at the turn of the present century.

24. Ibid., pp. 517–23.

25. Ibid., pp. 527–76. Baumgartner continued the missionary history to 1939; he concluded that 'the urgent need for acclimatization and decolonization in terms of spirit and religion did not surface to the level of awareness until the era of political colonialism approached its end' (p. 569.)

2. From the General to the Particular: Early Modern Europe 1500–1800

1. R.J. Evans, 'Religion and Society in Modern Germany', in *European Studies Review*, July 1982, p. 253.

2. See A. G. Dickens, 'Intellectual and Social Forces in the German Reformation', in *The Urban Classes, the Nobility and the German Reformation*, ed. W. J. Mommsen, Stuttgart 1979: 'Nowadays we should surely all agree that the Reformation arose in force and thenceforth remained irrepressible because during the early and mid-twenties it became a popular movement in the German and Swiss walled cities' (p. 19).

3. Blickle, *The Revolution of 1525*, ET by T. A. Brady and H. Midelfort, London 1979.

4. Ibid., p. 161.

5. Thomas A. Brady, 'The Social History of Reformation' in W. J. Mommsen (ed.) *The Urban Classes, the Nobility and the German Reformation*. Brady had written *Ruling-Class, Regime and Reformation 1520–1555 at Strassbourg*, Leiden 1978. He had been criticized, wrongly in his opinion, for attempting to explain evangelical religion in terms of social classes and class relations. His critic was Bernhard Moeller, who had written *Imperial Cities and the Reformation*, 1962, ET 1972, in a not dissimilar mood, attacking the Luther-cult and the neglect of urban history, but who was now suspicious of what he saw as 'sociologism', the reduction of religious history to social terms. Marxism, of course, is just as open to criticism for imposing 'ideas' upon the sequence of events, and for believing in the logical continuity of history.

6. The comment was made in his book on Strasbourg, p. 11.

7. A good example is *Catholicity, A Study of the Conflict of Christian Traditions*

in the West, 1947, ed. G. Dix and A. G. Herbert: the Reformation destroyed Christian unity and led to secular, liberal individualism.

8. The group took its name from its periodical, *Les Annales*.

9. For further discussion, see, for example, S. Clark, *Past and Present*, 1983.

10. Peter Burke, *Popular Culture in Early Modern Europe*, 1978, p. 234.

11. See, for example, R. Mandrou, *Introduction à la France moderne*, Paris 1974; R. Muchembled, *Culture populaire et culture d'élites*, Paris 1978. Descriptions of an alleged peasant mentalité (actually much more in the nature of hypotheses than is always conceded) go back indirectly to historians like Lucien Fèbvre, who argued, in *Le problème de l'incroyance au xvie siècle: La religion de Rabelais*, Paris 1942, reprinted 1968, that the sixteenth-century mind, including the mind of Rabelais, was structurally incapable of atheism. This assertion seems to have been taken quite seriously for a generation.

12. See n. 11 above.

13. For comment on this use of 'acculturation' see *Religion and Society in Early Modern Europe 1500–1800*, ed. K. von Greyerz, 1984, especially 'Against the Acculturation Thesis', by Jean Wirth, pp. 66–78.

14. Delumeau, *Catholicism between Luther and Voltaire*, Paris 1971, ET 1977, p. xvii.

15. M. Vovelle, 'Dechristianization in Year 11', in K. von Greyerz (ed.), op.cit., p. 89. Vovelle underlined the temporary transference from God (masculine) and the King (masculine) to the Goddess of Reason (usually, Vovelle said, symbolized by a perfectly respectable young woman, not the prostitute of Catholic legend).

16. Ibid., p. 92.

17. In England, where the French Revolution was never quite copied (to the historical confusion of E. P. Thompson), a Catholic historian like Professor Scarisbrick has built up a similar view of the English (Henrician) Reformation: this was not a response to the widespread rejection of Catholicism, but the work of an acquisitive minority which, led by the Crown in Parliament, imposed Protestantism by force on an unwilling majority. Sociologically, this revisionist position reflected the changing balance of power between Catholic and Protestant in England after 1945.

18. Delumeau, op.cit., p. 230.

19. G. le Bras, ' "Déchristianization", terme fallacieux', in *Cahiers d'Histoire*, Lyons, ix 1, 1964, pp. 92–97: see Delumeau, op.cit., p. 227.

20. Jean Delumeau, *Le Christianisme, va-t-il mourir?*, Paris 1977, p. 187.

21. Ginzburg, op. cit., p. 128.

22. See 'Reverence and Profanity in the Study of Early Modern Religion' by R. C. Trexler, in K. von Greyerz (ed.), op.cit., pp. 245–269.

23. The shock of defeat in Vietnam, and fear of Soviet Communism, made American intellectuals particularly anxious about ways of creating a loyal community. Rituals of communal solidarity which would generate self-sacrifice had an evident attraction.

24. See, for example, The Library of Christian Classics, which published a selection of Calvin's *Theological Treatises*, edited by J. K. S. Reid, 1954, and of his *Commentaries and Letters*, edited by J. Haratounian, 1958; J. T. McNeill

edited Calvin's *Institutes of the Christian Religion*, 1961. *Reformed Dogmatics*, edited by J. W. Beardslee, contained translated material from continental Calvinists, Wollebius (1586–1629), Voetius (1589–1687) and Turretin (1623–1687), but these needed more introductory material to make them useful to the general reader.

25. Wendel, *Calvin*, ET 1963, p. 97. Old ways of thought die hard. In the *Oxford Dictionary of the Christian Church*, ed. F. L. Cross, 1966, the entry for Servetus began firmly: 'physician and heretic'. Carlo Ginzburg argued for a link between the ideas of Servetus and the notions of Menocchio (see above p. 35) Similar discussion of the ruthless attitude of Luther to the peasants in 1525 can be found in P. Althaus, *Luther's Haltung im Bauernkrieg*, Darmstadt 1971[4]; H. Bornkamm, *Luther in der Mitte seines Lebens*, Göttingen 1979, ET 1983, saw Luther as the victim of circumstances.

26. There was an interesting Catholic study of Calvin by Alexander Ganoczy, *Le Jeune Calvin, genèse et évolution de sa vocation réformatrice*, Wiesbaden, 1966.

27. Quentin Skinner summarized his important argument in 'The Origin of the Calvinist Theory of Revolution', in *After the Reformation: Essays in Honour of J. R. Hexter*, ed. Barbara Malament, Pennsylvania 1980, pp. 309–330. His revision of older views affected both secular and committed accounts of the history of political thought in the West.

28. Hence the translations which appeared: for example, Luther's commentary on *Galatians*, edited from a brilliant Elizabethan version by P. S. Watson, 1953; *Lectures on Romans*, 1962; *Early Theological Works*, edited by T. Torrance, 1962; *The Reformation Writings of Martin Luther*, B. L. Woolf, 2 vols, 1953–56; *Martin Luther*, an excellent compendium by John Dillenberger, 1961. Under the auspices of American Lutheranism an English version of the complete works, edited by J. Pelikan, was begun in 1958.

29. See also Maritain's richly naive political theory, *True Humanism* (ET 1938, from lectures published in Spain in 1934), where the Renaissance and the Reformation together stand for a catastrophic past event which only a return to a Catholic political order can reverse. This was the older style of Catholic apologetic, before it was discovered that the Reformation was really part of a 'Catholic' evangelization of Europe, which foundered on the Enlightenment. Like other Catholic thinkers, Maritain blundered throughout the 1920s and 1930s, because he did not grasp the balance of forces between the Vatican, Catholic liberalism, and Fascism, including Nazism.

30. This sentence is constructed from the description of Luther to be found in *The Oxford Dictionary of the Christian Church*, ed. F. L. Cross, 1957. By this time a critical orthodoxy had established itself. The extreme concentration on Luther's personality was the psychoanalytical study, *Young Man Luther* by Erik Erikson, 1958, on which the playwright John Osborne relied in writing his *Luther*. However, Erikson did not overcome the technical problems of applying psychoanalysis to someone dead for centuries, nor did he solve the problems created by the lack of reliable information about Luther's personal life. The gradual change in Catholic attitudes was fostered by Joseph Lortz (*Die Reformation in Deutschland*, Freiburg 1939, ET 1968) and his pupils.

31. Delumeau, *Catholicism between Luther and Voltaire*, pp. 4–9. See also *Naissance et affirmation de la Réforme*, Paris 1965. More recently he has elaborated his view of modern Catholic history as a self-purifying process in *La Peur en Occident*, Paris 1978. An earlier, underrated version of the same themes was *La restauration catholique 1563–1648*, by L. Willaert, Paris 1960. One course of Delumeau's approach to Luther was *Un destin, M. Luther*, by Lucien Febvre, Paris 1927, where the existential triumphed over the theological in non-Kierkegaardian fashion. Kierkegaard, of course, rejected any possibility of Luther's spiritual case becoming the basis for a 'mentality' – for him 'collective Christianity' was a contradiction in terms.

32. H. Jedin, *Katholische Reformation oder Gegenreformation?*, Lucerne 1946, had distinguished between a 'Catholic Reform' and a 'Counter-Reformation'. But German church historians ignored the problem on the whole. For Italian historians, who have usually followed the French, see E. Cochrane, 'The Transition from Renaissance to Baroque', *History and Theory*, 1980.

33. No final agreement has been reached, and scholars as serious as W. J. Cargill-Thompson thought that it was never likely to be reached, on the date of Luther's so-called 'tower-experience', when he realized the full significance of 'justification by faith': the different dates suggested imply distinct interpretations of the origins of the Reformation.

34. See R. Trexler, 'Reverence and Profanity in the Study of Early Modern Europe', in *Religion and Society in Early Modern Europe 1500–1800*, ed. Kaspar von Greyerz, 1984, pp. 245–269. Trexler's *Public Life in Renaissance Florence*, New York 1980, applied his Durkheimian principles to the Renaissance. Although Trexler's critical perception is keen, he does not analyse his own position critically.

35. G. Strauss, *Luther's House of Learning*, p. 299. Thomas Brady pointed out that Strauss had not covered the bigger Lutheran cities, but that at the very least he had shown how far Lutheranism was an unsuccessful attack by urban religious élites on popular religion; see *Reformation Europe, A Guide to Research*, ed. Steven Ozment, St Louis 1982, pp. 171–2. Janine Garrisson-Estebe has produced similar results in what has been a rare social study of French Protestantism: *Protestants du Midi 1559–1598*, Toulouse 1980: southern French Calvinism was urban and the peasants rejected it. *Rouen during the Wars of Religion*, by Philip Benedict, 1981, threw light on Catholic as well as Calvinist attitudes, and once again confirmed that Protestantism survived or disappeared in terms of its hold on large towns.

36. Strauss, op.cit., p. 136.

37. Ibid., p. 302.

38. Le Roy-Ladurie, *Les Paysans de Languedoc*, Paris 1966, ET Urbana, Illinois 1974, p. 207. Ladurie was writing about France.

39. For Pietism, see especially F. E. Stoeffler, *The Rise of Evangelical Pietism*, Leiden 1965; *German Pietism in the Eighteenth Century*, Leiden 1973; and Stoeffler (ed.), *Continental Pietism and Early American Christianity*, Grand Rapids, Michigan 1976. There is no modern edition of the *Pia Desideria*. Note that later eighteenth-century Pietism is often now called Neo-Pietism.

40. Erb, *Pietists*, p. 25. It is interesting that although Erb attributed much

historical misrepresentation of Pietism to the influence of Albrecht Ritschl's 'negative' *Geschichte des Pietismus*, 3 vols, Bonn 1880–86, Ritschl reflected the sort of criticism of Pietism which Erb himself was making in the passage quoted. Ritschl's book was never translated, unfortunately.

41. John Stroup, *The Struggle for Identity in the Clerical State*, Leiden 1984, p. 190.

42. An excellent example of the survival of the old attack on Lutheran political quietism can be found in Rita Thalmann's moving book, *Protestantisme et Nationalisme en Allemagne de 1900 à 1945*, Paris 1976. Thalmann followed the careers of four representative German Protestants, Gustav Flenssen, Walter Flex, Jochen Klepper and Dietrich Bonhoeffer: only the last, in her opinion, had broken with a Lutheran tradition which had persuaded them to sacrifice their critical powers and their desire for human freedom in the belief that blind political submission was the key to eternal happiness. Thalmann was seeking to explain the emergence of Fascism as a *mass* movement: she made the Lutheran ethos dominant in Germany (a doubtful assertion) and thus the mid-wife to the birth of a *popular* party of reaction. Once again one encounters the idea that the attraction of nationalism has to be explained, that it is not attractive in itself.

3. Early Modern England: Was there Anything like the English Reformation?

1. C. Haigh, 'Some Aspects of the Recent Historiography of the English Reformation', in *The Urban Classes, the Nobility and the Reformation*, ed. H.J. Mommsen, Stüttgart 1979, p. 88.

2. J. J. Scarisbrick, *Henry VIII*, 1968, pp. 388f.

3. See articles by Margaret Aston, 'Lollardy and Literacy', in *History*, 1977, pp. 347–71, and 'Lollard Women Priests?', in *Journal of Ecclesiastical History*, 1980, pp. 441–61; Anne Hudson (ed.), *Selections from English Wycliffite Writings*, 1978; and articles by Michael Wilks, 'Misleading Manuscripts, Wycliffe and the non-Wycliffite Bible', in *Studies in Church History*, vol. 11, ed. D. Baker, 1975, pp. 147–61, and 'Royal Priesthood, the Origins of Lollardy', in *The Church in a Changing Society*, Uppsala 1978, pp. 63–70.

4. Thomas, *Religion and the Decline of Magic*, 1971, p. 87.

5. Witch-hunting has been part of the unacceptable face of church-history; between 1400 and 1700 about 100,000 witches may have been executed, about 80,000 of them women. Norman Cohn, in *Europe's Inner Demons*, New York, 1975, and Richard Kieckhefer, in *European Witch Trials, Their Foundation in Popular and Learned Culture*, 1976, both showed that the documents which historians had used as evidence of witch hunting in the fourteenth century were forgeries; this broke the link between the Albigensians and alleged early witchcraft, and wrecked the interpretation of witchcraft as a Christian heresy, involving repudiation of baptism and a pact with the devil. The witch-cult was really a sub-theological invention, whose existence tells us something about the state of the elite or learned culture, but little about a popular culture. The major witch persecutions seem to have begun in France in the fifteenth century and to have spread through Europe to reach a climax

between 1550 and 1650. What caused the intensity of the persecution is not agreed, but Robert Muchembled, in *La sorciere au village: xve-xviiie siecles*, Paris 1979, agreed with Jean Delumeau (see above Ch 2. n. 14) that the Protestant and Catholic evangelizing drive through Early Modern Europe must bear much of the responsibility. For England, apart from Thomas (see above no. 4), see Alan Macfarlane, *Witchcraft in Tudor and Stuart England*, 1970, where he stressed the part played by social change, including the widespread disappearance of Catholicism, in stimulating resource to local magic; but compare his *Origins of English Individualism*, 1979, where he seemed to reject his previous position.

6. See above p. 43.

7. A. J. Krailsheimer (ed.), *The Continental Renaissance 1500–1600*, 1971, p. 395.

8. J. Phillips, *The Reformation of Images, Destruction of Art in England 1535–1660*, University of California Press 1973.

9. Ibid.

10. Phyllis Mack Smith, *Calvinist Preaching and Iconoclasm in the Netherlands*, 1978, p. 38.

11. As far as the Civil War is concerned, there has been a recent swing of opinion away from the view that the causes of the war were social, economic and administrative (with Charles as the martyr of a misunderstood government): there is now more willingness to admit that religion, without being an autonomous force, may well have generated the hysteria which made violent conflict break out. See for example, D. Beales, G. Best (eds.), *History, Society and the Churches*, where Dr Morrill discusses this, pp. 102–25.

12. Natalie Davis, *Society and Culture in Modern France*, 1975, p. 186.

13. Phyllis Mack Crew, op.cit., p. 30.

14. Phillips, op.cit., p. 81.

15. Natalie Davis, op.cit., p. 157.

16. Ibid. Natalie Davis concluded her discussion of this subject by saying: 'The rites of violence are not the rites of violence in any absolute sense. They simply remind us that if we try to increase safety and trust within a community, try to guarantee that the violence it generates will take less destructive and cruel forms, then we must think less about pacifying 'deviants' and more about changing the central values' (p. 187). Alarm at the increasing ferocity of conflict in the twentieth century is one of the reasons why historians of religion have at last turned serious attention on the religious, and specifically Christian, roots of conflict in the past. Much is said about the need for spiritual and religious revival, as though religious renewal would reduce the risk of conflict, but the history of religion suggests that a shift from the apparently secular to the overtly 'religious' is as likely as not to sanctify cruelty.

17. G. Elton, *England under the Tudors*, 1955, pp. 273–74.

18. John Bossy, *Christianity in the West 1400–1700*, 1985, p.97.

19. Ibid., p. 95.

20. Ibid., p. viii. Bossy's case in *Christianity in the West* was not over plausible. Whatever the theoretical value of late medieval Catholicism as the instrument of an enhanced sociability, Europe in the fifteenth century showed every sign

of social collapse from war to major corruption, and late medieval Augustinian theology simply failed to cope with the perceptions of the new Humanism. Anyone accustomed to recent writing on English Catholic history would hardly be surprised to learn that whereas Erasmus was to blame for the troubles of the sixteenth century, Thomas More was a glorious, martyred apologist of an ideal social order.

4. Baroque to Secular: Religion in England

1. G. V. Bennett, *The Tory Crisis in Church and State 1688–1730, The Career of Francis Atterbury, Bishop of Rochester*, 1975, p. 295.

2. R. E. Sullivan, *John Toland and the Deist Controversy*, New York 1982: this is a fascinating study of English Deism, which goes further than many previous works to make a much-needed case for the positive value of Hanoverian Anglicanism, as a religious institution which recognized the limits of its capacity for doing good.

3. Bela K. Kiraly, 'The Hungarian Church', *Church and Society in Catholic Europe of the Eighteenth Century*, ed. W. J. Callahan and D. Higgs, 1979, p. 113.

4. Bennett, op.cit., p. 309.

5. Ibid., p. 308.

6. David Edwards, *Christian England*, 3 vols 1981–84; from vol. 3: *From the Eighteenth Century to the First World War*, preface.

7. Kenneth Thompson, *Bureaucracy and Church Reform 1800–1965*, 1970, has an excellent discussion on Weberian lines. See also Geoffrey Best, *Temporal Pillars*, 1964, on the history of the Church Commissioners.

8. P. A. Welsby, *A History of the Church of England 1945–1980*, 1984, pp. 289–90. An incisive, internal criticism of the overall complacency of the Establishment can be found in *Church and Politics Today: The Role of the Church of England in Contemporary Politics Today*, ed. G. Moyser, Edinburgh 1985, a symposium which covered a much wider ground than its title suggested.

9. Geoffrey Best, *Shaftesbury*, 1964, pp. 65–66.

10. Correlli Barnett, *The Collapse of British Power*, New York 1972, pp. 22–41, 43–45, 62–63. Compare Ian Bradley, *The Call to Seriousness: The Evangelical Impact on the Victorians*, 1976, who said that Evangelical principles suited the demands of the new industrial society; this failed to take seriously the Evangelical retreat from that society in an anti-modernizing phase after 1870, and the dominance of Holiness teaching, with its offshoots in purity organizations which opposed any relaxation of a hard-line attitude to most forms of sexual behaviour.

11. M. Hennell, 'Evangelicalism and Worldliness 1770–1870', *Popular Belief and Practice, Studies in Church History* vol. 8, ed. G. Cuming and D. Baker, 1972, p. 229. Hennell was consciously describing Anglican Evangelicals, whereas Doreen Rosman (*Evangelicals and Culture*) used evidence from Anglican, Methodist and Dissenting sources to build her picture of 'Evangelicalism'. Hennell neglected the social history of Anglicanism, which explained the Evangelical withdrawal. W. R. Ward, *Religion and Society in England 1790–1850*, 1972, shifted the emphasis from ideas to events, but 1850 was not useful

stopping-place in this field. See also the present writer's *Holding the Fort: Studies in Victorian Revivalism*, 1978, for another view of Evangelical history.

12. Another source of this approach was Ford K. Brown's *Fathers of the Victorians: The Age of Wilberforce*, 1961, which argued that while John Wesley failed to reform English society, Wilberforce organized a pressure-group which saved the Victorian age from persisting in the morals and manners of the Regency.

13. For this review, see *Victorian Studies*, 1983, pp. 458–59.

14. K. Thompson, op.cit., pp. 26–55.

15. W. G. Peck, *The Social Implications of the Oxford Movement*, 1933, pp. 315–16.

16. Owen Chadwick, *The Victorian Church*, Part I, 1966, p. 231.

17. E. A. Knox, *The Tractarian Movement 1833–45*, 1933, pp. 356–57.

18. Ibid., p. 364.

19. James Bentley, *Ritualism and Politics in Victorian Britain*, 1978, p. 128.

20. The history of nineteenth-century 'liberalism' has not yet been written: it would have to combine the study of an academic group of intellectuals chiefly concerned about freedom of enquiry, with that of another group whose liberalism was more social and which prolonged into the nineteenth century the Hanoverian, Enlightenment anxieties about the survival of civility, toleration, and moral sensitivity. (One has to remember that early eighteenth-century High Churchmen insisted that the so-called Toleration Act of 1689 did not include the word 'toleration'.) Arthur Stanley (1815–81) was the archetypal Victorian religious liberal. A. M. G. Stephenson, *The Rise and Decline of English Modernism*, 1984, was an unsatisfactory, anecdotal and short-sighted book, based on material about the Modern Churchmen's Union, whose history could be traced back to *c.* 1898/9. Stephenson wanted to assert the orthodoxy of these Anglican Modernists, as distinct from the 'radicalism' of the 'Myth of God Incarnate' Anglicans of the 1970s.

21. Cowling, *Religion and Public Doctrine in Modern England*, 1980, pp. 420–21.

22. Ibid., p. 426.

23. G. Bennett, in *Essays in Modern Church History*, ed. G. Bennett and J. Walsh, 1966, preface.

24. Norman Sykes, *Church and State in England in the Eighteenth Century*, 1934, pp. 144–45.

25. The extent to which Anglo-Catholicism was part of the institutional, rather than the religious history of the Church of England has been ignored. If it is true that many of the troubles of the twentieth-century Roman Catholic Church spring from its inability to accept that the French Revolution happened, it is equally true that the modern Church of England has never come to terms with the quasi-legalization of Dissent or Nonconformity in 1689. See especially Anthony Dyson, 'Reflections on Four Church and State Reports', *Church and Politics Today*, ed. G. Moyser, 1985, pp. 282–312.

26. Geoffrey Rowell, *The Vision Glorious*, 1983, p. 219.

27. D. Edwards, *Christian England*, vol. 3, 1984, p. 180.

28. See Callahan and Higgs, *Church and Society*, note 3 above.

29. American writers sometimes study eighteenth-century religion as part

of eighteen-century culture: for example, R. D. Stock, *The Holy and Demonic from Sir Thomas Browne to William Blake*, Princeton 1982, tried to use literature for the study of religious experience.

30. John Stroup, *The Struggle for Identity in the Clerical Estate*, Leiden 1984, p. 57.

31. See above pp. 51–2.

32. Bernard Semmel, *The Methodist Revolution*, 1974, p. 7.

33. Jean Orcibal, 'The Theological Originality of John Wesley', *History of the Methodist Church in Great Britain*, ed. R. Davies and G. Rupp, vol. 1, 1965, p. 102. The argument quoted may be found in G. C. Cell, *John Wesley's Theology*, Abingdon Cokesbury 1950, pp. 361f. Cell's formula was charmingly ecumenical, but relied on the assumption that the synthesis was *necessarily* acceptable in both directions; in fact, Wesley's doctrine of holiness was more eccentric than he implied.

34. John Lawson, 'The People Called Methodists: "Our Discipline" ', in *History of the Methodist Church*, vol. 1, p. 183. This 'Catholic synthesis' belonged to the ecumenical politics of the mid-twentieth century, not to the eighteenth century.

35. R. Davies, 'The People Called Methodists: "Our Doctrine" ', in *History of the Methodist Church*, vol. 1, pp. 145–179. The final quotation is from Lawson, ibid., p. 185, where he claimed that 'the Church of England and the Nonconformists shared fully in the national spiritual renewal': there was no *national* spiritual renewal, unless that is what one means by Regency.

36. V. H. H. Green, *John Wesley*, 1964, pp. 72–3.

37. Brian Harrison, *Drink and the Victorians: The Temperance Question in England 1815–72*, 1971, was the first important book on teetotalism. He was clear that the teetotal movement failed to tackle the nineteenth-century drink problem effectively. His general conclusion was the 'voluntary associations (like the teetotal organizations) helped British democrats to shed that anti-government tendency which continues to bedevil French democratic parties: Alliance agitation enabled all prohibitionists, whatever their subsequent course, to shed their sense of inferiority: in this way, it helped to heal the wound that had been festering in English society since 1662' (p. 386). The divisions of the anti-Conservative parties in the 1980s suggested that this conclusion was optimistic.

38. For the Free Churches, see, for example, John Briggs and Ian Sellers, *Victorian Nonconformity, Documents of Modern History*, 1973. For the earlier period, see G. I. T. Machin, *Politics and the Churches in Great Britain 1832 to 1868*, 1977; this was very much the view from Westminster.

39. William Strawson, in *History of the Methodist Church*, vol. 3, 1983, p. 230.

40. C. Welch, *God and the Incarnation in Mid-Nineteenth-Century German Theology*, 1965, p. 9. Compare his later discussion in *Protestant Thought in the Nineteenth Century: vol i, 1799–1870*, 1972, where he described the British kenoticism as 'hesitant'.

Nineteenth-century christology has been made more accessible by the publication of a series of new translations: H.S. Reimarus, *Fragments*, ed. C. H. Talbert, 1965; D. F. Strauss, *The Life of Jesus Critically Examined*, ed. P. C.

Hodgson, 1972; F. Nietzsche, *The Antichrist*, ed. R. J. Hollingdale, 1968; J. Weiss, *Jesus's Proclamation of the Kingdom of God*, ed. R. H. Hiers and D. L. Holland, 1971; and W. Herrmann, *The Communion of the Christian with God*, ed. R.T. Voelkel, 1972.

41. A. Kenny, *Faith and Reason*, 1983, p. 60.

42. Owen Chadwick, *The Victorian Church, Part II*, 1970, p. 110.

43. There was a useful account of the controversy at the political level in Machin, *Politics and the Churches*, etc.

44. Note the wider, European context of the Roman Catholic Marian revival after 1815, in which submissiveness also became the keynote of the feminine.

45. See Ann Douglas, *The Feminization of American Culture*, New York 1978, for the way in which the role of the American Protestant minister was restated in 'feminine' terms as his intellectual status declined in the nineteenth century.

46. Olive Banks, *The Faces of Feminism*, 1981, p. 23.

47. The best detailed discussion of the role of women in Victorian charity is in F. K. Prochaska, *Women and Philanthropy in Nineteenth-Century England*, 1980. Prochaska thought that Josephine Butler's part in the repeal of the Contagious Diseases Acts had been exaggerated.

48. For a useful discussion of the problems, see *Feminist Interpretations of the Bible*, ed. Letty M. Russell, 1985. All the contributors were American. One quotation suggests the crisis: 'What warrant is there, someone will ask, for extending the Bible's general critique of oppression to a critique of patriarchy that is not in the text and seems even to be counterindicated by much of the text?' (p. 64.)

5. Illustrative Interludes

1. See, e.g., D. Blackbourn, G. Eley, *Mythen Deutschen Geschichtsschreibung*, Ullstein 1980. Blackbourn also contributed 'The Problem of Democratization, German Catholics and the Centre Part', to R. J. Evans (ed.), *Society and Politics in Wilhelmine Germany*, 1980.

2. This is true of otherwise excellent books like Jeffrey Herf's *Reactionary Modernism: Technology, Culture and Politics in Weimar and the Third Reich*, 1984. Herf analyses the way in which Nazism combined reactionary politics with technological modernization, but he ignored the extent to which the resulting ideology seemed plausible because so many of its themes, such as 'anti-materialism', 'anti-Judaism', 'nationalism' etc. were already part of the outlook of the Protestant and Catholic Churches. Karl Barth was wide of the mark when he spoke of the Nazis 'bewitching' Christians in Germany, and Thomas Mann's exculpatory appeal to demonic forces was equally irrelevant: ideologically, the decisive steps had been taken long before: the churches had bewitched themselves.

3. A similar movement of consolidation took place after 1815 in the Protestant subculture, dominated by the conservative, pietist tradition; see, for instance, F. Spotts, *The Churches and Politics in Germany*, Middletown, Conn. 1973, and R. M. Bigler, *The Politics of German Protestantism: The Rise of the*

Protestant Church Elite in Prussia 1815–48, Berkeley 1972. Schleiermacher won the intellectual battle, but conservatives controlled the institutions.

4. J. Sperber, *Popular Catholicism in Nineteenth-Century*, Princeton 1984, p. 71.

5. Ibid., p. 151.

6. Ibid., p. 152.

7. For the Kulturkampf, see especially, M. Anderson, *Windhorst*, 1982.

8. Sperber, op.cit., p. 216.

9. Ibid., p. 218.

10. Ibid., p. 297.

11. Ibid., p. 283.

12. Ellen Lovell Evans, *The German Centre Party*, Southern Illinois 1981, p. 283.

13. S.A. Stehlin, *Weimar and the Vatican 1919–33*, Princeton 1983. Stehlin presented the Vatican as unable to refuse the Nazi offer of 1933. 'Unfortunately, for the Vatican, the new government which brought the Weimar Republic to an end was soon to disregard the Concordat, treating it as a mere scrap of paper' (p. 452). For the other important concordat of this period, see J. E. Pollard, *The Vatican and Italian Fascism 1929–32*, 1985: Pollard has a much more balanced and critical view of the compromising Pope, Pius XI.

14. G. Levy, *The Catholic Church and Nazi Germany*, 1964, p. 99.

15. See, O. Dibelius, *In the Service of the Lord*, Stuttgart 1961, ET 1964.

16. Daniel Borg, *The Old Prussian Church and the Weimar Republic*, University Press of New England, 1984, p. 199.

17. Ibid., p. 200. See also J. P. Wright, *Above Parties: The Political Attitudes of the German Protestant Church Leadership 1918–33*, 1974.

18. K. Barth, *The German Church Conflict*, 1965, English version of Barth's commentaries on the German situation between 1933 and 1939.

19. Dansette wrote an account of the worker-priest movement, *Le destin du Catholicisme français 1925–56*, Paris 1959; Emile Poulat's *Naissance des Prêtres ouvriers*, Paris 1965, replaced this; there was a valuable German study, *The Church and Industrial Society*, ET 1965 by Gregor Siefer. For English readers Dansette's textbook replaced C. S. Phillips, *The Church in France 1815–1907*, 2 vols, 1929, 1936. T. Zeldin, *France 1848–1945*, (2 vols, 1973–77), though widely praised, lacked coherence on religious subjects. The standard Catholic history is A. Latreille, and R. Remond, *Histoir du Catholicisme en France*, vol. 3, from the eighteenth century to the present, Paris 1962.

20. See below, pp. 216–20.

21. See also E. Léonard, *Le Protestant français*, Paris 1955: Léonard was the best-known Protestant historian of his generation; more recently Jean Baubérot has written widely on nineteenth-century French Protestantism, including *Un Christianisme profane?*, Paris 1978, a study of the Protestant Christian-socialist periodical, *L'Avant-Garde*, which flourished between 1899 and 1911, advocating a religious style free from dogma and ritual, and looking for connections with the socialist working classes.

22. See *Chouannerie and Counter-Revolution: Puisaye, the Princes, and the British Government in the 1790s*, by Maurice Hutt, 2 vols, 1983, the latest in a series of studies which put religion, sociology and immense research into the analysis

of resistance to the Revolution: compare C. Tilly, *The Vendée*, 1964, and D. Sutherland, *The Chouans, the social origin of popular counter-revolution in upper Brittany 1770–1796*, 1982; equally important for resistance in the south of France was G. Lewis, *The Second Vendée: the continuity of counter-revolution in the Department of the Gard 1789–1815*, 1978. Interest in revolutionary movements, guerrilla warfare, and peasant risings, rather than in religious matters, predominated in all these.

23. See G. Lewis, *The Second Vendée*.

24. An excellent illustration of this was J. McManners, *French Ecclesiastical Society under the Ancien Régime*, 1961, based on the cathedral town of Angers in the eighteenth century. The fury with which a section of French urban society turned on the church is impressive: at the height of the struggle 264 priests from the Angers area were shipped to Spain, and another 100, old or unfit, were later deliberately drowned at Nantes. For another, more restrained version, see Olwen Hufton, *Bayeux in the late Eighteenth Century*, 1967. This material has to be balanced against the more recent emphasis for Catholicism tended, however, to be stimulated by the Revolution, and to disappear again, quite quickly, after the Restoration of 1815.

25. See also his essay, 'Dechristianization in the Year Two', in K. von Greyerz, op.cit., pp. 79–94.

26. Ibid., p. 91. He was thinking especially of 'goddesses of reason', who were in general not the prostitutes of popular anti-revolutionary propaganda, but respectable young women.

27. Olwen Hufton, 'The French Church', in W. Callahan and D. Higgs, *Church and Society in Catholic Europe in th Eighteenth Century*, 1979, p. 31.

28. The classic study was by Ernest Sévrin, *Les Missions religieuses en France sous la Restauration (1815–1830)*, vol. 1, *Le Missionaire et la mission*, Saint-Mandé, Seine 1948; vol. 2, *Les Missions 1815–1820*, 1959. The Protestant revivals, and Protestant reaction to Catholic missions, was discussed in Daniel Robert's *Les Églises reformées en France 1800–1830*, Paris 1961.

29. René Rémond, *The Right-Wing in France from 1815 to de Gaulle*, 1968, ET from *La Droite en France*, Paris 1963[3]: 'the relativism of any statement of the liberal point of view directly offended the absolute position of Catholicism and seemed a defiance of its authority' (p. 119).

30. Edward Berenson, *Populist Religion and Left-Wing Politics in France*, Princeton 1984, p. 73.

31. Ibid., p. 214.

32. H. Macquan, *Trois jours au pouvoir des insurgés*, 1852.

33. E. Tenot, *La Provence en décembre 1851, étude historique sur le Coup d'État*, 1865.

34. Maurice Agulhon, *The Republic in the Village*, London-Paris 1982, p. 291.

35. Ibid., p. 252.

36. Ibid., p. 253.

37. See above pp. 32–6.

38. Eugen Weber, *Peasants into Frenchmen*, 1977, p. 495.

39. Ibid.

40. Ibid, p. 356.

41. Many efforts have been made in recent years to defend the record of the Papacy in this century: Anthony Rhodes, *The Vatican in the Age of the Dictators*, 1973; Francis Murphy, *The Papacy Today*, 1981; Derek Holmes, *The Papacy in the Modern World*, 1981; and Peter Nichols, *The Pope's Divisions*, 1982. The leadership which the Popes provided, however, did not justify the claims made for the significance of the office.

42. Peter Ackroyd, *T. S. Eliot*, 1984. Eliot dedicated a pamphlet on Dante to Charles Maurras in 1929.

43. William Warren Sweet (1881–1959), produced *The Story of Religion in America* in 1930. He was a Methodist, and much of his work was devoted to establishing Methodism in the religious history of the United States.

44. Sydney E. Mead, born in 1904, published *The Lively Experience: The Shaping of Christianity in America* in 1963. A much more professional historian than the rather sentimental Sweet.

45. Perry Miller (1905–1963), a romantic historian of ideas, chief architect of the revision and revival of Puritan myth in American historical writing. He expounded the old Puritan Boston to the new, Catholic Boston. His best single book was *Jonathan Edwards*, 1948; but he wrote the intellectual history of New England in *Orthodoxy in Massachusetts, 1630–1650*, 1933, *The New England Mind, the Seventeenth Century*, 1939; and *The New England Mind from Colony to Province*, 1953. He took up the line indicated in Samuel Morison's *Builders of the Bay Colony*, 1930. At this academic level Puritanism has been accepted as part of the American national tradition, whereas in England the survival of Anglican dominance relegated Puritanism and its heirs to the rank of dubious outsiders.

46. See Chapter 7, pp. 177–202.

47. Revivalism in America has been well covered: See especialy, Whitney Cross, *The Burned-Over District: the Social and Intellectual History of Enthusiastic Religion in Western New York 1800–1850*, New York 1950; James F. Findlay, *Dwight L. Moody, American Evangelist 1837–99*, Chicago 1969, fine for facts, and the best biography available; John Kent, *Holding the Fort*, 1978, and Richard Carwardine, *Transatlantic Revivalism, Popular Evangelicals in Britain and America, 1790–1865*, both deal with the overlap between Britain and America; William G. McLoughlin, *Modern Revivalism from Finney to Billy Graham*, 1959. I suspect that I am the only one of these writers who has spent as much time on the message as on the methods of the professional revivalists.

48. For the open-ended nature of American Methodism, see Albert Outler, 'Do Methodists have a doctrine of the Church?', in D. Kirkpatrick (ed.), *The Doctrine of the Church*, New York 1964, pp. 11–28.

49. Several have been mentioned. E. R. Sandeen's *The Roots of Fundamentalism, British and American Millenarianism 1800–1930*, Chicago 1970, was a trailblazing study; more characteristic would be Larzer Ziff, *Puritanism in America: New Culture in a New World*, 1973. Revision of the view that Puritanism was never more than one interesting byway in American history is long overdue.

50. S. Ahlstrom, *A Religious History of the American People*, 1972, p. 10. It was illuminating that Ahlstrom called his synthesis something other than 'church

history'. This is a better overall account than Robert T. Handy, *A History of the Churches in the United States and Canada*, 1976; both have excellent bibliographies. For Catholic history in the United States there is a recent, revised bibliography, John T. Ellis and Robert Trisco, *A Guide to American Catholic History*, Santa Barbara, 1982[2].

51. See Chapter 7, for some account of the American scholarship which explored the collapse of Chinese missionfields, and note that some American scholars analysed the weaknesses of European missionaries in Africa at the same time.

52. George Marsden, *Fundamentalism and American Culture*, New York 1980, p. 228.

53. Ibid., p. 230.

54. Ahlstrom, op.cit., pp. 1079–1097. Even so, Ahlstrom interpreted American history since 1945 as a gradual emergence from a 'Puritan Epoch', in which the United States had thought of itself as 'the almost chosen people'. Outside America, however, he admitted that 'the present time of crisis is linked, not with Puritanism, but more broadly with the rise and fall of Western imperialism, colonialism, and capitalism', (p. 1095).

6. *Newman and Catholic Modernism*

1. J. C. H. Aveling, *The Handle and the Axe: The Catholic Recusants in England from Reformation to Emancipation*, 1976, discussed Newman's view on p. 354.

2. Ibid., pp. 356–58.

3. James Hennessey, *American Catholics: A History of the Roman Catholic Community in the United States*, 1981: see p. 217; 'The post-*Pascendi* years in American Catholicism were marked by intellectual retreat and theological sterility. A thoroughgoing and immensely effective educational police action isolated the theological reaches of the Catholic community from the contemporary world with which tentative contact had been so recently established. The combination of Americanist and Modernist crises, and particularly the powerful integrist reaction which set in after 1907, effectively put an end for the next fifty years to further development of Catholic thought in authentic American dress'.

4. Victorian anti-Catholicism has not been adequately studied; E. R. Norman, *Anti-Catholicism in Victorian England*, 1968, had a useful selection of documents, but the introductory material was thin.

5. E. R. Norman, *The English Catholic Church in the Nineteenth Century*, 1984. Norman changed the usual balance of the story from Newman to Wiseman, the elder Ward, Manning and Vaughan; the result was not quite an ultramontane handbook, but Norman certainly contemplated the Roman taming of the English Catholic community with some satisfaction.

6. See above, Chapter 1, pp. 17–18, 24–5.

7. Lewis Watt (ed.), *The Doctrines of the Modernists (The Encyclical Pascendi of Pope Pius X) and Modernist Errors (The Decree Lamentabili of July 4, 1907)*, Catholic Truth Society 1937.

8. Norman, op.cit., p. 334.

9. Ibid., p. 341.

10. Norman, one feels, aspired to join the succession of 'Anglican reactionaries' established by Maurice Cowling in *Religion and Public Discourse in Modern England*, a line in which he included Charles Smyth, who wrote *Simeon and Church Order*, 1940, and Edwyn Hoskyns who, with F. N. Davey, produced a kind of High Church-Barthian commentary on *The Fourth Gospel* (also in 1940). These men represented Anglicanism at its dogmatic worst, denouncing all forms of liberalism, as though energetic contradiction was proof of thought. Cowling confused this position with that of historians like Edward Welbourne of Emmanuel College, Cambridge, whose historical nominalism was one root of the liberal relativism which Hoskyns and Smyth hated so much.

11. Bernhard Hasler, *How the Pope became Infallible*, 1981, published after the author's death, with a foreword from Hans Küng, himself in trouble with Roman authority, was an unconvincing attempt to destroy Pius IX personally, in order to impugn the proclamation of infallibility at Vatican I.

12. See above pp. 159–60.

13. Derek Holmes, *More Roman than Rome*, 1978, p. 240.

14. For which see T. M. Loome, *Liberal Catholicism*, Matthias Grünewald Verlag, Mainz 1979, p. 409.

15. See above p. 166.

16. For Wilfred Ward, see M. Ward, *The Wilfrid Wards and the Transition*, 2 vols, 1934–38, though the scale inflated Ward's importance.

17. Quoted in T. Loome, op.cit., p. 412.

18. William J. Schoenl, *The Intellectual Crisis in English Catholicism*, New York 1982, p. 203.

19. See also John Kent, 'Religion and Science', *Nineteenth-Century Religious Thought in the West*, ed. N. Smart, J. Clayton, S. Katz and P. Sherry, 1985, pp. 1–37.

20. Loome, op.cit., p. 196.

21. But Bishop was right in his insistence that for Rome itself the central issue was that of authority, and especially that of authority over the laity, a question which dominated Pius IX's mind, and was settled decisively in the *Römerbrief* of 1863, which warned off scientists and other would-be lay theologians from the sphere of ecclesiastical doctrine. There was an older English tradition of lay independence (see Bossy, op.cit.) which was sternly called to heel after 1850, and which had not commonly trespassed on doctrinal matters.

22. Alec Vidler, *A Variety of Catholic Modernists*, 1970, p. 54.

23. Reardon, in *Nineteenth-Century Religious Thought in the West*, vol. 2, p. 173.

24. Ibid.

25. Ibid., p. 172.

7. Failure of a Mission: Christianity Outside Europe

1. 'I should consider myself worse than despicable if I failed to declare my firm conviction that the British Army and Navy are today used by God for the accomplishment of His purpose': a Wesleyan missionary quoted by

Geoffrey Moorhouse in *The Missionaries*, 1973, p. 281); he was quoting from Dennis Kemp, *Nine Years at the Gold Coast*, 1898.

2. The watchword of the Student Volunteer Missionary Movement of the later 1890s. The best account of this world is in *Red Tape and the Gospel, A Study of the significance of the ecumenical missionary struggle of William Paton (1886–1943)*, by Eleanor M. Jackson, Birmingham 1980.

3. John R. Mott (1865–1955) was an American Methodist lay evangelist who specialized in raising money and people for the missionary movement.

4. For Fairbank, see his autobiography, *Chinabound, A Fifty Year Memoir*, New York 1982. With D. Twitchett he edited the *Cambridge History of China*, vols. 10–12, 1976, 1980, 1982, which covered the years 1800–1949.

5. The *Nemesis* was the British warship whose adventures signalled the commencement of the Victorian invasion of China; see also *Peter Parker and the Opening of China*, by Edward V. Gulick, Harvard 1973, about the American part in the process.

6. For the Taipings, see, for example, *Christian Influence upon the Ideology of the Taiping Rebellion*, E. Boardman, Madison 1952; *China and Christianity 1860–70*, Paul Cohen, Harvard 1963; and *The Last Stand of Chinese Conservatism 1862–74*, by Mary C. Wright, Stamford 1957, which was also concerned with the massacre of Christians in Tientsin in 1870.

7. Fairbank, loc.cit., p. 221.

8. For Catholicism, see the *Jesuits at the Court of China*, by A. Rowbotham, Berkeley 1942, and *Apostolic Legations in China in the Eighteenth Century*, Pasadena 1948, by A. S. Rosse, both on the Rites Controversy and Cardinal Tournon's journey to Peking in 1705. For the later period, *La Politique missionaire de la France en Chine 1842–1856*, Wei Tsing Sing, Paris 1960.

9. For the Boxers, see Victor Purcell, *The Boxer Uprising*, 1963; Charles Tan, *The Boxer Catastrophe*, Columbia 1955; Paul A. Varg, *Missionaries, Chinese and Diplomats: the American Protestant Missionary Movement in China 1890–1952*, Princeton 1958.

10. In a fascinating book, *China and the Christian Impulse*, Paris 1982, ET Janet Lloyd, 1985, Jacques Gernet argued, in terms of the seventeenth-century controversies between Catholic missionaries and Chinese intellectuals, that the philosophical structure which controlled Christian theology had no natural equivalent in Chinese, so that mutual understanding was nearly impossible.

11. Irwin T. Hyatt, *Our Ordered Lives Confess; Three Nineteenth-Century Missionaries in East Shantung*, Harvard 1976. Compare Ellsworth C. Carson, *The Foochow Missionaries 1847–1880*, Harvard 1974.

12. S. L. Thrupp (ed.), *Millenial Dreams in Action*, The Hague 1962, p. 143.

13. J. M. R. Owens, *Prophets in the Wilderness: The Wesleyan Mission to New Zealand 1819–1827*, Auckland 1974.

14. K. P. S. Gupta, *The Christian Missionaries in Bengal 1793–1833*, Calcutta 1971, pp. 164–65.

15. Sundararaj Manickam, *The Social Setting of Christian Conversion in South India*, Wiesbaden 1977, pp. 257–8.

16. *Handbuch der Kirchengeschichte*, ed. Hubert Jedin and John Dolan, vol. x, 1981, pp. 777–94.

17. Max Warren, *Social History and Christian Mission*, 1967, p. 129.

18. See Adrian Hastings, *A History of African Christianity 1950–1975*, 1979.

19. J. H. Boer, *Missionary Messengers of Liberation in a Colonial Context*, Amsterdam 1979, p. 472.

20. Elliott Kendall, 'The Missionary Factor in Africa' in E. Fasholé-Luke et. al., *Christianity in Independent Africa*, 1978, pp. 16–25.

21. Boer, op.cit., p. 465.

8. Ecumenism, the Light that Failed

1. George Bell, *Christian Unity, The Anglican Position*, 1948, p. 152.

2. Ibid., p. 167.

3. See above pp. 205 and 207.

4. Ogbu Kalu, 'Church Unity and Religious Change in Africa' in E. Fasholé-Luke, R. Gray, A. Hastings and G. Tasie (eds), *Christianity in Independent Africa*, 1978, p. 164.

Bibliography

Peter Ackroyd, *T. S. Eliot*, Abacus, Hamish Hamilton 1984.

M. Agulhon, *The Republic in the Village: The People of the Var from the French Revolution to the Second Republic*, Plon, Paris 1970, ET 1982.

S. Ahlstrom, *A Religious History of the American People*, Yale University Press, New Haven and London 1972.

J. F. A. Ajayi, *Christian Missions in Nigeria 1841–1891 – The Making of a New Elite*, Longman 1965.

A. M. Allchin, *The Silent Rebellion: Anglican Communities 1845–1900*, SCM Press 1958.

P. Althaus, *Luther's Haltung im Bauernkrieg*, Darmstadt 1971.

M. Anderson, *Windhorst*, Oxford, Clarendon Press 1981.

Perry Anderson, *Arguments within English Marxism*, Verso Editions, London 1980.

P. F. Anson, *The Call of the Cloister*, 1955, revised edition by A. W. Campbell, 1964.

A. Armstrong, *The Church of England, the Methodists and Society 1700–1850*, University of London Press 1973.

B. Armstrong, *Calvinism and the Amyraut Heresy: Protestant Scholasticism and Heresy in Seventeenth Century France*, Madison 1969.

R. F. Atkinson, *Knowledge and Explanation in History*, Macmillan 1978.

J. F. C. Aveling, *The Handle and the Axe: The Catholic Recusants in England from Reformation to Emancipation*, Blond and Briggs 1976.

E. A. Ayandele, *The Missionary Impact on Modern Nigeria 1842–1914*, Longman 1966.

G. R. A. Balleine, *A History of the Evangelical Party in the Church of England*, Longman Green 1908.

S. Berger, *Religion in West European Politics*, Frank Cass 1982.

C. Binfield, *So Down to Prayers: Studies in English Nonconformity 1780–1920*, Dent 1977.

D. Blackbourn, *Mythen Deutschen Geschichtsschreibung*, Ullstein, Frankfurt 1980.

—— *The Peculiarities of German History*, Oxford University Press 1984.

J. Boel, *Christian Mission to India*, Graduate Press, Amsterdam 1975.

J. H. Boer, *Missionary Messengers of Liberation in a Colonial Context*, Rodopi, Amsterdam 1979.

D. Borg, *The Old Prussian Church and the Weimar Republic: A Study in Political Adjustment 1917–1927*, University Press of New England, Hanover, New Hampshire, 1984.

J. Bossy, *The English Catholic Community 1570–1850*, Darton, Longman and Todd, 1975.

—— *Christianity in the West 1400–1700*, Oxford University Press 1985.

I. Bradley, *The Call to Seriousness: The Evangelical Impact on the Victorians*, Jonathan Cape 1976.

T. A. Brady, *Ruling-Class, Régime and Reformation 1520–1555 at Strassbourg*, Brill, Leiden 1978.

Briggs, J. and Sellers, I., *Victorian Nonconformity: Documents of Modern History*, Edward Arnold 1973.

E. Bristow, *Vice and Vigilance: Purity Movements in Britain since 1700*, Gill and Macmillan, Dublin 1977.

P. Brooks (ed.), *Christian Spirituality*, SCM Press 1975.

O. Brose, *Church and Parliament: The Reshaping of the Church of England 1828–60*, Oxford University Press 1959.

F. K. Brown, *Fathers of the Victorians: The Age of Wilberforce*, Cambridge University Press 1961.

P. Burke, *Popular Culture in Early Modern Europe*, Temple Smith, London 1978.

P. Butler, ed., *Pusey Rediscovered*, SPCK 1983.

H. Butterfield, *Christianity and History*, George Bell 1953.

R. Byrnes, *Antisemitism in Modern France*, vol. I, Rutgers University Press, New Brunswick 1950.

R. Caillois, *Les Jeux et les hommes, le masque et le vertige*, Gallimard, Paris 1967.

W. J. Callahan and D. Higgs, *Church and Society in Catholic Europe of the Eighteenth Century*, Cambridge University Press 1979.

R. Carwardine, *Transatlantic Revivalism: Popular Evangelicalism in Britain and America 1790–1865*, Greenwood Press, Westport, Connecticut 1978.

G. C. Cell, *The Rediscovery of John Wesley*, Abingdon Cokesbury 1935.

W. O. Chadwick, *The Victorian Church, Part 1 /2*, A. and C. Black, 1966, 1970; reissued SCM Press 1987.

—— *The Popes and European Revolution*, Oxford History of the Christian Church, Oxford University Press 1981.

—— *The Secularization of the European Mind in the Nineteenth Century*, Cambridge University Press 1975.

—— *The Mind of the Oxford Movement*, A. and C. Black 1960.

—— *From Bossuet to Newman: The Idea of Doctrinal Development*, Cambridge University Press 1957.

G. K. Clark, *The Making of Victorian England*, Methuen 1962.

—— *Churchmen and the Condition of England 1832–1885*, Methuen 1973.

N. Cohn, *Europe's Inner Demons*, Chatto, New York 1975.

P. Cohen, *China and Christianity 1860–1870*, Harvard University Press 1963.

J. S. Conway, *The Nazi Persecution of the Churches 1933–45*, Weidenfeld and Nicholson 1968.

M. Cowling, *Religion and Public Doctrine in Modern England*, Cambridge University Press, vol. I 1980, vol. II 1985.

W. de Craemer, *The Jamaa and the Church*, Oxford University Press 1977.

G. Cragg (ed.), *The Works of John Wesley Volume 11: The Appeals to Men of Reason and Religion*, Oxford University Press 1975.

M. Creighton, *Historical Lectures and Addresses*, Longmans Green 1903.

F. L. Cross (ed.), *Oxford Dictionary of the Christian Church*, Oxford University Press 1966.

W. Cross, *The Burned-Over District: The Social and Intellectual History of Enthusiastic Religion in Western New York 1800–1850*, Cornell University Press, Ithaca, New York 1950.

D. Crummey, *Priests and Politicians, Protestant and Catholic Missions in Orthodox Ethiopia 1830–68*, Oxford University Press 1972.

V. Cunningham, *Everywhere Spoken Against: Dissent in the Victorian Novel*, Oxford University Press 1975.

R. Currie, *Methodism Divided: A Study in the Sociology of Ecumenicalism*, Faber and Faber 1968.

M. L. Daeel, *Old and New in Southern Shona Independent Churches*, 2 vols, Brill, The Hague 1971, 1974.

G. Daly, *Transcendence and Immanence: A Study in Catholic Modernism and Integralism*, Clarendon Press, Oxford 1980.

A. Dansette, *The Religious History of Modern France*, Herder and Nelson, 2 vols, Freiburg-London 1961.

D. Davie, *A Gathered Church: The Literature of the English dissenting interest, 1700–1930*, Cambridge University Press, 1976.

J. Davies, *The History of the Tahitian Mission*, Hakluyt Society 1961.

R. Davies, E. G. Rupp (eds.), *A History of the Methodist Church in Great Britain*, Epworth Press, 3 vols, 1965, 1978, 1983.

N. Z. Davis, *Society and Culture in Early Modern France*, Duckworth 1975.

J. Delumeau, *Le Catholicisme entre Luther et Voltaire*, Nouvelle Clio, Paris 1971, ET 1977.

—— *La Peur en Occident*, Fayard, Paris 1978, ET.

—— *Le Christianisme, va-t-il mourir?* Hachette, Paris 1977.

A. G. Dickens, *The English Reformation*, Batsford 1964.

—— *The Counter-Reformation*, Thames and Hudson 1968.

A. Douglas, *The Feminization of American Culture*, Avon Books, New York 1978.

M. Drabble, *The Oxford Companion to English Literature*, Oxford University Press 1985.

E. Durkheim, *Socialism*, Collier Books, New York 1967.

D. L. Edwards, *Leaders of the Church of England 1828–1944*, Oxford University Press 1971.

—— *Christian England* vol. 3, *From the Eighteenth Century to the First World War*, Collins 1984.
L. E. Ellsworth, *Charles Lowder and the Ritualist Movement*, Darton, Longman and Todd 1982.
E. G. Elton, *England under the Tudors*, Methuen 1955.
—— *Reformation Europe 1517–1599*, Fontana, Collins 1963.
—— *Policy and Police: The Enforcement of the Reformation in the Age of Thomas Cromwell*, Cambridge University Press 1972.
—— *Reform and Reformation in England, 1509–1558*, Edward Arnold 1977.
A. Embree, *Charles Grant and British Rule in India*, Allen and Unwin 1962.
F. Engels, *Der Deutsche Bauernkrieg*, 1850, ET, Lawrence and Wishsart 1956.
F. Erb, *Pietists (Classics of Western Spirituality)*, SPCK 1983.
E. Erikson, *Young Man Luther*, Faber and Faber 1959.
J. Estèbe-Garrisson, *Les Protestants du Midi 1559–1598*, Privat, Toulouse 1980.
E. Evans, *The German Centre Party*, Southern Illinois University Press 1981.
H. O. Evenett, *The Spirit of the Counter-Reformation*, Cambridge University Press 1968.

J. Fairbank, *The Missionary Enterprise in China and America*, Harvard University Press 1974.
O. Fatio, *Méthode et Théologie, Lambert Daneau et les débats de la scholastique Réformée*, Travaux d'Humanisme et la Renaissance, Geneva 1976.
L. Febvre, *Le Problème de l'incroyance au xvie siècle: la religion de Rabelais*, Albin Michel, Paris 1942, repr. 1968.
—— *Un destin, Martin Luther*, Presses Universitaires de France, Paris 1952.
J. F. Findlay, *Dwight L. Moody, American Evangelist 1837–99*, Chicago University Press 1969.
L. Fischer, *A Documentary History of the Faith and Order Movement 1927–63*, Bethany Press, St Louis 1963.
R. N. Flew (ed.), *The Catholicity of Protestantism*, Lutterworth Press 1950.
D. B. Forrester, *Caste and Christianity: Attitudes and Policies on Caste of Anglo-Saxon Missions in India*, Curzon Press 1980.
M. Fulbrook, *Piety and Politics: Religion and the Rise of Absolutism in England, Wurttemberg and Prussia*, Cambridge University Press 1983.

A. Ganoczy, *Le Jeune Calvin, genèse et évolution de sa vocation réformatrice*, Wiesbaden 1966.
A. D. Gilbert, *Religion and Society in Industrial England: Church, Chapel and Social Change 1740–1914*, Longman 1976.
C. Ginzburg, *The Cheese and the Worms*, Routledge and Kegan Paul 1980.
J. Godechot, *La Contre-Révolution, doctrine et action 1789–1804*, 1961, ET Routledge and Kegan Paul 1972.
V. H. Green, *John Wesley*, Nelson 1964.
K. von Greyerz (ed.), *Religion and Society in Early Modern Europe 1500–1800*, Allen and Unwin 1984.
J. R. Griffin, *The Oxford Movement 1833–1933*, Pentland Press, Edinburgh 1984.

K. P. S. Gupta, *The Christian Missionaries in Bengal 1793–1833*, Calcutta 1971.
R. Gutteridge, *Open Thy Mouth for the Dumb: The German Evangelical Church and the Jews 1870–1914*, Blackwell, Oxford 1976.
J. Guy, *The Cardinal's Court*, Harvester Press, Brighton 1980.

E. Halévy, *A History of the English People in 1815*, tr. E. I. Watkin and D. A. Barker, T. Fisher Unwin 1924.
—— *A History of the English People 1830–41*, T. Fisher Unwin 1927.
—— *The Birth of Methodism*, ed. B. Semmel, Chicago University Press, 1971.
R. T. Handy, *A History of the Churches in the United States and Canada*, Oxford University Press 1976.
J. Haratounian (ed.), *Calvin's Commentaries and Letters*, SCM Press 1958.
A. Hardelin, *The Tractarian Understanding of the Eucharist*, Uppsala 1965.
B. Harrison, *Drink and the Victorians: The Temperance Question in England 1815–72*, Faber and Faber 1971.
J. F. C. Harrison, *The Second Coming: Popular Millenialism 1780–1850*, Routledge and Kegan Paul 1979.
A. B. Hasler, *How the Pope became Infallible: Pius IX and the Politics of Persuasion*, Doubleday, New York 1981.
A. Hastings, *A History of African Christianity 1950–1975*, Cambridge University Press, 1979.
—— *A History of English Christianity 1920–1985*, Collins 1986.
M. Hennell (ed.), *Charles Simeon (1759–1836)*, SPCK 1959.
J. Hennessey, *American Catholics: A History of the Roman Catholic Community in the United States*, Oxford University Press, New York 1981.
J. Herf, *Reactionary Modernism: Technology, Culture and Politics in Weimar and the Third Reich*, Cambridge University Press 1984.
C. Hill, *Society and Puritanism in Pre-Revolutionary England*, Oxford University Press 1964.
M. Hill, *The Religious Order, A Study of virtuoso religion and its legitimation in the Nineteenth Century Church of England*, Heinemann 1974.
C. Hinrichs, *Preussentum und Pietismus*, Vandenhoeck and Ruprecht, Gottingen 1971.
E. J. Hobsbawm, *The Age of Revolution 1789–1848*, Mentor, New American Library, New York and Toronto 1962.
J. D. Holmes, *More Roman than Rome: English Catholicism in the Nineteenth Century*, Burns and Oates, 1978.
—— *The Papacy in the Modern World*, Burns and Oates 1981.
J. D. Holmes and B. W. Bickers, *A Short History of the Catholic Church*, Burns and Oates 1983.
W. A. Visser't Hooft, *The Genesis and Formation of the World Council of Churches*, World Council of Churches, Geneva 1982.
P. Hughes, *A Popular History of the Church*, Sheed and Ward 1939.
—— *Rome and the Counter-Reformation*, Sheed and Ward 1942.
—— *The Reformation in England*, 3 vols, Burns and Oates, Oxford 1950–1954.
O. Hufton, *Bayeux in the Late Eighteenth Century*, Oxford: Clarendon Press 1967.

—— *Europe, Privilege and Protest 1730–1789*, Fontana, Glasgow 1980.

M. Hutt, *Chouannerie and Counter-Revolution: Puisaye, the Princes, and the British Government in the 1790s*, 2 vols, Cambridge University Press 1983.

F. A. Iremonger, *William Temple, Archbishop of Canterbury: his Life and Letters*, Oxford University Press 1948.

F. A. Isambert, *Christianisme et classe ouvrière*, Casterman, Tournai 1961.

E. Jackson, *Red Tape and the Gospel*, Selly Oak Colleges, Birmingham 1980.

P. Jagger, *Clouded Witness: Initiation in the Church of England in the Mid-Victorian Period 1850–75*, Pickwick Publications, Pennsylvania 1982.

R. C. D. Jasper, *George Bell, Bishop of Chichester*, Oxford University Press 1967.

E. Jay, *The Religion of the Heart: Anglican Evangelicalism and the Nineteenth Century Novel*, Oxford University Press 1979.

—— *The Evangelical and Oxford Movements*, Cambridge University Press 1983.

H. Jedin, *A History of the Council of Trent*, 2 vols, Nelson 1957–61.

—— *The Crisis and Closure of the Council of Trent*, 1967.

H. Jedin and J. Dolan (eds.), *Handbuch der Kirchengeschichte*, 10 vols, Freib-urg-im-Breisgau: ET as *History of the Church*, in which volumes 5–10 deal with the modern period, Burns and Oates 1980–81.

S. Campbell-Jones, *In Habit: An anthropological study of working nuns*, Faber and Faber 1979.

G. Josipovici, *The Lessons of Modernism*, Macmillan 1977.

A. Kenny, *Faith and Reason*, Columbia University Press, New York 1983.

J. Kent, *Holding the Fort: Studies in Victorian Revivalism*, Epworth Press 1978.

—— *The End of the Line? The Development of Christian Theology in the Last Two Centuries*, SCM Press 1982.

—— *'Religion and Science 1860–1914', Nineteenth-Century Religious Thought in the West*, ed. Ninian Smart et al., Cambridge University Press 1985, vol iii, p. 1–37.

I. Kershaw, *Popular Opinion and Political Dissent in the Third Reich*, Bavaria 1933–45, Oxford University Press 1983.

R. Kieckhefer, *European Witch Trials, Their Foundation in Popular and Learned Culture*, Routledge and Kegan Paul 1976.

M. D. Knowles, *The Religious Orders in England*, Cambridge University Press, 3 vols, 1950–59.

E. A. Knox, *The Tractarian Movement 1833–45*, Putnam 1933.

S. Koss, *Nonconformity and Modern British Politics*, Batsford 1975.

A. J. Krailsheimer (ed.), *The Continental Renaissance 1500–1600*, Penguin Books 1971.

A. Kreider, *English Chantries, The Road to Dissolution*, Harvard University Press 1979.

H. Küng, *Infallible?*, Fontana 1971.

—— *The Church Maintained in Truth*, SCM Press 1980.

—— *On Being a Christian*, Collins 1977.

R. Ladous, *L'Abbé Portal et la campagne anglo-romaine*, Université de Lyon, Lyon 1973.

D. Lagergren, *Mission and State in the Congo*, Uppsala 1970.

D. Laslett, *The World We Have Lost*, University Paperbacks 1965.

K. S. Latourette, *A History of the Expansion of Christianity*, 7 vols, Eyre and Spottiswoode 1938–46.

—— *Christianity in a Revolutionary Age*, 5 vols, Eyre and Spottiswoode 1959–63.

G. Le Bras, *Études de sociologie religieuse*, 2 vols, Presses Universitaires de France, Paris 1955–6.

E. Leonard, *Histoire générale de Protestantisme*, 3 vols: *La Réformation*, Paris 1961; *L'Établissement*, 1961; *Déclin et renouveau*, 1964: the first two were translated into English in 1966 and 1967.

A. TH. Van Leeuwen, *Christianity in World History*, Edinburgh House Press 1964.

G. Lewis, *The Second Vendée: the continuity of counter-revolution in the Department of the Gard 1789–1815*, Oxford University Press 1978.

G. Lewy, *The Catholic Church and Nazi Germany*, Weidenfeld and Nicholson 1964.

I. Linden, *The Church and Revolution in Rwanda*, Manchester University Press 1977.

A. Loisy, *L'Évangile et L'Église*, chez l'auteur, Bellevue (S.-et-O.) 1903.

J. Lortz, *Die Reformation im Deutschland*, Freiburg-im-Breisgau 1939, ET 1968.

E. Fasholé-Luke, *Christianity in Independent Africa*, Rex Collings 1978.

A. Macfarlane, *Witchcraft in Tudor and Stuart England, a regional and comparative Study*, Routledge and Kegan Paul 1970.

—— The *Origins of English Individualism: the family, property and social transition*, Blackwell, Oxford 1978.

—— *The Family Life of Ralph Josselin, a 17th century clergyman*, Cambridge University Press 1970.

B. Malament (ed.), *After the Reformation: Essays in Honour of J. R. Hexter*, Pennsylvania University Press 1980.

R. Mandrou, *Introduction à la France moderne, 1500–1640*, Paris 1974. ET, E. Arnold 1975.

S. Manickam, *The Social Setting of Christian Conversion in South India*, Wiesbaden 1977.

J. Maritain, *True Humanism*, Geoffrey Bles, The Centenary Press, 1938.

—— *Three Reformers*, Plon, Paris 1925; Sheed and Ward 1950.

M. Markowitz, *Cross and Sword*, Stanford University Press, California 1973.

G. Marsden, *Fundamentalism and American Culture: The Shaping of Twentieth Century Evangelicalism 1870–1925*, Oxford University Press, New York 1980.

D. Martin, *A General Theory of Secularization*, Basil Blackwell, Oxford 1978.

—— *The Breaking of the Image*, Basil Blackwell, Oxford 1980.

J.-M. Mayeur (ed.), *L'Histoire religieuse de la France, 19e-20e siècles: Problèmes et méthodes*, Beauchesne, Paris 1975.

H. McLeod, *Religion and the People of Western Europe*, Oxford University Press 1981.

J. McCracken, *Politics and Christianity in Malawi 1875–1940*, Cambridge University Press 1977.

W. G. McLoughlin, *Modern Revivalism: Charles Grandison Finney to Billy Graham*, Ronald Press, New York 1959.

—— *Billy Sunday was his Real Name*, Chicago University Press, New York 1955.

—— *Revivals, Awakenings and Reform: An Essay on Social Change in America 1607–1977*, University of Chicago 1978.

J. McManners, *French Ecclesiastical Society under the Ancien Régime*, 1961.

—— *The French Revolution and the Church*, SPCK 1969.

—— *Death and the Enlightenment, changing attitudes to death among Christians and Unbelievers in Eighteenth century France*, Oxford, Clarendon Press 1981.

J. T. McNeill, *Calvin's Institutes of the Christian Religion*, SCM Press 1961.

E. S. Mead, *The History of Christianity in America*, Harper and Row, New York 1963.

T. Metcalfe, *The Aftermath of Revolt in India 1857–1870*, Princeton University Press 1964.

P. Miller, *Jonathan Edwards*, William Sloane Associates, New York 1949.

—— *The New England Mind: From Colony to Province*, Harvard University Press 1953.

—— *The New England Mind: The Seventeenth Century*, Macmillan, New York 1939.

J. N. Molony, *The Emergence of Political Catholicism in Italy: Partito Popolare 1919–1926*, Croom Helm 1977.

T. Moloney, *Westminster, Whitehall and the Vatican: The Role of Cardinal Hinsley 1935–43*, Burns and Oates, Tunbridge Wells 1985.

W. J. Mommsen, *Stadburgertum und Adel in der Reformation*, Klett-cotta, Stüttgart 1979.

R. Moore, *Pitmen, Preachers and Politics*, Cambridge University Press, 1974.

J. R. H. Moorman, *A History of the Church in England*, A. and C. Black 1953.

—— *The Anglican Spiritual Tradition*, Darton, Longman and Todd 1983.

G. Moyser (ed.), *Church and Politics Today: The role of the Church of England in contemporary politics*, T. and T. Clark, Edinburgh 1985.

R. Muchembled, *Popular Culture and Elite Culture in France 1400–1750*, Louisiana State University Press, Baton Rouge 1985.

K. N. Mufuka, *Missions and Politics in Malawi*, Ontario 1977.

B. Moeller, *Imperial Cities and the Reformation*, ET Fortress Press, Philadelphia 1972.

F. X. Murphy, *The Papacy Today*, Weidenfeld and Nicholson 1981.

J. Murphy, *Church, State and Schools in Britain 1800–1970*, Routledge and Kegan Paul 1971.

P. Nichols, *The Popes' Divisions*, Faber and Faber, 1981.

R. Niebuhr, *The Nature and Destiny of Man*, Scribner, New York 1941.

—— *Faith and History: A Comparison of Christians and Modern Views of History*, Scribner, New York 1949.

F. Nietzsche, *Twilight of the Idols and The Antichrist*, tr. R. J. Hollingdale, Penguin Books, Harmondsworth 1968.

E. R. Norman, *Church and Society in England 1770–1970*, Clarendon Press, Oxford 1976.

—— *The English Catholic Church in the Nineteenth Century*, Oxford University Press 1984.

—— *Anti-Catholicism in Victorian England*, Allen and Unwin 1968.

J. Obelkevich, *Religion and Rural Society: South Lindsey 1825–75*, Oxford University Press 1976.

G. Oddie, *Social Protest in India: British Protestant Missionaries and Social Reform 1850–1900*, Manohar Publications, New Delhi 1979.

W. A. Oliver, *Prophets and Millenialists: The Uses of Biblical Prophecy in England from the 1790s to the 1840s*, Auckland University Press 1978.

A. C. Outler, *John Wesley*, Oxford University Press, New York, 1964.

J. Owens, *Prophets in the Wilderness, The Wesleyan Mission to New Zealand 1819–27*, Auckland University Press, 1974.

S. Ozment, *Reformation Europe, A Guide to Research*, Centre for Reformation Research, St Louis 1982.

—— *The Reformation in the Cities: the appeal of Protestantism to 16th and 17th Germany and Switzerland*, Yale University Press 1975.

R. R. Palmer, *The Age of the Democratic Revolution*, Princeton University Press 1959.

K. Panikkar, *Asia and Western Dominance*, Allen and Unwin 1953.

W. G. Peck, *The Divine Society: Christian Dogma and Social Redemption*, SCM Press 1925.

J. D. Y. Peel, *Aladura, A Religious Movement among the Yoruba*, Oxford University Press 1968.

J. Pelikan and H. J. Lehmann (eds), *Luther's Works*, Fortress Press, Philadelphia, 55 volumes altogether, 1943–.

C. S. Phillips, *The Church in France 1789–1848*, Mowbray 1929.

W. Pickering (ed.), *A Social History of the Diocese of Newcastle*, Oriel Press, Routledge and Kegan Paul 1981.

P. Pierrard, *Juifs et Catholiques français*, Fayard, Paris 1970.

M. Piette, John Wesley, La Réaction dans l'évolution protestante, Brussels 1926, ET *John Wesley in the Evolution of Protestantism*, Sheed and Ward 1937.

A. Pollard, and M. M. Hennell, *Charles Simeon 1759–1836*, SPCK 1959.

J. C. Pollock, *A Cambridge Movement*, 1953.

—— *The Keswick Story*, 1964.

—— *Billy Graham, the authorised biography*, Hodder and Stoughton, 1966.

E. Poulat, *Naissance des prêtre-ouvriers*, Casterman, Paris 1965.

—— *Histoire, dogme et critique dans la crise moderniste*, Casterman, Paris 1969.

—— *Alfred Loisy*, Editions du centre national de la recherche scientifique, Paris 1960.

—— *Intégrisme et Catholicisme intégral: Un réseau secret internationale antimoderniste, La Sapinière 1909–21*, Casterman, Paris 1969.

P. Pourrat, *La Spiritualité chrétienne*, ET 4 vols, Westminster, Maryland 1953–55.

F. K. Prochaska, *Women and Philanthropy in Nineteenth-Century England*, Oxford University Press 1980.

M. Ranchetti, *The Catholic Modernists: A Study of the Religious Reform Movement 1864–1907*, Turin 1963, ET Isobel Quigley 1969.

B. M. G. Reardon, *Roman Catholic Modernism*, A. and C. Black 1970.

—— *Liberal Protestantism*, A. and C. Black 1968.

—— *Liberalism and Tradition: Aspects of Catholic Thought in Nineteenth-Century France*, Cambridge University Press 1975.

—— *From Coleridge to Gore, A Century of Religious Thought in Britain*, Longman 1971.

J. K. S. Reid, *Calvin's Theological Treatises*, SCM Press 1954.

R. Remond, *La Droite en France*, Aubier, Paris 1963; ET *The Right-Wing in France from 1815 to De Gaulle*, 1968.

B. Reymond, *Une Église à croix gammée? Le protestantisme allemand au début du régime nazi 1932–35*, L'Age d'Homme, Lausanne 1980.

J. T. Reynolds, *The Evangelicals at Oxford 1735–1905*, Marcham Manor Press, Abingdon 1986.

A. Rhodes, *The Vatican in the Age of the Dictators 1922–45*, Hodder and Stoughton 1973.

D. Robert, *Les Églises Reformées* en France 1800–1830, Presses universitaires de France, Paris 1961.

D. Rosman, *Evangelicals and Culture*, Croom Helm 1984.

R. J. Ross, *The Beleaguered Tower: The Dilemma of Political Catholicism in Wilhelmine Germany*, Notre Dame University Press, 1976.

Ruth Rouse, and S. Neill (eds), *A History of the Ecumenical Movement 1517–1948*, The Westminster Press, Philadelphia 1954, second ed. 1967; continued in H. Fey (ed.) *The Ecumenical Advance 1948–68*, 1970.

R. Rotberg, *Christian Missionaries and the Creation of Northern Rhodesia 1880–1924*, Princeton University Press 1965.

—— *The Rise of Nationalism in Central Africa: The Making of Malawi and Zambia 1873–1964*, Harvard University Press 1965.

G. Rowell, *Hell and the Victorians: A study of the nineteenth-century theological controversies concerning eternal punishment and the future life*, Oxford University Press 1974.

—— *The Vision Glorious*, Oxford University Press 1983.

E. G. Rupp, *Luther's Progress to the Diet of Worms*, SCM Press 1951.

—— *The Righteousness of God*, Hodder and Stoughton 1953.

L. Russell (ed.), *Feminist Interpretations of the Bible*, Blackwell, Oxford 1985.

E. R. Sandeen, *The Roots of Fundamentalism: British and American Millenarianism 1800–1930*, Chicago University Press 1970.

J. J. Scarisbrick, *The Reformation and the English People*, Blackwell, Oxford 1984.

I. Scheiner, *Christian Converts and Social Protest in Meiji Japan*, California University Press 1970.

W. J. Schoenl, *The Intellectual Crisis in English Catholicism*: Garland, New York 1982.

T. Schoof (ed.), *The Schillebeeckx Case*, The Paulist Press, Ramsey, New Jersey 1984.

R. W. Scribner, *For the Sake of Simple Folk: Popular Propaganda in the Reformation*, Cambridge University Press 1981.

B. Semmel, *The Methodist Revolution*, Heinemann, 1974.

E. Sevrin, *Les Missions religieuses en France sous la Restoration 1815–1830*, t. i, *Le Missionaire et la mission*, Prêtres de la Miséricorde, St-Mande (Seine) 1948, t. ii, *Les Mission 1815–20*, J. Vrin, Paris 1959.

G. Shepperson and T. Price, *Independent African: John Chilembwe and the origins, setting and significance of the Nyasaland native rising of 1915*, Edinburgh University Press 1958.

K. M. de Silva, *Social Policy and Missionary Organisation in Ceylon 1840–55*, Longman 1965.

Q. Skinner, *The Foundations of Modern Political Thought: The Age of the Reformation*, Cambridge University Press 1978.

M. Smirin, *Die Volksreformation des Thomas Munzer und der grosse Bauernkrieg*, Berlin 1952.

B. A. Smith, *Dean Church, The Anglican Response to Newman*, Oxford University Press 1958.

H. M. Smith, *Pre-Reformation England*, Macmillan 1938.

M. L. Smith (ed.), *Benson of Cowley*, Oxford University Press 1980.

P. M. Smith, *Calvinist Preaching and Iconoclasm in the Netherlands 1544–69*, 1978.

C. Smyth, *Simeon and Church Order*, Cambridge University Press 1940.

J. Sperber, *Popular Catholicism in Nineteenth-Century Germany*, Princeton University Press 1984.

F. Spotts, *The Churches and Politics in Germany*, Middletown, Connecticut 1973.

J. Stehlin, *Weimar and the Vatican 1919–33*, Princeton University Press 1983.

A. M. G. Stephenson, *The Rise and Decline of English Modernism*, SPCK 1984.

Z. Sternhell, *Maurice Barrès et le nationalisme français*, Colin, Paris 1972.

F. E. Stoeffler, *The Rise of Evangelical Pietism*, Brill, London 1965.

—— (ed.), *Pietism and Early American Christianity*, Grand Rapids, Michigan 1976.

G. Strauss, Luther's *House of Learning: Indoctrination of the Young in the German Reformation*, John Hopkins University Press, Baltimore 1981.

J. Stroup, *The Struggle for Identity in the Clerical State: North-West German Opposition to the Absolute Policy in the Eighteenth Century*, Brill, Leiden 1984.

R. E. Sullivan, *John Toland and the Deist Controversy*, Harvard University Press, New York 1982.

B. Sundkler, *The Church of South India: the movement towards reunion 1900–47*, Lutterworth Press 1947.

—— *Bantu Prophets in South Africa*, Oxford University Press 1961.

D. Sutherland, *The Chouans, the Social Origin of Popular Counter-Revolution in Upper Brittany 1770–1796*, Clarendon Press, Oxford 1982.

W. W. Sweet, *The Story of Religion in America*, Harper's, New York 1950.

N. Sykes, *Church and State in England in the Eighteenth Century*, Cambridge University Press 1934.

—— *The Church of England Non-Episcopal Churches in the Sixteenth and Seventeenth Centuries*, 1948.

—— *Old Priest and New Presbyter*, Cambridge University Press 1956.

—— *William Wake, Archbishop of Canterbury*, 2 vols, Cambridge University Press, 1957.

—— *From Sheldon to Secker, Aspects of English Church History*, Cambridge University Press 1959.

U. Tal, *Christians and Jews in Germany 1870–1914*, Cornell University Press 1975.

J. V. Taylor, *The Growth of the Church in Buganda*, SCM Press 1958.

R. Thalmann, *Protestantisme et nationalisme en Allemagne 1900–45*, Klinkrieck, Paris 1976.

K. Thomas, *Religion and the Decline of Magic*, Weidenfeld and Nicholson, 1971.

E. P. Thompson, *The Making of the English Working Class*, Victor Gollancz 1963.

C. Tilly, *The Vendée*, Oxford University Press 1964.

K. A. Thompson, *Bureaucracy and Church Reform 1800–1965*, Oxford University Press 1965.

S. L. Thrupp (ed.), *Millenial Dreams in Action*, Brill, the Hague 1962.

P. Toon, *Evangelical Theology 1833–56: The Response to the Tractarians*, New Foundations Theological Library Series, John Knox 1979.

T. F. Torrance, *Luther, Early Theological Works*, SCM Press 1962.

R. Towler, *Homo Religiosus: Sociological Problems in the Study of Religion*, Constable 1974.

R. C. Trexler, *Public Life in Renaissance Florence*, Academic Press, New York 1980.

A. Vidler, *A Century of Social Catholicism 1820–1920*, SPCK 1969.

—— *Prophecy and Papacy: a Study of Lamennais, the Church and Revolution*, SCM Press 1954.

—— *A Variety of Catholic Modernists*, Cambridge University Press, 1970.

M. Vovelle, *Piété Baroque et déchristianisation en Provence au xviiie siècle*, Plon, Paris 1973.

—— *Religion et révolution: la déchristianisation de l'an II*, Hachette, Paris 1976.

W. Walkowitz, *Prostitution and Victorian Society*, 1980.

M. Walzer, *The Revolution of the Saints: A Study in the Origins of Radical Politics*, Harvard University Press 1966.

W. R. Ward (ed.), *The Early Correspondence of Jabez Bunting 1820–29*, Royal Historical Society, Camden Fourth Series volume 11, 1972.

—— *Early Victorian Methodism: The Correspondence of Jabez Bunting*, Oxford University Press 1976.

—— *Religion and Society in England 1790–1850*, Batsford 1972.

L. Watt, *The Doctrines of the Modernists and Modernist Errors*, Catholic Truth Society 1937.

E. Weber, *Peasants into Frenchmen: The Modernization of Rural France 1870–1914*, Stanford University Press 1976.

—— *Action Française*, Stanford University Press, 1962.

—— *Les Mystifications de Léo Taxil*, Paris 1964.

C. Welch, *God and the Incarnation in mid-nineteenth-century German Theology*, Oxford University Press 1965.

—— *Protestant Thought in the Nineteenth Century*, Yale University Press, *vol. 1 1799–1870*, 1972, and *vol. 2 1870–1914*, 1985.

P. A. Welsby, *A History of the Church of England 1945–1980*, Oxford University Press 1984.

L. Willaert, *La restauration catholique 1563–1648*, Paris 1960.

T. J. Williams, *Priscilla Lydia Sellon*, SPCK 1965.

A. N. Wilson, *Hilaire Belloc*, Hamish Hamilton, 1984.

B. Wilson, *Religion in Secular Society*, C. A. Watts 1966.

—— *Magic and the Millennium*, Heinemann 1973.

K. M. Wolfe, *The Churches and the British Broadcasting Corporation, 1922–56: The Politics of Broadcast Religion*, SCM Press 1984.

J. P. Wright, *Above Parties: The Political Attitudes of the German Protestant Church Leadership 1918–33*, 1974.

M. Wright, *German Missions in Tanganyika 1891–1941*, Oxford University Press 1971.

T. E. Yates, *Venn and Victorian Bishops Abroad*, Uppsala 1978.

S. Yeo, *Religion and Voluntary Organisations in Crisis*, Croom Helm 1976.

L. Ziff, *Puritanism in America: New Culture in a New World*, Oxford University Press 1973.

Index

DATE DUE

AUG 15 '90

HIGHSMITH #LO-45220